S0-AWR-339

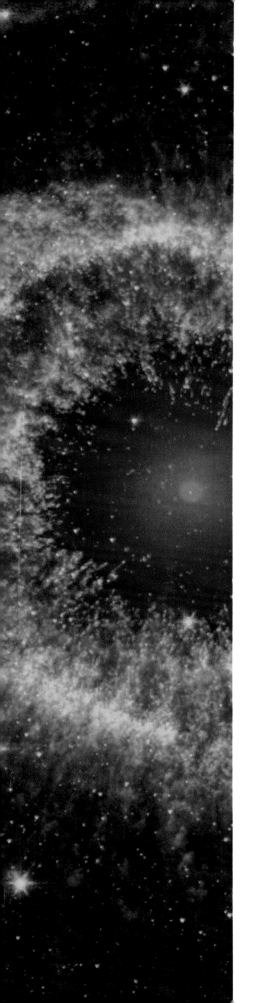

Student Edition

Bring Science Alive!
Exploring Science Practices

*NGSS is a registered trademark of Achieve. Neither Achieve nor the lead states and partners that developed the Next Generation Science Standards was involved in the production of, and does not endorse, this product.

Chief Executive Officer
Bert Bower

Chief Operating Officer
Amy Larson

Director of Product Development
Maria Favata

Strategic Product Manager
Nathan Wellborne

Senior Science Content Developer
Ariel Stein

Curriculum Consultants
Kim Merlino
Joan Westley

Program Editors
David Fraker
Mikaila Garfinkel
Edward Helderop
Rebecca Ou
Ginger Wu

Editorial Consultant
Glenda Stewart

Production Manager
Jodi Forrest

Operations & Software Manager
Marsha Ifurung

Designer
Sarah Osentowski

Art Direction
Julia Foug

Teachers' Curriculum Institute
PO Box 1327
Rancho Cordova, CA 95741

Customer Service: 800-497-6138
www.teachtci.com

Copyright © 2015 by Teachers' Curriculum Institute.
No parts of the publication may be reproduced without written permission from the publisher.
Printed in the United States of America.

ISBN 978-1-58371-983-1
2 3 4 5 6 7 8 9 10 -WC- 20 19 18 17 16 15

Manufactured by Webcrafters, Inc., Madison, WI
United States of America, May 2015, Job # 121653

SUSTAINABLE
FORESTRY
INITIATIVE

Certified Sourcing
www.sfiprogram.org
SFI-00617

Science Advisory Board

Marilyn Chambliss, Ph.D.
Associate Professor of Reading Education,
Emerita at the University of Maryland
University of Maryland, College Park

Angelo Collins, Ph.D.
Associate Dean
School of Education and Counseling Psychology
Santa Clara University
Santa Clara, CA

Ron Korenich, Ed.D.
Educational Consultant
Retired Coordinator of Elementary Education
for the Fox Chapel Area School District
Pittsburgh, Pennsylvania

Kathleen Peasley, Ph.D.
Assistant Superintendent for Academic Services
Grand Ledge Public Schools
Michigan

Steve Schneider, Ph.D.
Senior Program Director of Science, Technology,
Engineering, and Mathematics
WestEd

Jerome M. Shaw, Ph.D.
Associate Professor of Science Education
University of California, Santa Cruz

Andrew Shouse, Ph.D.
Associate Director of the Institute for Science
and Math Education and Assistant Research
Professor of Learning Sciences
University of Washington

Nancy Butler Songer, Ph.D.
Professor of Science Education and Learning
Technologies and Director of the Center for
Essential Science
University of Michigan

Donald B. Young, Ph.D.
Dean of the College of Education
and Professor of Science Education
University of Hawaii at Manoa

Science Content Scholars

Matthew Bobrowsky, Ph.D.
University of Maryland

John Czworkowski, Ph.D.
University of California, San Diego

Tanya Dewey, Ph.D.
University of Michigan

Andrew P. Norton, Ph.D.
*University of California,
Santa Cruz*

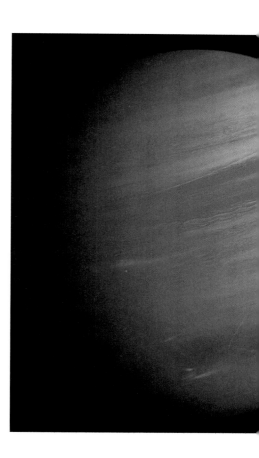

About the Next Generation Science Standards

What Teachers and Families Need to Know

The Next Generation Science Standards (NGSS) describe the science skills and knowledge all students need to know to succeed in college, careers, and citizenship. The standards were developed by a panel that collaborated with representatives from 26 lead states. They are based on *A Framework for K–12 Science Education*, which was written by a team of scientists, engineers, and science educators, and published by the National Research Council in 2012.

The NGSS were released in Spring 2013, and TCI's science instructional program, *Bring Science Alive!*, was developed to meet them.

Each performance expectation has three dimensions: disciplinary core ideas, scientific and engineering practices, and crosscutting concepts. Together, these describe what students should understand and be able to accomplish at each grade level.

What are performance expectations, and how does *Bring Science Alive!* prepare students to demonstrate mastery?

Performance expectations describe what all students should be able to do at the completion of a unit of study. They guide assessment and are supported by the details in the disciplinary core ideas, practices, and crosscutting concepts. Many performance expectations are followed by clarification statements and assessment boundaries. Clarification statements provide examples and details, and assessment boundaries limit what students should be tested on.

Performance expectation 4-LS1-1. has students construct an argument that internal and external structures function to support the survival, behavior, reproduction, and growth of plants and animals.

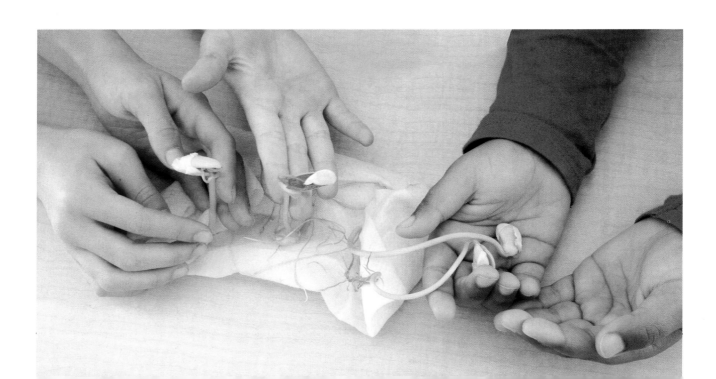

Bring Science Alive! prepares students to meet the performance expectations. Performance expectations are identified in the Student Text at the beginning of each unit and each lesson. They are also incorporated into the investigations in the online Presentations for students to practice.

How are the Next Generation Science Standards related to Common Core standards?

The NGSS are aligned to the Common Core State Standards for English Language Arts & Literacy in History/ Social Studies, Science, and Technical Subjects and Common Core State Standards for Mathematics.

Similarly, *Bring Science Alive!* is aligned to Common Core English and Mathematics. For example, all Reading Furthers in the Student Text align with the Reading Standards for Informational Text K–5. Interactive Tutorials address Common Core reading and writing standards. Lesson content and investigations are aligned with Common Core Mathematics, such as when students learn about measurement units and tools and graphing.

What are Disciplinary Core Ideas, and how does *Bring Science Alive!* meet them?

Disciplinary core ideas focus instruction on the foundational knowledge students need for success in each grade. Core ideas build from year to year, from Kindergarten to Grade 12, in learning progressions that revisit each topic several times, each time with greater depth and sophistication. Therefore, students are expected to understand the core ideas that were taught in previous grades.

For these reasons, teachers and parents may find fewer topics taught in each grade than they have seen previously. Additionally, many topics are taught in different grades than they were under previous standards. By limiting the content at each grade, students are able to learn with deeper understanding.

Bring Science Alive! guides students through these core ideas as they read their Student Text, complete Interactive Tutorials, carry out hands-on and online investigations, and write, draw, diagram, and calculate in their Interactive Student Notebooks.

One part of the disciplinary core idea PS2.A: Forces and Motion focuses on observing and measuring the patterns of an object's motion in different situations so that the object's motion can be predicted in future situations.

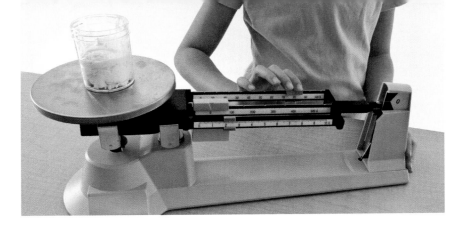

What are Science and Engineering Practices, and how does *Bring Science Alive!* meet them?

Science and engineering practices describe the abilities students should develop to engage in science and engineering. Students use these eight practices to master the principles described in the core ideas. The practices also help students understand how professional scientists and engineers answer questions and solve problems.

- (?) Asking questions and defining problems
- Developing and using models
- (Q) Planning and carrying out investigations
- Analyzing and interpreting data
- Using mathematics and computational thinking
- Constructing explanations and designing solutions
- (?!) Engaging in argument from evidence
- Obtaining, evaluating, and communicating information

The science and engineering practice Engaging in Argument from Evidence asks students to use data, evidence, and models to support an argument they make.

Every lesson in *Bring Science Alive!* develops several science and engineering practices in the online lesson Presentation. Practices are used explicitly and help teach the lesson's core ideas. Each of the eight practices is taught at every grade level with increasing sophistication from grade to grade.

What are Crosscutting Concepts, and how does *Bring Science Alive!* meet them?

The crosscutting concepts are used to organize students' understanding of science and engineering in the same way that scientists and engineers do. They give students specific ideas to consider when learning about a new topic. These ideas are intended to help students understand the topics at a deeper level.

In addition to supporting core ideas, the seven crosscutting concepts support one another. They are listed below with descriptions of their importance for all upper elementary students.

Patterns Recognizing patterns helps students sort and classify objects, describe rates of change and cycles, and make predictions.

Cause and Effect In their investigations, students observe patterns and then identify and test how two events may or may not be related.

Scale, Proportion, and Quantity Students recognize that objects and systems vary greatly in size and learn to measure using standard units.

Systems and System Models Describing and modeling systems helps students understand complex phenomena in terms of parts and their interactions.

Energy and Matter Students learn that matter is made of particles, that energy is transferred between objects, and that matter is neither lost nor gained when it changes.

Structure and Function Students explore identifying the smaller structures within larger ones and the functions of these structures.

Stability and Change Recognizing that change occurs at different rates helps students understand systems.

Each lesson is carefully developed to explain and integrate the crosscutting concept with core ideas.

While learning about the crosscutting concept Systems and System Models, students will discover how to describe a system using its components and interactions.

Connections to Engineering, Technology, and Applications of Science

The Next Generation Science Standards address engineering design as a process similar to, and just as important as, scientific inquiry. Engineering design is divided into three broad steps, each of which encompasses several of the science and engineering practices.

The steps are described by the grades 3–5 engineering design performance expectations, listed below.

- *3-5-ETS1-1. Define a simple design problem reflecting a need or want that includes specified criteria for success and constraints on materials, time, or cost.*

- *3-5-ETS1-2. Generate and compare multiple possible solutions to a problem based on how well each is likely to meet the criteria and constraints of the problem.*

- *3-5-ETS1-3. Plan and carry out fair tests in which variables are controlled and failure points are considered to identify aspects of a model or prototype that can be improved.*

Bring Science Alive! provides many opportunities for students to understand the work of engineers and use the engineering design process to solve problems relevant to the scientific knowledge they are simultaneously developing.

Engineering, Technology, and Applications of Science in the Investigations

Students learn how some engineers work to protect Earth's systems by reducing air pollution. While reading about this topic, they explore the process that engineers use when designing solutions to problems.

Engineering, Technology, and Applications of Science in the Student Text

Interactions of Science, Technology, Society and the Environment in the Student Text

While studying the structure and properties of matter, students learn how engineers, like the one pictured here, solve real-world problems by designing new materials.

Connections to the Nature of Science

The science and engineering practices describe how to engage in scientific inquiry. The disciplinary core ideas describe existing scientific knowledge. The crosscutting concepts provide a framework for connecting scientific knowledge. Students integrate these dimensions of learning when they learn what kinds of knowledge are scientific, how scientists develop that knowledge, and about the wide spectrum of people who engage in science.

Nature of Science in the Student Text

One of the basic understandings about the nature of science described in NGSS is that investigations use different tools, procedures, and techniques.

Nature of Science in the Investigations

How to Use This Program

1 The teacher begins each lesson with a **Presentation** that facilitates the lesson and the investigation.

2 In the Presentations, students participate in a hands-on **investigation** that blends the core ideas, science practices, and crosscutting concepts of NGSS.

3a In the online **Student Subscription**, students expand their knowledge through reading the Student Text, completing an Interactive Tutorial, and processing what they've learned in the **Interactive Student Notebook**.

3b Alternatively, students can read from the **Student Edition** and complete a consumable Interactive Student Notebook.

4 The lesson ends with students demonstrating their knowledge of each core idea, science practice, and crosscutting concept through a variety of paper and online **assessments**.

Literacy in Science

The Next Generation Science Standards were developed to work in tandem with the Common Core State Standards to ensure that students develop literacy skills through learning science. *Bring Science Alive!* builds on this synergy by emphasizing reading, writing, speaking and listening, and language skills while guiding students in developing their science knowledge.

Key Points from the ELA Common Core	*Bring Science Alive!*

Reading

Informational and literary texts are balanced with at least 50% of reading time devoted to expository texts.	CCSS changes the emphasis in reading from being based primarily on literary texts to being balanced between literary and informational texts. *Bring Science Alive!* reflects this balance in its text. Each lesson has several sections of purely informational text that explains the content of that lesson. Each lesson is followed by a Reading Further, which blends literary and informational style text to engage students with the content even further.
Establishes a "staircase" of increasing complexity in what students must be able to read as they move throughout the grades.	*Bring Science Alive!* is written with close attention paid to the text complexity to make sure it fits into the "staircase" of increasingly sophisticated text that students should read as they progress through the grades. However, within each grade's text, there is variation in the complexity to ensure that there is challenging text for all students.
Emphasizes the close reading of text to determine main ideas, supporting details, and evidence.	The digital Interactive Tutorials encourage close reading of the text. They require students to answer questions using evidence from the text. Answering the questions requires a clear understanding of the main ideas and other details provided in the section.

Writing

Three types of writing are emphasized from the earliest grades—writing to persuade, writing to inform/explain, and writing to convey experience.	NGSS and *Bring Science Alive!* require students to use all three types of writing emphasized by CCSS. In the investigations, students are often asked to construct written arguments to persuade their classmates of their explanation of a scientific concept. They also write accounts of their experiences in these activities and investigations, describing details of the experiment or design process. In the Interactive Student Notebook, students write explanations to demonstrate their understanding of the scientific concepts described in the text.
Effective use of evidence is central throughout the writing standards.	In all three types of writing, students are expected to use evidence appropriately to support their claims. They are given support in identifying key details which will serve most effectively as evidence. They also reflect on their use of evidence in various contexts to build an explicit understanding of the role evidence plays in science and argument in general.
Routine production of writing appropriate for a range of tasks, purposes, and audiences is emphasized.	Students routinely write in all of *Bring Science Alive!*'s curricula. The program emphasizes the flexibility and usefulness of writing to accomplish a variety of assignments. It also gives students exposure to the different expectations in writing for different purposes and audiences.

Key Points from the ELA Common Core	Bring Science Alive!

Speaking and Listening

Participation in rich, structured academic conversations in one-on-one, small-group, and whole class situations is emphasized in the standards.	Classrooms using *Bring Science Alive!* will regularly have structured science talks in which students reflect on their experiences and understanding of the investigations. They will also have regular discussions in smaller groups, ranging from discussions with a partner to groups of four or five students. These discussions are designed to build clear communication skills that are critical to success in science and all other fields of study.
Contributing accurate, relevant information; responding to and building on what others have said; and making comparisons and contrasts are important skills for productive conversations.	In all discussions, students are given support to help them learn to contribute relevant and accurate details and evidence. The cooperative tolerant classroom conventions emphasized throughout all of TCI's curricula encourage students to respond to and build on ideas and arguments presented by other students. *Bring Science Alive!* uses NGSS's crosscutting concepts to help students to compare and contrast relevant experiences across domains of science in discussions.

Language

Demonstrate command of the conventions of English when writing and speaking.	Throughout all the components of *Bring Science Alive!* students are expected to demonstrate command of the conventions of written and spoken English.
Acquire and use general academic and domain-specific words.	*Bring Science Alive!* has a progression of increasingly sophisticated vocabulary built into it with complexity suggested by the language used in NGSS. It is designed to emphasize key words used throughout a lesson or unit of study without overwhelming students with too many unfamiliar words. Every component of *Bring Science Alive!* makes use of the vocabulary and includes activities to help solidify comprehension.
Focus on developing skills to determine or clarify the meaning of unknown words or phrases.	Other science-related words which may be unfamiliar to students, but do not play a key role in the overall understanding of a concept, are put in italics and defined in context. This gives students ample opportunity and support in determining and clarifying the meaning of unfamiliar words using clues from the text.

Considerate Text

Sample Graphic Organizer

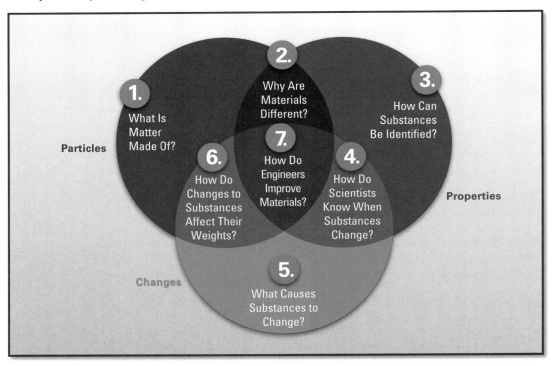

You are about to discover that *Bring Science Alive!* is both interesting and easy to understand. That's because our authors wrote it as a "considerate text," which is another way of saying that it makes readers want to read it. Here are some ways this book is considerate for all levels of readers:

- Each unit is carefully mapped out so that one lesson builds on the next. So, you will find a clear graphic organizer, like the one above, in each unit opener. The graphic organizer shows how all the lessons in the unit relate to one another. A **purple** lesson is the main idea, **blue** stands for lessons that support the main idea, and **green** and **red** lessons take those ideas even further.

- Short lessons make it easier for you to understand and remember what each one is about.

- Each section has a subtitle that provides an outline for your reading and is written with a clear focus. Information is presented in easy-to-manage chunks for better understanding.

- Important new words are in bold type. These words are defined in the glossary in the back of the book.

- Photos, illustrations, and diagrams provide additional information about the topic on the page.

How To Read the Table of Contents

The **lesson title** is also the lesson's Essential Question.

The **unit name** tells you the overall topic of the unit.

Each lesson has a **crosscutting concept** or 'theme' associated with it.

Unit 1 | Living Things and Ecosystems

1 What Is an Ecosystem? ....
Systems and System Models
Developing and Using Models
Reading Further: Cave Creatures ....

Every lesson emphasizes one or more **science and engineering practice**. These are the skills you will master in this lesson.

Every lesson includes a **Reading Further**—a fun, high interest article that promotes literacy and helps students engage with the content even further.

Contents

Unit 1 Living Things and Ecosystems

Unit 2 Earth Systems

Unit 3 Changes in Matter

Unit 4 Earth, the Moon, and the Stars

Living Things and Ecosystems

In a forest, you may see trees, birds, insects, ferns, moss, and mushrooms. Some things may be hidden from view like earthworms. All living things, or organisms, live in an ecosystem. An ecosystem includes all the plants and animals, as well as nonliving things, in one area. In this unit, you will read about ecosystems and how they function. You will learn how organisms interact with each other and with nonliving things to meet their needs.

Unit Contents

Unit 1 Overview

Graphic Organizer: This unit is structured to develop the concept of an **ecosystem** and then introduces **matter and energy's movement** in an ecosystem and changes in ecosystems over time.

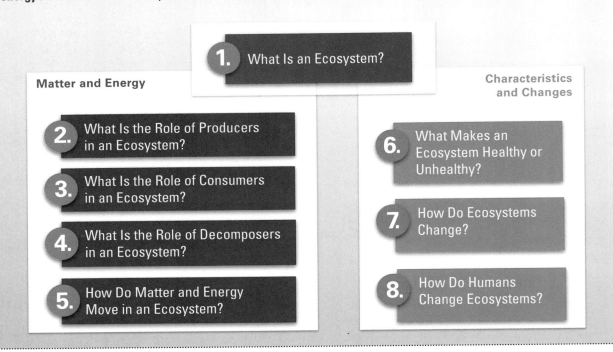

1. What Is an Ecosystem?

Matter and Energy

2. What Is the Role of Producers in an Ecosystem?

3. What Is the Role of Consumers in an Ecosystem?

4. What Is the Role of Decomposers in an Ecosystem?

5. How Do Matter and Energy Move in an Ecosystem?

Characteristics and Changes

6. What Makes an Ecosystem Healthy or Unhealthy?

7. How Do Ecosystems Change?

8. How Do Humans Change Ecosystems?

NGSS Next Generation Science Standards

Performance Expectations

5-PS3-1. Use models to describe that energy in animals' food (used for body repair, growth, motion, and to maintain body warmth) was once energy from the sun.

5-LS1-1. Support an argument that plants get the materials they need for growth chiefly from air and water.

5-LS2-1. Develop a model to describe the movement of matter among plants, animals, decomposers, and the environment.

Disciplinary Core Ideas

PS3.D: Energy in Chemical Processes and Everyday Life • The energy released from food was once energy from the sun that was captured by plants in the chemical process that forms plant matter (from air and water).

LS1.C: Organization for Matter and Energy Flow in Organisms • Food provides animals with the materials they need for body repair and growth and the energy they need to maintain body warmth and for motion.
• Plants acquire their material for growth chiefly from air and water.

LS2.A: Interdependent Relationships in Ecosystems • The food of almost any kind of animal can be traced back to plants. Organisms are related in food webs in which some animals eat plants for food and other animals eat the animals that eat plants. Some organisms, such as fungi and bacteria, break down dead organisms (both plants or plants parts and animals) and therefore operate as "decomposers." Decomposition eventually restores (recycles) some materials back to the soil. Organisms can survive only in environments in which their particular needs are met. A healthy ecosystem is one in which multiple species of different types are each able to meet their needs in a relatively stable web of life. Newly introduced species can damage the balance of an ecosystem.

LS2.B: Cycles of Matter and Energy Transfer in Ecosystems • Matter cycles between the air and soil and among plants, animals, and microbes as these organisms live and die. Organisms obtain gases, and water, from the environment, and release waste matter (gas, liquid, or solid) back into the environment.

Crosscutting Concepts

Systems and System Models • A system can be described in terms of its components and their interactions.

Energy and Matter • Matter is transported into, out of, and within systems. • Energy can be transferred in various ways and between objects.

 **Developing and Using Models**

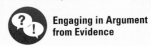 **Engaging in Argument from Evidence**

Have you ever wondered...

All living things need food to survive, though they obtain their food in different ways. Organisms in the same area interact with each other to meet their needs. This unit will help you answer these questions and many others you may ask.

How do different kinds of animals get what they need to survive?

How do plants get the food they need?

How do different organisms interact with each other in a food web to get the energy they need?

What Is an Ecosystem?

Science Vocabulary

ecosystem

Why do you think some species of grasses live in meadows and not in deserts? All organisms live where their needs are met. Ecosystems are composed of all the living and nonliving things that interact in an area. In this lesson, you will discover that there are similarities and differences among ecosystems.

NGSS | **5-LS2-1.** Develop a model to describe the movement of matter among plants, animals, decomposers, and the environment.

LS2.A. The food of almost any kind of animal can be traced back to plants. Organisms are related in food webs in which some animals eat plants for food and other animals eat the animals that eat plants. Some organisms, such as fungi and bacteria, break down dead organisms (both plants or plants parts and animals) and therefore operate as "decomposers." Decomposition eventually restores (recycles) some materials back to the soil. Organisms can survive only in environments in which their particular needs are met. A healthy ecosystem is one in which multiple species of different types are each able to meet their needs in a relatively stable web of life. Newly introduced species can damage the balance of an ecosystem.

Systems and System Models
A system can be described in terms of its components and their interactions.

Developing and Using Models

1. Organisms and Their Environment

Suppose you hike down into the Grand Canyon. At the top of the canyon, you notice many wildflowers and tall pine trees. The soil is damp from a recent rain. You see many birds and squirrels. As you descend into the canyon, you pass through an area of shorter trees. Most of the plants in this environment are small bushes and cactuses. Lizards move over the dry soil. The air is hot and dry.

Each environment is part of the Grand Canyon *ecosystem*. An **ecosystem** is all the living and nonliving things that interact with each other in an area. For example, all the pine trees, wildflowers, birds, squirrels, soil, and air are part of the Grand Canyon ecosystem.

Recall that an *organism* is any living thing. Organisms must meet their needs in an ecosystem, or they cannot survive there. They must have enough food and water. They require a temperature that is neither too hot nor too cold. They need places for their young to grow. Plants require enough sunlight to make food to stay alive. The living things depend on each other to survive. For example, in a forest ecosystem, a woodpecker might eat insects living in the bark of a tree. It might also build a nest in that tree. The woodpecker, insects, and the tree all interact in a forest ecosystem.

Air, water, and sunlight are nonliving things. Organisms depend on nonliving parts of their ecosystem for survival. For example, some trees need strong light and a lot of water to survive. They must live in moist, sunny ecosystems.

An ecosystem is all the living and nonliving things that interact in an area. This is the Grand Canyon in Arizona. Trees, birds, soil, and air are parts of the ecosystem here.

This tapir lives in a tropical rainforest, where it can meet its needs. Animals and plants can only live in the parts of ecosystems where their needs are met.

2. A Tropical Rainforest Ecosystem

Have you heard of the Amazon rainforest? It is a large, tropical rainforest surrounding the Amazon River of South America and the rivers that feed into it. Many organisms live there, like monkeys, large snakes, and brightly colored birds. Why do these animals not live everywhere?

Many of these animals can only meet their needs in this rainforest ecosystem. Other ecosystems might not have enough food, water, or heat. Likewise, plants and animals from a desert ecosystem could not meet their needs in the Amazon rainforest ecosystem. The rainforest would be too wet for those organisms.

Tropical Rainforests Are Wet and Warm

Heavy rainfall, constant heat all year long, and strong sunlight are the main features of these rainforests. Tropical rainforests are hot because they are found near Earth's equator, where there is a lot of sunlight. The large amounts of rainfall make the air very humid. All this moisture and warmth allow trees and other plants to grow quickly all year.

Tropical Rainforests Have Four Layers

You can think of the Amazon rainforest as having four layers, from the forest floor up to the highest treetops. Each layer has its own species of plants and animals. The *forest floor* is the bottom layer of a rainforest. It is dark and cool because very little light reaches the ground through the dense trees. Only certain plants can grow well in this shade, but earthworms, beetles, snakes, and larger animals, such as tapirs and jaguars, can be found. Large amounts of dead leaves and plant material fall onto the forest floor.

The second layer of a rainforest is called the *understory*. Many mammals, snakes, lizards, and insects live here. Plant leaves are much larger, so they can catch the small amount of sunlight that reaches this layer.

The next layer of a rainforest, called the *canopy*, contains most of the rainforest life. Tall trees grow with straight trunks. Their leaves are found only at the top, where sunlight falls. Other plants grow on the branches of trees to reach light. The canopy is home to monkeys and many species of colorful birds. Many insect species also live in the canopy.

The tops of the tallest trees make up the top layer of the rainforest, called the *emergent layer*. These tall trees are scattered through the forest and stretch above the canopy. They produce leaves only at the top. The treetops provide homes for eagles, parrots, butterflies, and other insects.

A tropical rainforest has four layers. Different kinds of plants and animals live in each layer. Each type of organism lives where it can meet its needs.

A Tropical Rainforest Has Many Species

Because each layer of a tropical rainforest has unique features, a huge number of species can meet their needs in at least one layer. In fact, the number and variety of plants and animals here is greater than in any other kind of ecosystem. The large numbers of plant species provide food for many animal species. The dense branches and leaves in the canopy provide shelter and nesting places for many species of birds and other animals.

The Layers of a Tropical Rainforest

Emergent layer

Canopy

Understory

Forest floor

These long plants are cattails. Many North American ponds have cattails growing along their edges. Cattails depend on many of the nonliving parts of a pond ecosystem to survive.

3. A Pond Ecosystem

Ecosystems come in different sizes. Some are large, like rainforests. Others are much smaller, like a pond. Ponds are small bodies of fresh water. Ponds are found in natural areas, on farms, and in city parks.

Pond Plants Depend on Nonliving Things

Plants need air, water, sunlight, and nutrients to live. Recall that *nutrients* are similar to food, but do not provide energy. Instead, nutrients keep a plant healthy. Plants get many nutrients they need from soil. The plants that live in and around a pond depend on its nonliving parts to meet these needs. Reeds and cattails grow around the pond. Their roots dig into the moist soil at the pond's edge. They also grow in the muddy bottom of the pond, where they take in nutrients. Water lilies also live in ponds. The leaves of these water plants float on the water's surface so that they can absorb sunlight and take in air. The roots of the water lilies take in nutrients from the muddy bottom of the pond.

Sunlight also affects the pond in another way. It warms the water and the air above the water, so roots and the leafy parts of plants can grow in the temperature range they need.

Plants depend on all these nonliving things to survive in the pond ecosystem. They need access to water, to soil, and to the sun. The plants might not be able to live in a different ecosystem.

Pond Animals Depend on Plants and Other Animals

The animals that live in a pond ecosystem depend on plants and other animals to meet their needs. Animals must eat food. Fish eat smaller fish and insects. Ducks nibble on duckweed. A frog catches a water bug with its long, sticky tongue. A turtle eats small pond plants and fish. Water birds, such as herons, also eat fish. Female fish lay eggs among the cattail roots at the edge of the pond. They will be sheltered and protected there until they hatch. After they hatch, the baby fish hide in the cattail roots until they can protect themselves from turtles and larger fish.

Algae are tiny plantlike organisms that are food for many pond animals. The green algae float on the water's surface and also underwater where there is still some light. Algae may even cover the pond surface completely. Algae are eaten by tadpoles, snails, and insects.

Almost all animals need air. Pond water has air in it that fish and tadpoles take in through their *gills*. Gills are a structure that some animals have that lets them get air underwater. The animals that live around the pond or on its surface breathe air directly.

Organisms that live in a pond ecosystem can survive there because their needs are met. In a different ecosystem, they might not survive. Soil, temperature, and the amount of available water might not meet a pond plant's needs. Different plants might not be suitable food for pond animals.

Duckweed is a small plant that floats on the pond surface. It is food for animals that live in this ecosystem, such as ducks.

Animals in a pond depend on other organisms in the pond to survive. This frog eats insects that it finds flying over the water.

Nature of Science

4. How Scientists Study Ecosystems

Now that you have learned about several ecosystems, you might wonder how scientists learn about the interactions between living and nonliving things in an ecosystem.

Ecology is the study of how living and nonliving things interact with their environments. Scientists that study ecosystems and teach other people about them are called *ecologists*. They answer questions about the environment in several ways. Suppose the government wants to build a dam across a river near a forest. Scientists might do experiments in the area to find out how the dam would affect the organisms that live there. They would try to learn how the dam might change the water flow in the river and how the change would affect living things. Based on the results of the research, the government might change its plans for the dam.

Ecologists study the ways living things interact in natural systems. Some look at the activities of animals by tagging the animals with small radios. The radios let these ecologists track the animals' movements. They can see where the animals go and when they move.

Not all natural events can be studied directly. For example, some impacts of a dam on wildlife cannot be observed before it is built. Scientists use models to study nature. Some models show which animals interact with other animals in an ecosystem. They can help scientists learn about and predict changes in ecosystems.

Ecologists study nature in many ways. This scientist is using his computer to produce a model of the forest ecosystem he is sitting in.

What Is an Ecosystem?

1. Organisms and Their Environment   An ecosystem is all the living and nonliving things that interact in an area. Air, soil, water, and sunlight are some nonliving things in an ecosystem. Organisms that live in an ecosystem must meet their needs there, or they will not survive. Many organisms that live in an ecosystem could not survive in another ecosystem.

2. A Tropical Rainforest Ecosystem   Tropical rainforests are wet, warm ecosystems with four layers. These are the forest floor, the understory, the canopy, and the emergent layer. Many different species of organisms live in rainforests, and each layer also houses different types of living things. Beetles, snakes, lizards, monkeys, and parrots are some organisms in these rainforests.

3. A Pond Ecosystem   Ponds are smaller ecosystems than tropical rainforests. Many organisms live there and interact with each other to meet their needs. Duckweed, water lilies, frogs, fish, turtles, and herons are some pond organisms. They need many of the nonliving parts of a pond ecosystem, such as the water, air, sunlight, and nutrients in the muddy soil.

4. How Scientists Study Ecosystems   Scientists who study the environment are called ecologists. Many ecologists study how ecosystems work. They track animals so they can see where the animals go and what they do. Ecologists teach others and answer questions about ecosystems. They also use computers to model ecosystems so that they can learn more.

Cave Creatures

On land, in the air, and under water—you can find living things everywhere on Earth. Some creatures even spend their entire life cycle below Earth's surface in caves. What type of creatures live in a cave ecosystem?

Wearing warm, waterproof clothes and carrying flashlights, ecologists explore the complete darkness of a cave. They wear gloves to protect their hands from cold temperatures, constant moisture, and rough surfaces. They wear helmets to protect their heads from low ceilings. What will these adventurers find?

A cave is a natural opening in Earth's surface. Many animals find their way into a cave. Some live just inside the opening, while others live miles from the entrance. If a cave has enough water, it may support its own unique ecosystem. And, the deeper you get from Earth's surface, the stranger life gets!

Cave ecosystems are different from ecosystems such as forests, grasslands, and lakes. Plants and other producers grow well on Earth's surface, using sunlight for the energy they need to survive. Many other living things in an ecosystem use either plants or plant eaters as their source of food. But the inside of a cave gets little or no light from the sun. So, cave ecosystems usually have no plants.

At Earth's surface, temperatures tend to change a lot, depending on the weather and amount of sunlight. But some caves extend far away from the surface, with little or no sunlight coming inside. Thus, in many caves, temperatures tend to stay the same all year round. Cave creatures are adapted to live in this type of environment.

Many types of bats live in caves, natural openings in Earth's surface. Bats only spend some of their time in caves, but other animals spend their whole lives there.

Cave crickets are part of some cave ecosystems. They find food and water in a cave and may become food for other cave animals.

Away from the Sun

Where a cave creature lives within a cave depends on its needs. Caves form in different ways and can be many sizes. The type of rock and the amount of water affect what animals can live there and where they live.

Animals such as bears, skunks, snakes, and moths live only in the outer part of a cave, near the opening. They may use caves for shelter, but they go outside to get most of the food and water they need. They are not specially adapted to living their whole lives in caves. If a major change occurred in the cave ecosystem, they might simply leave and find new shelter. Even so, these animals are an important part of a cave ecosystem, because they bring in food or nest materials. They may shed hair, leave waste, and die inside the cave. In these ways, they provide food for other living things that make the cave their home.

Some light enters the cave near the entrance, but deeper in the cave there is little light even during the day. Here, temperatures change less, and there may be pools of water or small streams. Bats often live deeper in these dim parts of caves. They cling to the ceiling to sleep and fly out of the cave to find food at night. Deeper in the cave may live crickets, rats, and salamanders. These animals may spend their whole lives in the cave, but they could survive on the surface, too. If the cave ecosystem changes, these individuals might come to harm. But other members of their species would continue to live elsewhere.

In the Dark

There are places in a cave where it is always totally dark. There, ecologists come across animals that are found nowhere else. These often include species of crickets, salamanders, or even small fish that are specially adapted to the cave environment.

Most animals use their eyes to find food and watch for predators. In a cave environment, where it is always dark, being able to see is not useful for survival. Blind crickets can survive better than ones that can see, because they may have other traits that help them survive without vision. They pass these traits on until all of the crickets in the deep cave are blind.

Many animals that live entirely in caves have no color in their skin or shells. When an explorer's flashlight shines on them, they appear white. On Earth's surface, having a colorful outer skin or coat helps many animals hide from predators. For example, a fawn's spots help it blend in with grass or shadows and be safe from a mountain lion. But in the darkness of a cave, color cannot help. This is because no animal can see where there is no light.

A third trait many cave-dwellers share is that they move and live slowly. Their hearts beat slowly, and they do not need to eat often. So, they stay still a lot. These traits allow them to live where it is cold and food is not plentiful. The animals that are adapted to cave life in these ways cannot survive outside their cave ecosystem.

Olms are blind and colorless amphibians that live in caves. Olms are adapted to live in the darkness of a cave ecosystem.

Cave slime oozes down from the roof of Cueva de Villa Luz, a cave in Mexico. Cave slime is produced by microbes that make their home in caves.

Cave Slime

Not all of the creatures unique to caves are animals that crawl, fly, or swim. Some are tiny organisms that live in a slime that covers the walls of caves.

Just what kind of creature makes cave slime its home? Some kinds of organisms are too small to be seen unless you use a microscope. Scientists call these living things *microbes*. Cave slime is created by certain kinds of microbes. The microbes that produce cave slime can even live in caves where the air contains acids that are poisonous to animals. The slime helps to protect the microbes from the air. The microbes take in the acids, some of which they later release into the slime as waste. The acids in the slime dissolve the rock around it.

Whether they are as large as a bear or as small as a slime microbe, all living things need water and a place to live. Most need air, too. The unique nature of a cave ecosystem teaches us that not all living things need to live in sunlight.

Often the species that are specially adapted to the deepest parts of caves are found in only one cave in the world. This means that if their ecosystem is destroyed, the species would die out. Therefore, when ecologists study these unique ecosystems, they are careful to not damage the living or nonliving things in them. Ecologists and other cave explorers must suit up to avoid being harmed by the rough cave environment. They must also take care not to do harm. That's why even cave slime should be treated with care!

What Is the Role of Producers in an Ecosystem?

Science Vocabulary

carbon dioxide

oxygen

photosynthesis

producer

Producers are the organisms in ecosystems that make their own food. Almost all plants are producers that use water, air, and energy from sunlight to make their own food. Most plants store excess food in their roots or stems. Water and a gas in the air provide the matter that producers use to make food and grow new parts.

NGSS

5-PS3-1. Use models to describe that energy in animals' food (used for body repair, growth, motion, and to maintain body warmth) was once energy from the sun.
5-LS1-1. Support an argument that plants get the materials they need for growth chiefly from air and water.

LS1.C. Plants acquire their material for growth chiefly from air and water.
PS3.D. The energy released from food was once energy from the sun that was captured by plants in the chemical process that forms plant matter (from air and water).

Energy and Matter
• Matter is transported into, out of, and within systems.
• Energy can be transferred in various ways and between objects.

Developing and Using Models

Engaging in Argument from Evidence

1. Producers Make Food

Producers make things. A company that produces cars makes cars. A bakery that produces baked goods makes bread and cakes. Plants are producers. What does a plant make?

Producers are the parts of an ecosystem that capture the energy in sunlight. They use this energy to produce their own food. When producers make their own food, the energy that came from sunlight is stored in their bodies. They use this energy to grow, develop, and reproduce. Plants are producers. So are green algae, the small plantlike organisms that sometimes grow on pond surfaces. Some bacteria, tiny organisms that cannot be seen without a microscope, are also producers. Thus, in an ecosystem, a **producer** is any organism that produces, or makes, its own food.

Since producers make their own food, where do you think they get the matter they need? *Matter* is everything around you that has weight and takes up space. Like energy, matter cannot be created. So, producers get the matter they need from the air and water that surround them. Matter moves into ecosystems, like when the water in a stream flows into a pond ecosystem. Matter also moves out of ecosystems, like when the pond water flows out of the pond. Matter also moves within an ecosystem. This can happen when producers use raw materials in an ecosystem to make food. Both raw materials and food are kinds of matter. Next, you will learn what raw materials producers use to make food and what happens to this food.

This river is covered in green algae. Green algae are producers that grow on the surface of ponds, rivers, and lakes. They make their own food using the energy in sunlight.

The leaves of plants contain the factories where food is produced by photosynthesis. Carbon dioxide and water are the raw materials producers need for photosynthesis.

2. Photosynthesis Uses Both Matter and Energy

You can think of the green leaves of a plant as factories that produce a product. The product of these factories is food.

Plants Need Matter to Make Food

A factory must take in raw materials to do its job and make its product. The raw materials plants need to make food are air and water, which are kinds of matter. Plants need air partly because it contains **carbon dioxide,** a gas found in air. The process of using carbon dioxide and water to make food is called **photosynthesis**.

Photosynthesis takes place in most plants' leaves, so the raw materials must be delivered to the leaves. Plant leaves have tiny openings to take in air with carbon dioxide. The openings are too small for you to see without a microscope. Most plants live on land and grow in soil. Soil contains the water that a plant needs to make food. The roots of a plant grow down into the soil and take in water. The water travels up the stems of the plant and into the leaves.

The leaf factories now have both of the raw materials they need for photosynthesis: carbon dioxide and water. However, a factory cannot produce its product without energy. Energy is needed to power the equipment and machines that make the product. The leaf factories also need energy. Where does this energy come from?

Plants Need Energy to Make Food

Energy enters most ecosystems as sunlight. Some of this energy is captured by producers and used to power the leaf factories that make food. The energy in sunlight is captured by *chlorophyll*, a green substance found in leaves and other green parts of a plant. Plants need the right amount of sunlight to survive. This is one of the reasons why plants can live only in certain ecosystems. Too much sunlight burns a plant's leaves and turns them brown, so they cannot make food. Plants that get too little sunlight cannot make food because they capture too little energy.

Now that the leaf factory has a supply of energy, it can begin to make food. Using the energy in sunlight, the leaf combines carbon dioxide and water in a process that makes sugar. Sugar is food for the plant. All parts of the plant need sugar. If the plant grows new leaves or flowers, it uses sugar as its energy source. Some plants also use sugar to turn their stems and leaves toward the sun to get more energy.

In addition to sugar, the leaf factory also produces oxygen. **Oxygen** is another gas found in air. The oxygen produced by photosynthesis is a waste material. It moves out of the plant through the same tiny openings in the leaves that the carbon dioxide went in and goes into the air. You will read more about photosynthesis and oxygen later.

In photosynthesis, carbon dioxide and water are used to form sugar and oxygen. Sugar is food for the plant. Oxygen is a waste product. Energy from sunlight is needed to power photosynthesis.

Photosynthesis

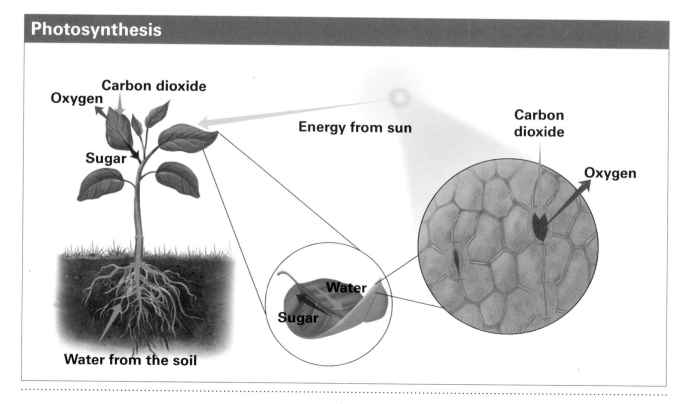

Oxygen
Carbon dioxide
Energy from sun
Carbon dioxide
Oxygen
Sugar
Water
Sugar
Water from the soil

3. Producers Store Excess Food

Plants produce large amounts of food during photosynthesis. What do you think happens to it all?

Most of the food plants produce is used immediately to provide energy for the plant's life processes. Food provides energy and building materials that allow the plant to make more leaves and longer stems and roots. The food that plants make in their leaves is transported by water to all parts of the plant. Apple trees and geraniums use food to make flowers, fruits, and seeds for reproduction, while spruce and pine trees use food to make cones and seeds. Plants use food for movement. Although a plant cannot move from place to place, its parts can move—leaves move to face the sun so they can capture the sun's energy, and flowers open during the day.

However, not all food is used as soon as it is made. Plants store some of the food for use when the plant cannot perform photosynthesis, such as at night or when the growing season ends. When the growing season ends, the leaves of most plants fall to the ground. The plant no longer produces food. It survives by using stored food.

Plants turn sugar into starch for storage. Some plants store starch in their roots. Carrots and turnips are examples. Other plants store starch in their stems or other structures. Potatoes are specialized stems that grow underground. When animals eat potatoes or carrots, they get energy from this stored food.

These roots, stems, and other plant structures store extra food for the plant until it is needed. The plant uses the stored food when it cannot perform photosynthesis, like at night.

All the green plants you can see in this image are carrying out photosynthesis. They release oxygen into the air and animals, like the goat, can breathe it in.

4. Photosynthesis Produces Waste

Every factory that makes a product also makes wastes. Cans of waste may pile up in corners of the factory floor. What do factories do with these wastes? They throw them away or recycle them.

You have read that photosynthesis produces oxygen gas as a waste and that this oxygen is released into the air through openings in the plant's leaves.

Look at the word equation for photosynthesis:

carbon dioxide + water + light $\longrightarrow$ sugar + oxygen

The materials on the right side of the arrow, sugar and oxygen, are the products that form. Sugar is not a waste because this food is used by the plant for energy. But most of the oxygen made is not used by the plant. It is a waste that the plant "throws away" through the leaf openings and out into the air.

Almost all living things, including plants and other producers, need oxygen to power their life processes. For example, you take in oxygen when you breathe in and use it in your body. But plants make much more oxygen through photosynthesis than they need. Most of it is released into the air and is available for animals to breathe in. You can think of this oxygen as being recycled in an ecosystem. It is made by all the producers that live there and used by almost all the living things. Thus, oxygen gas moves from the living parts of the system to the nonliving parts and back again.

5. Where the Matter for Photosynthesis Comes From

You now know that plants mostly use water and carbon dioxide for the matter they need to grow. But more than 300 years ago, most scientists thought that plants got food from soil and that soil caused a plant to grow.

Jan van Helmont, an early Belgian scientist, questioned this idea of "soil-eating" plants. He did an experiment in which he showed that the matter needed for plant growth came from water, not soil. He planted a 2.3 kg (5 lb) young willow tree in a pot with 91 kg (200 lb) of soil that he had dried in an oven. For five years, he gave the tree only rainwater. After five years, van Helmont took the tree out of the pot. It had grown large with many new leaves, branches, and roots. He weighed the tree and found that it weighed 77 kg (170 lb), a weight increase of 74.7 kg (165 lb). Then he dried and weighed the soil, and its weight had hardly changed at all! Where did the matter to grow this big plant come from?

The tree had gotten much heavier, but the soil was still about the same weight. So, van Helmont concluded that the matter the plant used for growth could not have come from the soil. He thought that the matter must have come from water alone since water was all that he gave the tree during its five years of growth. His experiment is an early example of using scientific evidence to support an idea. Van Helmont's works were published in 1648 after his death.

But you learned that he was only half right. Do you remember where the matter for plant growth comes from? It also comes from carbon dioxide. More than 150 years later, in 1804, another scientist named Nicolas-Théodore de Saussure proved that the large amounts of matter plants need to grow also come from carbon dioxide in the air.

This is a willow tree, like the one van Helmont used in his experiment. He thought that plants only gained weight from water, but we now know that they get a lot of their weight from carbon dioxide in the air, too.

What Is the Role of Producers in an Ecosystem?

1. Producers Make Food   Producers are organisms in an ecosystem that make their own food. They almost always use sunlight as energy to do this, and most producers are plants. They use the sun's energy to turn matter in their environment into food. Most producers get matter for their growth from the nonliving components of their ecosystem.

2. Photosynthesis Uses Both Matter and Energy   Photosynthesis is the process that most plants use to make their own food. Plants use energy from sunlight, water, and carbon dioxide from the air to make sugar, which they use as food. They also produce oxygen as a waste product, which they release into the air.

3. Producers Store Excess Food   Most food from photosynthesis is used immediately by the producer. However, some food is stored for use when plants cannot perform photosynthesis. When it is nighttime or if a plant has no leaves in winter, it uses its stored food to survive. Most plants store their food in their stems or roots.

4. Photosynthesis Produces Waste   Factories produce wastes as well as useful products. Plants produce food through photosynthesis. But like factories, they also produce wastes, such as oxygen. Even though plants do need some oxygen, they produce far more than they use. Plants release the extra oxygen into the air through leaf openings as a waste.

5. Where the Matter for Photosynthesis Comes From   A scientist named Jan van Helmont performed an experiment in the 1600s to find out where the matter came from for photosynthesis. He thought that the matter came only from water. Scientists now know that it also comes from carbon dioxide in the air.

Animal Producers

The green leaves of land plants are the main producers of their ecosystems. Producers make food from carbon dioxide and water through photosynthesis. But are there any animals that can do this?

These reef-building corals are animals that have tiny algae living inside their bodies. Although the coral seem to make food, it is really the algae that do.

Basically all the animals you encounter are not producers because they do not make their own food. But a group of animals called reef-building corals seem to make their own food. Reef-building corals are small ocean animals that live together in groups. The corals produce a hard outer covering that is similar to the shell of a clam. This covering supports and protects the coral's body. When many groups of hard corals grow together, they form a rocky underwater structure called a reef. These reefs grow best in warm, shallow, clear seawater.

Reef-building corals eat tiny sea animals that they catch with their tentacles. But corals also seem to make their own food. So, are they producers? Like land plants, they have chlorophyll in their bodies that lets them perform photosynthesis. However, it turns out that corals do not really make food by themselves. Their bodies contain small, plantlike organisms called algae. Algae are photosynthetic, which means they perform photosynthesis. So, algae also make food using carbon dioxide and water in their environment. This lets them trap the energy carried by sunlight. In exchange for the coral's hospitality, the algae provide food for their host.

This giant clam is another animal that seems to make its own food. But, in fact, it is the algae that live in the clam's colorful mantle that actually make food for themselves and for the clam. Only the blue edge of the mantle can be seen in this photo.

Giant Clams

Another animal that seems to be a producer is the giant clam. Giant clams live in shallow parts of the Pacific Ocean and the Red Sea, usually anchored to coral reefs. Once they attach themselves to a reef, they stay there for the rest of their lives. A giant clam may be almost 1.5 m (5 ft) across, or about the height of a typical fifth grader. But that very same clam may weigh about as much as five fifth graders put together because of its thick, hard shell.

Giant clams have a colorful structure called a *mantle*. The mantle covers the clam's insides beneath its shell. It also acts as a habitat for algae.

Giant clams live in a relationship with the algae they harbor, just as reef-building corals do. The algae live inside the clam's body, where they are protected from animals that would eat them. The clam supplies the needed carbon dioxide and nutrients to the algae. In exchange, the algae make food by photosynthesis and provide it to the clam.

During the day, a giant clam opens its double shell. It spreads its mantle out of its shell so that the algae in the mantle can trap sunlight. The algae need the sunlight to perform photosynthesis. Algae make most of the food the clam needs. The rest of the clam's food comes from tiny animals that the clam filters out of the seawater. Having two sources of food allows a giant clam to grow to a very, well, *giant* size!

This solar-powered sea slug can make some of its own food. Its green color is from chlorophyll that it got by eating algae.

Solar-Powered Green Sea Slugs

For a long time, scientists thought there were no animals that were true producers. But as scientists explored and studied life, they discovered photosynthetic sea slugs! These small, green invertebrates don't just have algae living inside them. They actually have their own chlorophyll!

Because these sea slugs are animals, they cannot make chlorophyll when they first hatch. So, they have to get it from somewhere else. When a slug eats a meal of green algae, its body breaks down the algae into parts. Instead of digesting the parts of the algae that contain chlorophyll, the slug saves them in its intestine. Usually an organism needs special genes to keep the photosynthesis factories working. But some species of these sea slugs continue to perform photosynthesis for many months after their last algae meal. Do the sea slugs have their own genes to keep the chlorophyll working? Scientists think so, but they are still figuring out exactly how they can do this.

The story got even stranger when other scientists did an experiment. The sea slugs they studied were from a species that had chlorophyll inside their bodies. But the slugs didn't seem to be using the food it made! What was going on? Why would an animal make food and not use it? Is this true for other species of solar-powered sea slugs as well? Part of the reason science is so interesting is that its puzzles can be hard to solve. Scientists will keep looking for more evidence to try to solve this puzzle.

Solar Salamanders

Animal producers aren't just found in the ocean. At least one land animal is solar powered, too. Spotted salamanders live in forests, where they spend most of their time underground. So, you might not expect these animals to perform photosynthesis. They only come above ground in order to eat and mate. Then they lay their eggs in pools of water. They have to pick where they lay their eggs carefully. If the pond contains fish, the fish will eat the eggs before they hatch!

The small eggs sit on underwater plants in clumps surrounded by a clear jelly. The jelly coating makes it hard for the eggs to get oxygen. But if there are algae inside the jelly, the algae can perform photosynthesis. The algae take carbon dioxide that the eggs produce and turn it into food and oxygen. The eggs with algae grow larger and stronger than eggs without algae.

Most of the algae are gone by the time the salamander grows up. But some adult salamanders still have algae inside of them. Scientists think that the algae might be continuing to perform photosynthesis, making the salamander food from inside its body!

No one knows how many other animal producers scientists will discover in the future. Their understanding of what a producer is, what a consumer is, and how they relate to each other may change with new evidence. Perhaps even you could discover the evidence that shows that animals can be producers!

A spotted salamander is another animal producer. A scientist found that structures inside the salamander's body were producing food.

LESSON 3

What Is the Role of Consumers in an Ecosystem?

Science Vocabulary

circulation

consumer

digestion

Animals are consumers, organisms that eat other organisms to get food. Most cannot make their own food. The energy that consumers use in their lives comes from the food they eat. Producers first make food using the energy in sunlight. Then consumers eat those producers or other consumers to get their own energy.

5-PS3-1. Use models to describe that energy in animals' food (used for body repair, growth, motion, and to maintain body warmth) was once energy from the sun.

PS3.D. The energy released from food was once energy from the sun that was captured by plants in the chemical process that forms plant matter (from air and water). **LS1.C.** Food provides animals with the materials they need for body repair and growth and the energy they need to maintain body warmth and for motion.

Energy and Matter
Energy can be transferred in various ways and between objects.

Developing and Using Models

28   Unit 1 Living Things and Ecosystems

1. Consumers Eat Other Organisms

A hawk sits high in a tree watching the ground. It sees a small mammal. Quickly, the hawk swoops down and captures the animal with its sharp claws. It brings the animal to its nest to feed its babies.

A hawk is a **consumer,** an organism that gets energy by eating other organisms. Consumers, like producers, are living parts of an ecosystem. All animals are consumers. Unlike most plants, nearly all animals are unable to make their own food. Instead, consumers get the matter and energy they need by consuming food. The energy in their food was once energy from the sun that was captured by producers during photosynthesis.

Food provides animals with the materials they need for body repair and growth. Food also provides the energy animals need to move and maintain other body functions. For example, when a wolf goes hunting in the winter, it is using energy. It needs energy to run after deer. It also needs energy to stay warm. Many animals need energy to keep themselves warm, especially if they live in a very cold place!

Animal species vary greatly in the food sources they use to meet their needs. Some animals, such as hawks and lions, eat only meat from other animals. Deer, rabbits, and land snails are some animals that eat mostly plant material. Most animals eat both plant and animal material. For example, brown bears eat fish, insects, berries, and nuts. Humans can eat both plants and animals.

Hawks are consumers that only eat other animals. Although hawks have no teeth, their sharp claws and beaks help them capture and eat their food.

2. Digestion Breaks Down Food to Release Energy

Bricks, steel, and wood are used to build houses, schools, and barns. You can think of the matter in food as the building materials that are used to make body parts.

Why is food so important to an animal? Food gives animals the building materials and energy they need to grow and survive. The animal uses the matter to grow larger, to repair body parts, and to reproduce. Growth, repair, and reproduction also require energy. Mammals and birds need energy to keep their bodies warm. In fact, everything an animal does uses energy.

Mice have digestive systems like yours. Food is taken in through their mouths. The food is then broken down to provide the simple materials and energy that the body can use.

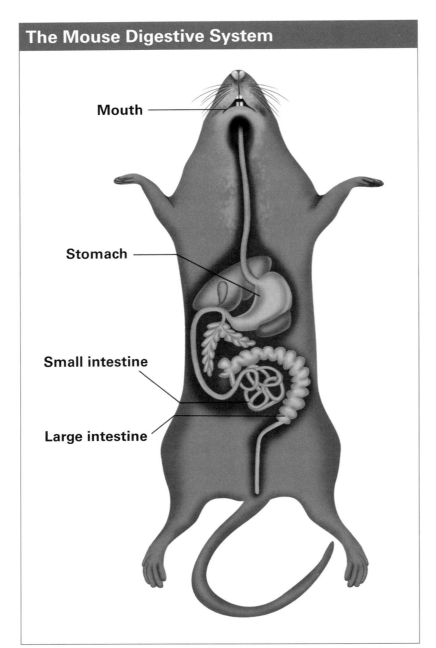

The Mouse Digestive System

Mouth

Stomach

Small intestine

Large intestine

Food Must Be Digested

Consumers cannot use the building materials and energy in food right away. The food must first be digested. **Digestion** is the process that breaks down food into simple materials that an animal's body can use. Most animals have a digestive system where digestion takes place. A mouth, stomach, small intestine, and large intestine are some of the parts of a mammal's digestive system. Other animals such as clams and worms do not have all these parts, but they still digest the food they eat.

Think about a mouse that has eaten a meal. The mouse's body needs to break down the food in the meal to use it. When the mouse eats, the food is broken down in two ways. First, the mouse chews the food up into small pieces. Then, the food is mixed with digestive juices that break it down into simple materials for the mouse.

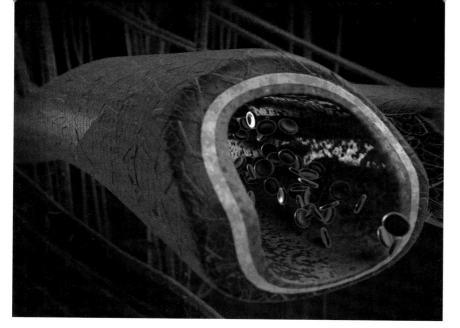

This model shows what a mouse's blood vessel might look like. The blood carries useful materials like digested food and oxygen throughout the mouse's body. It also moves wastes.

Materials Must Be Distributed

There is one more step in digesting the meal. The broken down materials pass through the walls of the mouse's small intestine and move into the blood. The blood carries them to all parts of the mouse's body. **Circulation** is the process of moving blood in a large, complicated loop through the body. Mice, as well as many other animals, have a circulatory system that is made up of a heart, blood vessels, and blood. The digestive and circulatory systems work together to supply all parts of the body with the materials and energy that they need.

Blood moves inside blood vessels. The heart acts like a pump to circulate the blood. You can think of the blood vessels as a highway system that moves materials in the mouse's body. The blood vessels form a large loop in its body, so the blood moves around in a continuous cycle. The blood picks up a supply of materials as it passes the small intestine. It also picks up oxygen as it passes through the lungs. Then, like trucks on a highway, the blood drops off these materials to the rest of the mouse's body. When it makes another trip past the small intestine, it picks up a new supply of materials to take to body parts. In the body parts, the materials are further broken down using oxygen to release the energy they contain. As the food and oxygen are used up, the blood continuously supplies more of both. Thus, the mouse's body always has a supply of the things it needs.

As the blood drops off building materials, it picks up wastes that the body parts must get rid of. You will read about how the mouse's body gets rid of the wastes it makes.

3. Consumers Store Excess Food

Many birds migrate thousands of kilometers to warmer areas. About two weeks before they leave, they begin a feeding frenzy. How do you think the birds store all of the food they eat before they go?

Suppose a bird eats a large meal. It digests the food in that meal into simple building materials. However, the bird does not immediately need all the materials and the energy in them. Instead, it stores the materials and energy to use later, when it cannot find other food.

Most of this excess food is stored in a bird's body as fat. The farther a bird migrates, the more fat it must store. A bird traveling a long distance may double its weight before it leaves. It will rarely eat during the trip.

How does the bird's body prepare for this journey? When an animal eats more food than it needs right away, its body stores the extra food energy for later. An animal stores the extra energy for short periods of time in the form of sugar. The materials can be stored for longer periods of time as fat. When an animal needs energy between meals, it sends a signal releasing the stored sugar or fat into the blood. The blood carries the sugar to all parts of the body. There, it is broken down to free the energy it contains.

By storing food, animals can survive when they cannot find other food to eat. They can use the stored food to repair body parts, move, and stay warm. Animals always need a supply of energy, so they either must be eating or using stored food all of the time.

This Blackpoll Warbler doubles its weight before flying thousands of miles from Canada to South America each autumn. It stores extra food that it eats as fat, which it uses as energy during the trip.

When this horse breathes out, some of the water its body produces freezes in the cold air. Carbon dioxide waste is also breathed out by the horse, but you cannot see it. The water and carbon dioxide that were part of a living organism are once again nonliving parts of the ecosystem.

4. Consumers Produce Wastes

Recall that a plant is similar to a factory and that all factories produce wastes. An animal's body is like a busy factory, too. Many processes take place in the body. Food is digested and energy is released from it. The animal grows and repairs damaged body parts. Muscles move the arms and legs. The heart beats and pumps blood. All these processes create wastes.

During digestion, much of the matter in food is broken down into materials that the body needs. But some of the matter cannot be used. This matter is waste. The large intestine removes the digestive waste from the body. These solid wastes go into the ecosystem.

What happens to the food in the bloodstream? The simple materials from digested food are further broken down in the body using oxygen from the air. This releases energy, but more wastes are made. One of these wastes is carbon dioxide gas. It is picked up by the blood and removed from the body when the animal breathes out. It goes back into the air.

Wastes also are made when an animal dies. The once-living matter from the animal's body is broken down and passes into the soil and air.

What happens to all these wastes? They become part of the nonliving things in an ecosystem—the air, soil, and water. The once-living matter goes back into the environment to be used again by other organisms. Producers reuse the carbon dioxide to make food and grow. Thus, matter is recycled in an ecosystem.

Just like other animals, humans are consumers. After humans eat food, their bodies digest it, and their circulatory system moves the materials throughout their bodies.

5. Humans Are Consumers

When you are hungry, you look for something to eat. You might choose an apple or a piece of cheese. When you are thirsty, you might pour a glass of juice or milk. Cheese and milk were once part of an animal. An apple and juice are plant products. You decide what kind of food you want to eat and what you want to drink. You may decide that you will eat only plant products or that you want to eat all kinds of food.

You have other needs as well. You need a place to live and a family to take care of you. You need clean air to breathe and clean water to drink. You need food energy to keep warm and to power all the activities your body does. You use that energy to move, to breathe, to repair body parts, and to stay warm. You are even using energy while you sleep!

Humans, like all other animals, are consumers that have needs that must be met if they are to survive. You have a digestive system that breaks down food into materials that your body can use. You have a circulatory system with a heart that pumps the blood in your blood vessels. Your blood delivers needed materials so that your body can grow larger and repair itself. Like other consumers, all of the food energy that humans use once came from the sun. Even though humans cannot perform photosynthesis, the energy in their food came from a plant at some point. That plant got its energy from the sun.

You are one of the living parts that make up the ecosystem where you live. You interact with the other living things and with the nonliving things in your ecosystem.

What Is the Role of Consumers in an Ecosystem?

1. Consumers Eat Other Organisms   Consumers are the organisms in an ecosystem that eat other organisms. Unlike producers, most consumers cannot make their own food, so they eat other organisms. This food provides them with the energy and matter they need for growth, repair, movement, and everything else they do.

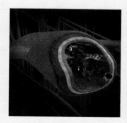

2. Digestion Breaks Down Food to Release Energy   When consumers eat food, their bodies must break it down before they can use it. Many consumers have digestive systems that mash up food and produce juices that break it down. They also have circulatory systems that move the digested food throughout their bodies.

3. Consumers Store Excess Food   Consumers need to be able to store extra food so they have energy and matter available when they are unable to eat. Many consumers store food as sugar in their blood for short periods of time. They often also store food as fat for long periods of time. Animals like birds use these reserves during migration.

4. Consumers Produce Wastes   A consumer cannot digest all parts of its food, so solid wastes are left behind. Other wastes, like the gas carbon dioxide, are produced as an organism uses its stored energy. Many animals get rid of this waste by breathing. All of these wastes are deposited into the environment and become nonliving parts of their ecosystems.

5. Humans Are Consumers   Like all animals, humans are consumers. Humans must find and eat food, since they cannot make food like plants can. The human body digests food and breaks it down so its energy and matter can be used. Humans use this energy for everything their bodies do.

Dropping Clues

Wild animals tend to avoid humans, but sometimes humans want to know what animals are nearby. One way to identify which animals are present is to look for what they leave behind. And what do all animals leave behind? Waste!

That's right! One way to track animals is by their droppings—also known as scat or pellets. Scientists, park rangers, and hikers in search of clues that animals are nearby commonly check for animal droppings. They can use scat to identify wild animals, when they passed by, and even how many live in an area! You may want to do this in order to learn about animal behavior. You may need to know if there are pests around. Or you may want to know what dangerous animals are in the area so that you can take extra precautions to stay safe.

One of the first things to know is not to touch droppings with your bare hands. After all, waste is anything an animal's body needs to get rid of. This often includes bacteria and viruses that can cause disease. Touching droppings or even breathing their dust might transmit those diseases to you. If you need or want to pick up droppings to study them, first learn how to do so safely from a guide or teacher.

Many people can use animal droppings to identify animals that live in or have passed by an area. Rabbit droppings like the ones shown are a sign that a rabbit has passed by recently.

Deer are herbivores that leave pellet droppings. Deer pellet droppings are oval-shaped, tend to be smooth, and are dark brown to black in color.

Herbivores Around Town

Even the animals living in a city leave droppings that can help you identify them. There are millions of different species of animals in the world, many of which live in cities.

Many of the wild animals you will see in a city or surrounding areas are herbivores. Herbivores are consumers that mainly, or only, eat plants. Often, whatever an animal eats does not get completely digested, so some plant pieces come out in their waste. Also, many plant eaters leave piles of small droppings called pellets. This means that a pile of small pellets with plant pieces is a clue that you have found herbivore droppings.

Mice, rabbits, and deer leave pellet droppings. All are common in cities and surrounding areas. Rodents such as mice have very small, tube-shaped droppings. Rodent droppings inside a building are a safety hazard, so it is good to be able to recognize them. In a park you won't always spot rodent droppings because they are so small. However, rabbit and deer droppings are common around towns and easy to spot.

Rabbits and deer leave pellet droppings that are similar in size, often about 1 cm (0.4 in) across. You can spot some differences between them, though. Rabbit droppings are round and have a rough texture and brown color. Deer droppings are more oval-shaped, and they tend to be smooth and have a dark brown to black color.

Carnivore scat often contains bits of bones and fur from the animals that the carnivore ate. Scat from wolves contains bits of fur from the animals they ate.

Carnivores in the Wild

If you live in or travel to someplace far from a city, you may be in places that carnivores live. For example, carnivores such as foxes, wolves, and mountain lions live in the wilder lands of forests and mountains. Most wild animals avoid humans, so you usually do not encounter them. But you still want to know if a mountain lion is nearby!

Animal droppings are often called scat. Since few carnivores are likely to be in a city, a nature center guide may show you models or pictures of scat. Your guide may also tell you ways to recognize scat in the wild.

Carnivores are consumers that mostly eat other animals for food. Like all animals, some of what they eat comes out in their waste. So, scat often contains bits of fur, bones, or other parts of animals the carnivore ate.

Carnivore scat comes in different shapes than the droppings of herbivores. Scat tends to occur as a few bigger, lumpy pieces. Also, the size of scat is related to the size of the animal that makes it. For example, wolves are much larger than foxes. So, as you may expect, wolf scat is usually bigger than fox scat.

Most predators, such as wolves, claim a territory. A *territory* is an area of land that an animal defends against other animals like it. Often animals do this to protect food sources. Many animals that have a territory use their scat and other waste to mark its boundaries. So, scientists may study and map scat to learn about animal territories.

Omnivores Here and There

Omnivores are consumers that can eat both plants and animals. Some animals that you may think of as meat eaters are actually omnivores. These include bears and some kinds of foxes, which are also wild animals that you are not as likely to see in or near a city.

Most omnivores can live in many places because they can eat so many different kinds of foods. For example, raccoons, skunks, and coyotes are common both in the wild and near places people live. Raccoons do well in several kinds of ecosystems, such as near ponds and in forests. You may also find them digging in your trash cans. So, you may find raccoon droppings in a city nature center or park.

Like all other animals, some of what an omnivore eats may end up in its droppings. Carnivore scat often has pieces of animals in it, and herbivore droppings have plant pieces. So, you can probably predict what droppings from a bear or other omnivore may contain. If you guess that bear scat can have both animal parts and berry bits in it, you would be right.

So, now you know a little bit more about animal waste. You know an animal's droppings tell you what it eats. You can figure out if the droppings belong to an herbivore, carnivore, or omnivore. You may also be able to guess what size the animal was. And, the next time you go to a park or nature center, impress your friends and family with all you know about animal droppings!

Omnivore droppings contain both animal and plant pieces. Droppings from bears contain bits of berries as well as animal parts like fish bones.

What Is the Role of Decomposers in an Ecosystem?

Science Vocabulary

bacteria

compost

decomposer

fungi

Mushrooms are a common sight in many forests. The mushrooms you see here are the reproductive structures of a fungus that is living inside the dead tree and using it for food. This fungus is one type of decomposer. Decomposers are an important part of ecosystems. By breaking down dead organisms, decomposers recycle matter so it can be used again. This is one important way that the living and nonliving parts of an ecosystem interact.

NGSS

5-LS2-1. Develop a model to describe the movement of matter among plants, animals, decomposers, and the environment.

LS2.A. The food of almost any kind of animal can be traced back to plants. Organisms are related in food webs in which some animals eat plants for food and other animals eat the animals that eat plants. Some organisms, such as fungi and bacteria, break down dead organisms (both plants or plants parts and animals) and therefore operate as "decomposers." Decomposition eventually restores (recycles) some materials back to the soil. Organisms can survive only in environments in which their particular needs are met. A healthy ecosystem is one in which multiple species of different types are each able to meet their needs in a relatively stable web of life. Newly introduced species can damage the balance of an ecosystem.

LS2.B. Matter cycles between the air and soil and among plants, animals, and microbes as these organisms live and die. Organisms obtain gases, and water, from the environment, and release waste matter (gas, liquid, or solid) back into the environment.

Systems and System Models
A system can be described in terms of its components and their interactions.

Developing and Using Models

1. Some Organisms Are Decomposers

A tree falls in a forest and lies on the forest floor. At first, it still looks like a fallen tree. But within a few years, its leaves and bark fall off. After many years, all that will remain is a patch of rich soil. Decomposers will have done their job.

You know that producers make their own food and consumers eat other organisms for food. Some organisms do not make their own food or eat other living organisms. These organisms are *decomposers*. A **decomposer** is an organism that breaks down dead organisms and their wastes. They use matter from dead plants, dead animals, and their wastes to live and grow. The decomposers that change a fallen tree into soil get matter and energy from the dead tree.

Many of the decomposers in an ecosystem are types of *fungi* or *bacteria*. **Fungi** are one group of living things that are neither plant nor animal. Some fungi are large, such as those that produce mushrooms growing on logs. Other fungi, such as yeast, are too small to be seen without a microscope. Some types of bacteria are decomposers, too. **Bacteria** are one group of organisms that are too small to be seen without a microscope. Soil contains huge numbers of bacteria.

Other kinds of organisms work with these fungi and bacteria to break down dead organisms and their wastes. Earthworms live in soil. They eat dead leaves and chunks of dead material and wastes found there. Some kinds of flies and beetles find dead animals lying above the soil. When they eat the dead animals, these invertebrates use the dead animal as a source of matter and energy.

Soil contains types of fungi and bacteria that use matter from dead plants and animals to live and grow. Earthworms also live in soil and work with these fungi and bacteria to break down dead materials and wastes.

Some fungi release digestive juices into the dead material they grow inside of. The material is broken down into simple materials that are absorbed by the fungus.

2. Decomposers Recycle Matter

Have you ever seen a clump of mushrooms growing in a forest area? Some of these clumps were probably growing out of a dead stump or log. The dead material is food for the fungus that produced the mushrooms.

Fungi Digest Their Food

Decomposers break down dead material and wastes into simple materials. They get the energy and matter needed to survive, grow, and complete their life cycles by decomposing these once-living things.

How do you think fungi digest food? They are not plants, so they do not make their own food. They do not have mouths, so they do not swallow food. Instead, fungi make juices that digest dead material. These juices are like the ones inside your digestive system! Typical fungi release the juices into the dead material they are growing in, and the dead material is broken down into simple materials. Then the simple materials are taken into the fungus, which gets the matter and energy it needs to survive from them.

However, a fungus cannot take in all the matter it digests. Some of the leftover matter enters the air and soil. This matter becomes a nonliving part of the ecosystem.

Decomposers Are Nature's Recyclers

Have you ever collected kitchen wastes for a garden? Fruit and vegetable scraps and other materials are added to a pile with soil. The bits and scraps of food are recycled into material that can be added to garden soil.

In the same way, decomposers recycle materials in an ecosystem. If decomposers did not recycle the materials used in an ecosystem, new organisms could not use them.

Without decomposers, none of the living things that die would break down. They and their wastes would pile up. Decomposers prevent this matter from piling up because they break it down. As they break down wastes, they also recycle the materials in waste matter. For example, a fungus that breaks down a dead tree returns the tree's matter to the air and soil. The matter is then taken up by grass and used to live and grow. The grass, in turn, may become food for deer. When the deer dies, decomposers will eat it and return that material to the soil and air. Thus, the cycle of life in an ecosystem continues.

You have read that large amounts of dead leaves and plant material fall onto the forest floor in a rainforest ecosystem. Many kinds of fungi, bacteria, and worms live on and in the forest soil because they like the hot, moist climate of a tropical rainforest. Worms break the large pieces of dead leaves and plants into tiny pieces as they feed. Then bacteria and fungi break down the tiny pieces to form simple materials that are taken up by the many plants that grow in the rainforest. All of these organisms recycle a lot of materials very quickly. The large amounts of recycled matter allow the rapid growth of plants in a rainforest.

Notice the small holes in this leaf lying on a rainforest floor. Decomposers are recycling the matter in the dead leaf. Then this matter can be taken up by rainforest plants.

3. Some Decomposers Can Store Excess Food

Have you ever left food like bread or a ripe piece of fruit out on the counter for a week? What did it look like when you came back? Most likely, it had molds growing on it. *Molds* are a group of small fungi that get energy by breaking down food. How do you think decomposers like molds store energy when they cannot find food?

You have learned that many consumers store excess food as both sugar and fat. Animals store food as sugar for short periods of time. They store food as fat for when they need energy over long periods of time, like when birds migrate. You have also learned that producers store excess food in the form of starch. Starch is stored in the roots and stems of plants.

Many decomposers also store food, at least for short periods of time. Fungi, such as molds, store excess food as sugar, just as animals do. However, fungi do not store food as fat.

Bacteria have no way to store excess food. To stay active, they have to live in an environment where they are surrounded by food sources. If there are not enough dead materials and wastes to break down, bacteria may die or become dormant. An organism that is *dormant* is still alive but is not growing or developing. When the environment has what the bacteria need, they can become active again.

Molds are a group of fungi that act as decomposers. These mold organisms are growing and getting energy from the orange they are living on. Excess food is stored in the molds as sugar.

When decomposers start digesting these fallen apples, they will return some substances to the soil. Those substances will be used by the apple trees to grow again the next season.

4. Decomposers Produce Wastes

It might seem surprising that decomposers—organisms that clean up wastes—also produce wastes of their own. But they do. All living things produce wastes.

Decomposers produce many of the same kinds of wastes that other organisms that eat food do. They produce carbon dioxide gas when they break down food to release energy. They produce wastes from the food they digest. They produce waste materials as they move and grow. When the decomposer dies, its once-living material becomes waste. All these wastes are released into the air, soil, and water of an ecosystem, where they will be available for use by other living things.

Wastes from decomposing matter include nutrients that plants need to grow. Plants take up these nutrients through their roots, from within the soil. They use them as building materials and to stay healthy. When decomposers break down dead organisms, they return many of these substances as wastes to the soil. Plants growing in the soil can use them again.

Several gases are made when decomposers break down matter. Carbon dioxide is released into the air. Carbon dioxide will be used by plants to make food by photosynthesis. Other gases are more harmful to the environment. Methane, for example, is another gas made by some bacteria when they break down dead material. Methane can be dangerous. It is poisonous to most other organisms and can even be lit on fire!

Kitchen waste, like egg shells and banana peels, can go in a compost pile. A compost pile alternates layers of plant matter with layers of soil. Water is added, and the decomposers in the soil break down the plant matter.

5. Humans Can Help to Decompose Wastes

Even though you are not a decomposer, you can help to decompose some wastes that your family usually puts out as garbage. By making a compost pile in your backyard or at your school, you help build an ecosystem that decomposers live in to break down some of your wastes. It is also a good way to make soil full of substances that plants need to grow.

Compost is a mixture of soil and decaying matter that provides the materials that plants need. If kitchen and yard wastes were not composted, they would end up in a landfill, where their nutrients cannot easily be used by plants.

A compost pile is a system with multiple layers of soil and plant matter that will decay. It also has decomposers and each of its parts interact to break down materials. Decomposers in the soil break down the plant matter. Adding water will keep it moist. The compost pile should be stirred with a shovel or pitchfork often. Earthworms can also help to stir the pile and break down materials.

Only plant and some animal matter should be added to a compost pile. Grass clippings, fruit and vegetable peels, leaves, eggshells, coffee grounds, and shredded newspaper all produce good compost. However, meat scraps do not. As the scraps decay, simple materials that plants need are produced. When the compost is finished breaking down, you can mix it with garden soil to grow vegetables and flowers. The plants will grow well in the rich soil. When humans make compost, they take advantage of natural processes to help return matter to their ecosystem.

What Is the Role of Decomposers in an Ecosystem?

1. Some Organisms Are Decomposers   Decomposers are organisms in ecosystems that get energy and matter by breaking down dead organisms. Many kinds of fungi and bacteria are decomposers. Some kinds of worms, flies, and beetles also help break down once-living materials.

2. Decomposers Recycle Matter   When decomposers break down dead organisms, they return their matter to the air and soil. This allows living organisms in that ecosystem to use that matter to continue to grow. Fungi that are decomposers recycle matter when they release digestive juices from their bodies into the dead materials around them.

3. Some Decomposers Can Store Excess Food   Some decomposers can store the food they eat as sugar. However, other decomposers cannot store food at all. To stay active, many bacteria must always be in an environment where they can take in food. If they cannot, the bacteria may go into a resting state or die.

4. Decomposers Produce Wastes   Decomposers get the matter that they need to survive from other organisms' wastes, but they also produce wastes of their own. Their wastes help to return matter to the air and soil of their ecosystem. Many of these waste substances are nutrients that plants need to grow.

5. Humans Can Help to Decompose Wastes   Humans can build compost piles to help decompose kitchen and yard wastes. The compost piles provide an environment that is good for many decomposers. Compost piles help return matter to ecosystems and produce rich soil that helps humans grow plants.

Decomposers to the Rescue

In March of 1989, the oil tanker *Exxon Valdez* was on its way to California when it hit an underwater reef. Millions of gallons of crude oil spilled into the clear waters of Prince William Sound in Alaska. How did decomposers come to the rescue?

Prince William Sound is located in a remote part of Alaska. Visitors can reach it only by helicopter, plane, or boat. The Sound is a wildlife paradise that is home to salmon, sea otters, seals, and seabirds.

After the wreck of the *Exxon Valdez*, environmental workers quickly realized that cleaning up the oil spill would be difficult. Not only did globs of sticky oil cover the sandy and rocky beaches of Prince William Sound, but thousands of seabirds, mammals, and other animals had been killed or severely injured. When feathers become coated with oil, birds cannot fly or swim. They are no longer waterproof, and they can drown. Feathers and fur also insulate an animal and keep it warm. So, an oil-coated animal can quickly freeze in Alaska's winter climate.

These workers are trying to clean up the oil spill by spraying oil-covered surfaces with steam. The method did not work well and was soon stopped.

As volunteers began to clean the oil-coated animals, government and industry workers tried to clean oil from the beaches and water. First, they used helicopters to spray a special mixture on the oil to try to dissolve it, but this did not work. Next, they set fire to the oil. This helped burn off some of the oil but a lot still remained. Bad weather forced the workers to stop the burning. They tried other methods such as using steam to clean rock surfaces. They all failed. It looked like they would need a new clean-up method.

Scientists grew bacteria that could break down oil in a lab. The scientists found that the bacteria grew faster when they added nitrogen fertilizer. Nitrogen is a nutrient that helps bacteria grow.

Bioremediation, a New Clean-up Method

The clean-up method that finally worked was bioremediation. *Bioremediation* is a process that uses decomposers and other living things to remove pollutants from an environment. Decomposers such as fungi and bacteria can come to the rescue when they are used for bioremediation. They can also clean up some toxic wastes produced by mining and factories.

In an ecosystem, bacteria, fungi, and other decomposers are constantly at work breaking down once-living material. Decomposers can break down and get energy from many different substances. Some materials, such as dead plant and animal matter, are found naturally in an environment. Other materials are not found naturally in most environments. Pollutants such as crude oil and toxic factory wastes are examples. But some decomposers have been found to thrive on such substances.

After the oil spill, engineers and scientists studied different bacteria and found a pollution-eating bacteria. The scientists found that adding nitrogen fertilizer, which provided extra nutrients, caused the bacteria to grow faster. The bacteria could then break down even more of the pollutant. Workers in Prince William Sound sprayed the oil slick with a mixture of nitrogen fertilizer and bacteria that could break down oil. Within a few days, the oil began to break down. Today, much of it is gone, but more oil still remains. Oil-eating bacteria still live on the beaches and are still hard at work continuing the cleanup.

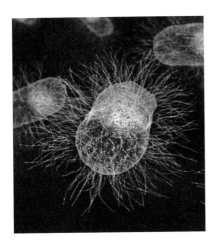

These bacteria can break down caffeine and prevent it from polluting the environment. This is another example of bioremediation.

Decomposers Clean up Other Pollution

Decomposers can clean up other substances, too. You have probably heard of caffeine, a substance in coffee, tea, colas, chocolate, and energy drinks that can keep many people awake.

Wherever people consume caffeine, it eventually ends up in an ecosystem. A lot of caffeine in rivers, lakes, and the ocean becomes a pollutant. How can decomposers help solve this problem? Scientists have found some kinds of bacteria and yeasts that naturally use caffeine as food. As they use the caffeine to grow, it is broken down into harmless substances. Some cities are already using these decomposers to treat wastewater. They can reduce the amount of caffeine to 1/20th of what it was before treatment!

Caffeine can also be a pollutant where coffee is grown. Growing and producing coffee beans leaves behind a lot of waste with caffeine and other pollutants. This waste is often dumped in rivers where it kills fish. What if this waste could be turned from a problem into something useful?

Scientists have found bacteria and fungi that live where coffee plants grow. There are high levels of caffeine in the environment, but the bacteria and fungi break it down. Scientists studying these decomposers hope to find ways to break down the caffeine in the huge amounts of coffee waste. Then the material could be used to feed animals instead of polluting the environment!

Coffee beans at the centers of these fruits are used to make coffee. The rest is usually thrown away. Scientists are working on ways to use decomposers to make the waste useful.

A Bioremediation Double Bonus

Bacteria can be incredibly helpful. Of course, the bacteria that can clean up toxic pollutants are valuable agents for environmental cleanup. There are also some bacteria that can generate electricity. Some of these powerhouse decomposers produce electricity from carbon dioxide and hydrogen gases. Others break down wastes from living things to produce electricity.

Now scientists have found a doubly helpful organism. A species of bacteria found in soil and in some factory wastes eats pollutants *and* generates electricity! These bacteria can generate enough electricity to power small electronic devices such as cell phones. The bacteria just need two things, a food source and an environment without oxygen. Then they can produce electricity 24 hours a day. When used in bioremediation, they clean up pollutants and generate power at the same time. Some cities are looking at using these bacteria in wastewater treatment plants, or factories that clean the water you use. The bacteria would help clean the water and also provide extra electricity for the plant!

Decomposers really *do* come to the rescue. They have rescued the environment many times in the past. They will continue to do so in the future. Hopefully, as long as research continues in bioremediation, scientists will discover new organisms and new ways for these organisms to help people.

Certain kinds of bacteria live in some of the most polluted environments on Earth. This photo shows water that is contaminated with oil. But bioremediation methods can help clean up environments such as this one.

How Do Matter and Energy Move in an Ecosystem?

Science Vocabulary

energy pyramid

food chain

food web

Matter and energy are always moving in an ecosystem. Matter moves in a cycle, while energy moves in one direction and is constantly being lost as heat by organisms. Food chains are models that show feeding relationships between organisms. Food webs are models that show all the different food chains of an ecosystem.

NGSS   **5-LS2-1.** Develop a model to describe the movement of matter among plants, animals, decomposers, and the environment.

LS2.A. The food of almost any kind of animal can be traced back to plants. Organisms are related in food webs in which some animals eat plants for food and other animals eat the animals that eat plants. Some organisms, such as fungi and bacteria, break down dead organisms (both plants or plants parts and animals) and therefore operate as "decomposers." Decomposition eventually restores (recycles) some materials back to the soil. Organisms can survive only in environments in which their particular needs are met. A healthy ecosystem is one in which multiple species of different types are each able to meet their needs in a relatively stable web of life. Newly introduced species can damage the balance of an ecosystem.

LS2.B. Matter cycles between the air and soil and among plants, animals, and microbes as these organisms live and die. Organisms obtain gases, and water, from the environment, and release waste matter (gas, liquid, or solid) back into the environment.

Systems and System Models
A system can be described in terms of its components and their interactions.

Developing and Using Models

1. Matter Remains in an Ecosystem

Recall that the matter organisms need comes from within the ecosystem. You can think of an ecosystem as a closed system. Most matter does not enter or leave the system. Instead, matter cycles among its different parts.

Living things obtain matter from their environment and release waste back into it. This matter moves in a cycle. Plants use air, water, nutrients, and sunlight to make food and grow. Some animals eat the plants and use their matter to grow. When those animals die, decomposers will grow using the matter from the animals' bodies. The decomposers release this digested matter back into the air and soil. The matter in an ecosystem is recycled.

Gases are a type of matter that moves through an ecosystem. For example, oxygen and carbon dioxide are cycled between organisms and the air. The producer in the diagram takes carbon dioxide from the air. It uses this gas and water to make sugar, releasing oxygen as waste. Then the consumer breathes in the oxygen and uses it in its body. It also eats the producer for food, represented as carbon in the diagram. The decomposer takes oxygen from the air and food from the consumer or producer. The consumer and decomposer make carbon dioxide, putting it into the air. When producers use it again, the matter is recycled.

Oxygen and carbon cycle through an ecosystem between producers, consumers, decomposers, and the air. Matter is recycled in an ecosystem.

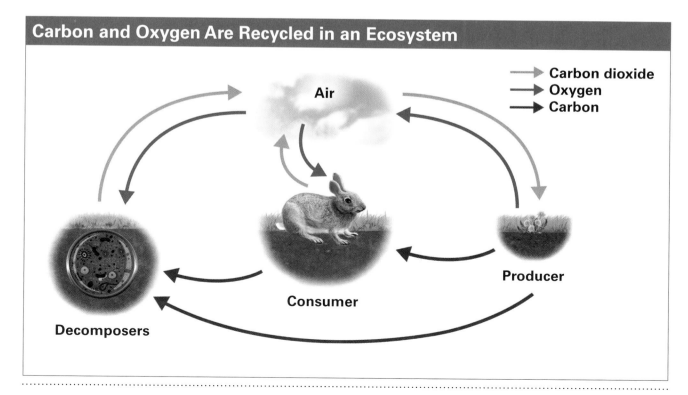

Carbon and Oxygen Are Recycled in an Ecosystem

→ Carbon dioxide
→ Oxygen
→ Carbon

Air

Consumer

Decomposers

Producer

2. Energy Is Lost from an Ecosystem

Energy enters almost all ecosystems carried by sunlight. Remember that matter cycles in an ecosystem. But unlike matter, energy moves in only one direction. It flows from the sun to producers—and from producers to consumers and decomposers. Here's an example of how energy moves through an ecosystem. Energy from light is captured by a dandelion plant during photosynthesis. The plant uses some of the captured energy to grow and make leaves. All living things use energy for their activities, and all activities produce heat. Some energy is stored in the plant's leaves as sugar. Some energy is lost as heat.

When a rabbit eats the dandelion, energy stored in the plant moves to the rabbit. But the amount of energy transferred to the rabbit is less than the amount stored by the dandelion. This is because the dandelion used some energy and lost it as heat. The rabbit is slowly losing energy as heat all the time.

Next, if the rabbit dies, decomposers will start to use the energy stored in the rabbit's body. But some energy has been lost as heat already. The decomposers will not get all the energy that the rabbit had, just like the rabbit did not get all the energy the dandelion had. Some energy is lost at each stage.

Finally, the decomposers die and their energy is lost as heat. Eventually, all the useful energy is used up. Energy moves one way in an ecosystem, not in a circle. Most of the energy is lost as heat at each stage.

Energy from the sun moves in only one direction in an ecosystem, from producers to consumers and to decomposers. All the energy is eventually lost as heat.

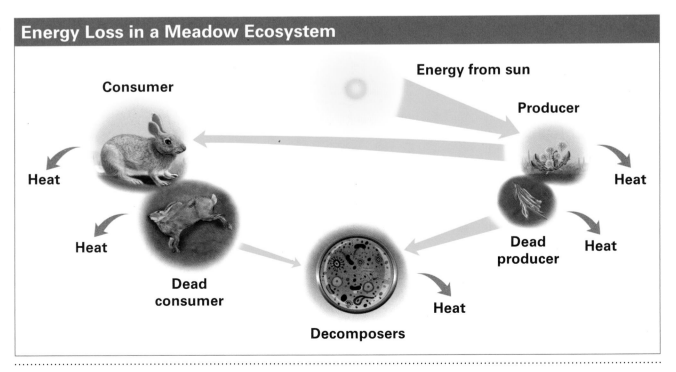

Energy Loss in a Meadow Ecosystem

Energy from sun

Consumer

Producer

Heat

Heat

Heat

Heat

Dead consumer

Dead producer

Decomposers

Heat

3. Energy Flows Through Food Chains

Think about the energy flow in the meadow ecosystem. The energy started from the sun and moved through different organisms. How do scientists know where the energy flows?

A **food chain** is a model of the path of energy through a series of organisms in an ecosystem. Mice eat grass seeds, and snakes eat mice, which are eaten by eagles. This food chain can be shown as a simple diagram. The arrows show the direction energy moves through the food chain.

$$\text{grass} \longrightarrow \text{mouse} \longrightarrow \text{snake} \longrightarrow \text{eagle}$$

A food chain always starts with a producer because they are the only organisms that can make their own food. The second organism in a food chain is always a consumer that eats the producer. These are called first stage consumers. Second stage consumers eat first stage consumers, like the snake in the food chain above. Finally, the eagle is a third stage consumer, because it eats second stage consumers.

An **energy pyramid** is a model that shows the amount of energy that is passed on at each level of a food chain. As you have learned, heat is lost at each level. So, each link of the chain receives less energy than the link before it had. Most food chains are made up of only three or four organisms. This is because so much energy is lost at each stage.

An energy pyramid shows that the bottom level, the producers, holds the most stored energy. Each level above producers holds less energy because most of the energy is lost as heat at each level.

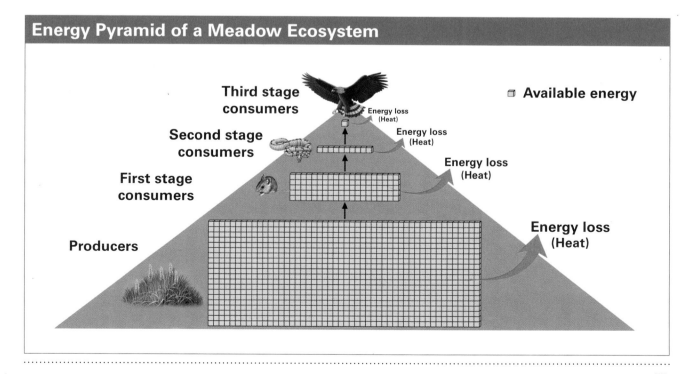

Energy Pyramid of a Meadow Ecosystem

Third stage consumers

Second stage consumers

First stage consumers

Producers

Available energy

Energy loss (Heat)

Energy loss (Heat)

Energy loss (Heat)

Energy loss (Heat)

4. Many Organisms Make up a Food Web

Do you always eat the same food? Of course not! Many organisms eat different foods, too. For this reason, feeding relationships in most ecosystems are far more complex than simple food chains.

Food Webs Have Many Connected Food Chains

Most food chains in nature overlap. Overlapping food chains form a food web. A **food web** is a model that shows the many connected food chains and feeding relationships.

In a meadow ecosystem, you may find grass and other producers, rabbits, grasshoppers, eagles, mice, foxes, and snakes. Grass uses sunlight to make food. Rabbits eat the grass. Eagles eat rabbits. What do you notice about the feeding relationships so far? They form a food chain.

However, mice and grasshoppers also eat grass. Snakes, eagles, and foxes eat mice. Eagles eat almost all the animals in the meadow. Now the food chains are a food web because several plants and animals are eaten by more than one thing. This food web is composed of several food chains that overlap. A food web shows how most consumers eat more than one kind of food and are themselves eaten by more than one kind of animal. Food webs show how energy moves through all the organisms in an ecosystem.

Most ecosystems have many food chains. The many overlapping food chains in this meadow ecosystem form its food web.

Food Web of a Meadow Ecosystem

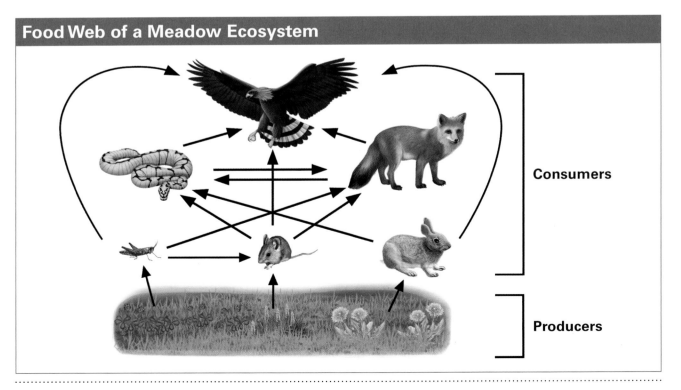

Consumers

Producers

Shark

Octopus

Manta ray

Eel

Food Webs Are Complex

Most ecosystems are very complex. Food webs usually have many different kinds of producers and consumers. For example, coral reef ecosystems can have thousands of species that meet their needs there. Most producers that live in a coral reef are different kinds of algae. Some algae live in the water, while others grow on dead corals or even *inside* living coral animals. All of these producers make food through photosynthesis.

There are also many different consumers in a coral reef. Parrotfish and some kinds of sea stars eat the coral. Manta rays swim around, filtering algae from the water. There are even more consumers that eat other consumers in a coral reef. Many octopuses, squids, and eels eat the fish. Different sharks might eat all of these animals.

A coral reef's food web is very complicated. There are many producers, many first-stage consumers, and even more higher-stage consumers. It is hard to sort out all the ways these species interact in their huge food web! So, even though energy only goes in one direction in an ecosystem, it goes through many different organisms along the way.

These are some of the organisms that make up a food web in a coral reef. Most ecosystems have many organisms living there, so their food webs are very complex.

5. Humans Are Parts of Food Chains and Food Webs

Think of some of the foods that you have eaten this week. Have you had fish or chicken? What about potatoes, lettuce, or spinach?

Humans are parts of many different food chains. When humans eat potatoes or lettuce, they are first stage consumers. When humans eat animals like chicken that eat plants, they are second stage consumers. When humans eat fish that eat other fish, such as tuna, they are third stage consumers or higher. Because no animals normally hunt humans, humans are at the top of all their food chains.

Most animals live in one ecosystem. They eat plants or animals in their own ecosystem, and their waste goes into that ecosystem. However, humans are different. They take food from many different ecosystems. Because humans can eat foods from many different ecosystems, they are part of many food webs. For example, tuna is a favorite food of many cultures around the world. Tuna is often caught in one part of the ocean and shipped around the world to feed people. Another example is chocolate. Many people around the world eat chocolate. But the plant chocolate comes from, the cacao tree, only grows in tropical ecosystems such as rainforests. So, cacao fruits are shipped to other parts of the world.

Most humans are not part of just one ecosystem. They do not spend their whole lives in a desert, a meadow, or in one part of the ocean. Instead, the whole Earth can be thought of as the ecosystem that humans live in. All of the foods humans eat can be found on Earth. And all of the waste humans make goes back to Earth.

Humans take food from different ecosystems all around the world. They are parts of many food chains and food webs.

How Do Matter and Energy Move in an Ecosystem?

1. Matter Remains in an Ecosystem   In an ecosystem, matter cycles. Producers use air, water, and sunlight to grow. Consumers eat those plants or other consumers to get matter for growth. Decomposers get matter for growth from dead producers and consumers. When decomposers die, the matter enters the air and soil, so plants can use it again.

2. Energy Is Lost from an Ecosystem   Unlike matter, energy does not cycle through an ecosystem. Instead, energy moves only one way, from the sun to producers, and on to consumers and decomposers. At each organism, most of the energy is lost as heat, so the next organism in the chain gets far less.

3. Energy Flows Through Food Chains   Food chains are models that show how energy moves in one part of an ecosystem. They demonstrate feeding relationships between species of organisms. Energy pyramids are models that show how much of the original energy is still available at each level of the food chain.

4. Many Organisms Make up a Food Web   Most kinds of plants and animals are eaten by more than one species. Food webs are models that show how all of the different food chains in an ecosystem are linked together. They show how matter and energy move throughout an entire ecosystem by tracking all of the feeding relationships among all the organisms.

5. Humans Are Parts of Food Chains and Food Webs   Humans are also parts of food chains and food webs. Which food webs humans are parts of depends on what they eat. Humans take food from many different ecosystems and are part of many food webs. The whole Earth can be thought of as the ecosystem that humans live in.

The Little Sub That Could

A tiny submarine slowly glides along the Pacific Ocean floor. Suddenly, the two scientists aboard the submarine see dark billowing clouds ahead and some unusual organisms. But sensors show that the nearby water is extremely hot. How can life exist in this harsh environment?

During this deep-sea dive in 1977, the scientists discovered a hydrothermal vent. Many vents are found in areas of the ocean floor that are pulling away from one another. When a crack forms in the floor, very hot seawater loaded with minerals pours out of the crack. When the hot water flows into the surrounding cold water, it cools down very quickly. Cooled minerals pile up around the vent opening, creating chimney-like formations. Dark black "smoke" pours out of them.

Hydrothermal vents are deep underwater and very hot, so how do scientists study them? They travel down to see them in tiny, sturdy submarines. Built in 1964, *Alvin* is one of the world's first submersible research vehicles. It is designed to carry a pilot and two scientists to study areas deep underwater. It is about 7 m (23 ft) long and nearly 4 m (12 ft) tall, and the metal sphere where the scientists sit is even smaller, almost 3 m (9 ft) wide. So, the scientists must sit very close together when they use this little submarine to explore the ocean.

Alvin is one of the world's first submersible research vehicles. Scientists aboard *Alvin* discovered the first hydrothermal vent in 1977. They have since discovered and studied many vent ecosystems.

Alvin may be small, but that does not mean it isn't helpful! *Alvin* is designed to dive as deep as 4.5 km (3 mi) under the water's surface. The submarine is made with a type of metal called titanium to keep it from being crushed by the huge pressure deep under the ocean. What else does *Alvin* need for scientists to study an ecosystem like a hydrothermal vent?

Scientific submarines let scientists study hydrothermal vent ecosystems up close. White crabs, transparent shrimp, and other strange creatures live at the base of these black smoker chimneys.

Studying a Vent Community

There is no sunlight or plant life at the bottom of the ocean. Yet, large numbers of unusual animals thrive near the vents. Red-tipped tubeworms, white crabs, blue-spotted mussels, and transparent shrimp are found nowhere else on Earth. How do scientists aboard *Alvin* study these ecosystems when there is no sunlight?

First, *Alvin*'s pilot makes the submarine dive with steel weights that make the vehicle heavier. That extra weight is left on the ocean floor when the sub needs to rise back to the surface. Each dive lasts between eight to ten hours. That way, scientists have plenty of time to study the underwater ecosystem. They take pictures and collect samples of living and nonliving things. They also study the interactions between the vent organisms and the nonliving parts of their ecosystem.

Alvin is equipped with both still cameras and video cameras. Scientists can also observe the environment with their own eyes through three round windows in the titanium sphere. But the ocean bottom is so dark, how can scientists see outside the submarine? *Alvin* carries powerful lights to light up the seafloor. *Alvin* also has two robotic arms that can manipulate instruments to collect samples or move objects. Each arm's basket can carry up to 181 kg (400 lbs) of tools and seafloor samples. Scientists can collect these samples and take them back to the surface to study them further.

Energy in a Hydrothermal Vent Community

Scientists study hydrothermal vents to answer questions about ecosystems. For instance, can the organisms in an ecosystem survive without photosynthesis? People used to think this was impossible. Plants and other organisms carry out photosynthesis using sunlight. Then animals eat the plants. Other animals and decomposers eat both plants and animals. So, all the energy in most food webs originally comes from sunlight.

But how do the animals in hydrothermal vent ecosystems get energy if no sunlight reaches their ecosystem? The answer is *chemosynthesis*, or the process of getting energy by breaking down minerals.

Alvin's scientists have collected samples of many vent animals and studied them. They had to learn how to keep the animals under conditions similar to those deep in the ocean. They discovered that the animals in a vent ecosystem cannot perform chemosynthesis. However, other organisms that live there can.

The scientists discovered huge numbers of bacteria in the mineral-rich hot water of a vent. These bacteria get energy by using chemosynthesis to break down the minerals in seawater. Vent animals depend on these bacteria for food and energy. Some vent animals, like tubeworms, cannot eat food because they have no mouths and no digestive systems. Instead, they absorb some of the food that is produced by the chemosynthetic bacteria living inside them. So, in a hydrothermal vent ecosystem, the energy comes from minerals, not the sun!

Alvin is equipped with many tools that allow scientists to study the organisms in a hydrothermal vent ecosystem. Some organisms, like these red-tipped tubeworms, absorb food produced by bacteria that live inside of them.

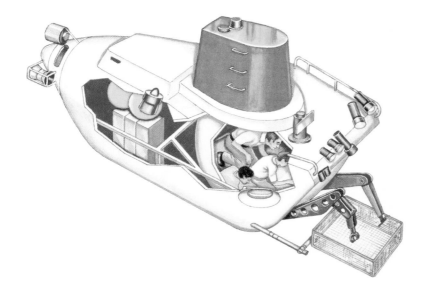

This illustration shows a cross-section of *Alvin*. Notice the scientists and pilot in the personnel sphere. During the upgrade, engineers are enlarging the sphere and making it safer and more comfortable.

Alvin's Upgrade

The more scientists study the ocean, the more they learn about ecosystems that exist deep underwater. In order to explore them, engineers are always working on building new research submersibles, and also improving old ones! For example, in 2006, engineers installed a brand new robotic arm on *Alvin*.

In 2011, the sub began undergoing a complete upgrade. Engineers worked on a new, larger, and more comfortable "personnel sphere"—the place where the passengers live and work. This new titanium metal sphere was designed to withstand greater pressures than the old sphere. It will allow *Alvin* to dive beyond its current 4,500 m (3 mi) limit.

Updated command and control systems allow *Alvin* to travel to more places more easily. Larger windows will help scientists see more of ocean ecosystems. Engineers have also installed new telephones.

As teams of engineers finish improving parts of *Alvin*, they reassemble the parts piece by piece. The engineers are also experienced submarine pilots. They have added their expertise through each part of the upgrade design process. The U.S. Navy, which owns *Alvin*, inspects every new part to make sure the new *Alvin* is safe and reliable. If you get to be the person riding *Alvin* to the bottom of the ocean to study new ecosystems, you'll agree that safety is the most important part of the upgrade!

What Makes an Ecosystem Healthy or Unhealthy?

Science Vocabulary

predator

prey

Ecosystems can be healthy or unhealthy. A healthy ecosystem meets the needs of many species of organisms. Because their needs are met, species living in a healthy ecosystem continue surviving there, and the web of life remains stable. Scientists commonly look at predator and prey relationships when they are studying ecosystem health.

NGSS

5-LS2-1. Develop a model to describe the movement of matter among plants, animals, decomposers, and the environment.

LS2.A. The food of almost any kind of animal can be traced back to plants. Organisms are related in food webs in which some animals eat plants for food and other animals eat the animals that eat plants. Some organisms, such as fungi and bacteria, break down dead organisms (both plants or plants parts and animals) and therefore operate as "decomposers." Decomposition eventually restores (recycles) some materials back to the soil. Organisms can survive only in environments in which their particular needs are met. A healthy ecosystem is one in which multiple species of different types are each able to meet their needs in a relatively stable web of life. Newly introduced species can damage the balance of an ecosystem.

Systems and System Models A system can be described in terms of its components and their interactions.

Developing and Using Models

1. Healthy Ecosystems

In an ecosystem, all the parts affect each other. Plants depend on the nonliving parts for making food, and animals depend on both plants and other animals for food. All living parts also depend on the nonliving parts for shelter, for water, and for air. A healthy ecosystem can meet the needs of all the species that are part of it.

In a healthy ecosystem, many kinds of living things can meet their needs in a web of life that is stable. Healthy ecosystems usually have many different kinds of organisms. Each one has a role to play. Producers make food, consumers eat producers or each other, and decomposers recycle the ecosystem's matter so it can be used again. Healthy ecosystems provide plenty of food and resources for many organisms. Each species in the ecosystem has enough of what it needs to continue surviving there.

Look at this simple pond food chain.

algae ⟶ tadpole ⟶ fish ⟶ turtle ⟶ heron

In this food chain, the fish, turtles, and herons capture and eat other animals for food. An animal that captures and eats other animals is a **predator**. The animal that is captured and eaten is the **prey**. The pond can stay healthy only when predator and prey numbers are balanced. If there are too few prey, the predators can starve. If there are too few predators, the number of prey can increase too much. Too many or too few of any one kind of organism destroys the balance.

In a healthy pond ecosystem, there are enough turtles and fish for herons to eat. If many turtles and fish died, however, the herons might starve if they could not find another food source.

Isle Royale is a large island in Lake Superior. Its forest ecosystem includes moose and wolves, which scientists have studied for many years.

2. A Healthy Forest Ecosystem on Isle Royale

Isle Royale is a remote island in Lake Superior, the largest of the Great Lakes. Wolves and moose make their home in its forest ecosystem. For many years, scientists have studied the relationship between wolves and moose on Isle Royale. This was easily done because almost no animals could enter or leave the island. So, it is a natural ecological experiment!

Studying the predators and their prey shows the importance of balance an ecosystem. Wolves are predators, and moose are their prey. On Isle Royale, wolves are the only predator of moose, and moose are the only prey for the wolves. When there are plenty of moose, the wolves have enough to eat. The wolves can survive and raise offspring.

When scientists first began to study the moose and wolves on the island, the ecosystem was healthy. Moose on the island ate fir, aspen, and birch trees. There was enough rain and good growing conditions, so the trees grew quickly and were plentiful. Even though the number of moose changed from year to year, there were still a healthy number of them. When the moose have enough to eat, they can reproduce more easily. A few more moose meant that wolves had a plentiful food supply. The forest ecosystem on Isle Royale was in balance and was healthy.

Moose are large animals that are prey for wolves. When the moose and wolf numbers are balanced, the Isle Royale ecosystem is healthy.

3. Unhealthy Ecosystems

Here is the same pond food chain you saw earlier.

> algae ⟶ tadpole ⟶ fish ⟶ turtle ⟶ heron

What changes in the pond ecosystem might cause the food chain to change?

Suppose too many algae grow in the pond. This can happen if too many nutrients enter the pond. When the algae start to die, bacteria in the pond water decompose them. The process of decay requires oxygen, and the bacteria use up most of the oxygen in the water when they decompose the algae. Fish need oxygen to survive. With less oxygen in the water, fish start to die.

Suppose many of the fish die. The turtles will have less to eat, and some will starve. If many turtles in this food chain die, what will happen to the herons that eat the turtles and fish? They might die too because they no longer have enough to eat. Fewer herons means that less turtles will get eaten. So, more will live to have offspring. This might increase the number of turtles in the pond. An increase in turtles may cause more fish to die again as the fish are eaten.

An ecosystem can be in trouble if even one kind of living thing dies out or becomes too common. In the above example, all the organisms have been affected by the growth of algae. The numbers of predators and prey in the pond are no longer balanced or stable. The number of species in the pond may decrease as some of those that are left cannot meet their needs. This pond ecosystem has become unhealthy.

Sometimes there can be a rapid growth of algae in a pond. When bacteria decompose the algae, oxygen in the water is used up. Fish that depend on this oxygen may die, and the ecosystem may become unhealthy.

Wolves like this one live on Isle Royale. If a lot of moose die, these wolves would starve since they cannot find enough other food, and the ecosystem becomes unhealthy.

4. An Unhealthy Forest Ecosystem on Isle Royale

Think back to the island of Isle Royale. Over the years, the Isle Royale ecosystem changed. You have seen how the numbers of organisms can change and become unbalanced when changes occur in an ecosystem. How did Isle Royale change? What caused it to become unhealthy?

Scientists observed that for a number of years, there were fewer moose than usual. When there are fewer moose, the wolves have less food and some die. Scientists also noted that the weather at Isle Royale during this time was warmer than usual. Warm weather caused an increase in the number of ticks, small organisms that suck blood. Ticks carry bacteria that cause disease in moose. The interaction between the weather and the ticks led to the death of many moose. Many wolves then died because they had less food. With fewer predators, the number of moose increased quickly.

Soon, there was a winter that was the coldest and snowiest in over a century. Moose had little to eat and many died. At first, the wolves fed on starving moose. Then the number of wolves began to decrease.

You can see how nonliving parts of an ecosystem cause changes in the living parts. Changes in weather often cause the balance between predators and prey to change, like when the number of ticks increased in hot weather. The balance is still changing on Isle Royale. Ecologists keep studying ecosystems to understand what makes them healthy or unhealthy.

What Makes an Ecosystem Healthy or Unhealthy?

1. Healthy Ecosystems   Healthy ecosystems are ones in which many different kinds of organisms can meet their needs. The web of life in a healthy ecosystem is stable. That means most of the species living there can continue to live there for a long time. Healthy ecosystems usually also have balanced predator and prey relationships.

2. A Healthy Forest Ecosystem on Isle Royale   Isle Royale is a huge island in Lake Superior. The island's isolation makes it a great ecological laboratory. Scientists study groups of wolves and moose that live on the island because they have an interesting predator and prey relationship. When the Isle Royale ecosystem is healthy, the numbers of wolves and moose are balanced.

3. Unhealthy Ecosystems   Ecosystems can be unhealthy if there are too many or too few of one type of organism. Occasionally too much algae grows in ponds or lakes. When many algae grow and then die, it can cause fish and other organisms to die. This upsets the ecosystem's balance. These kinds of changes can affect organisms further along the food chain as well.

4. An Unhealthy Forest Ecosystem on Isle Royale   Scientists observing Isle Royale have seen shifts in the health of the ecosystem. In one example, unusually warm weather conditions caused a problem. If the weather is very warm, more ticks are born, which kill the moose. With fewer moose, the wolves starved to death, and the animals were not in a stable balance.

The Ecosystem Inside You

Okay microscopic eco-tourists, all aboard for a trip in and around the human body! You will pass through several regions of the body, each with its own unique living and nonliving parts. Ready? Let's go!

You can think of the human body as an ecosystem with living and nonliving parts that interact. Each area of the body is a habitat to the organisms that live there. They are able to meet their needs because each habitat has its own unique environmental conditions.

Your tour starts outside the body. The first thing you see is the skin, the body's covering. Notice that different parts of the skin have different environmental conditions. Skin on the arms and legs is dry, but skin on the scalp, neck, and face is oily. As the conditions of the skin change from day to day, the kinds and numbers of of organisms living there also change.

Some of these organisms are blood suckers. See how head lice prefer the dark, oily environment found on the scalp. They poke tiny holes in the soft, moist skin of the scalp and feed on human blood. Fleas and bedbugs are not normal inhabitants of human skin but they can be temporary visitors there. Like lice, they get food and energy by sucking blood.

The pink animals in the photo are eyelash mites. They live at the base of hairs in the eyelashes and eyebrows. The mites get energy by eating dead skin and by sucking food from hair roots.

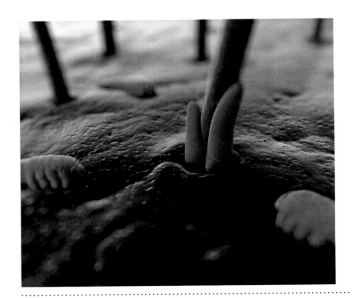

Next on your tour, you will see tiny pieces of dead skin piled up at the base of the eyelashes and eyebrows. Small, eight-legged eyelash mites find shelter and food here. They get food energy by eating dead skin and sucking food from hair roots.

Look at all the bacteria! Most are harmless. They help to keep their skin habitat healthy by fighting harmful bacteria over food. The harmless bacteria usually win. They are better adapted to living here.

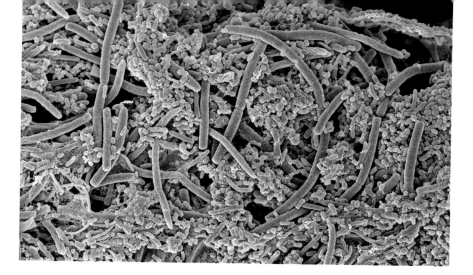

Bacteria in the human mouth produce a kind of glue that forms dental plaque. The bacteria seen here as green, purple, and blue rods use the plaque they make to hold themselves in place.

Into the Mouth

Now our tour of the body moves into the mouth. Put on your raincoats and grab flashlights, because this habitat is much darker, warmer, and wetter than the skin habitat. The teeth are covered with a thick, sticky layer of bacteria. These organisms are adapted to living in the moist, dark mouth. The bacteria that live on teeth get energy by breaking down the sugars present in the mouth. They produce a kind of glue that forms dental plaque. Even if you brush regularly, some bacteria will still be there.

Did you know that scientists have found that each person has a unique combination of mouth and throat bacteria? It's true, but the numbers and kinds of bacteria change as environmental conditions change. They change according to what a person eats and drinks. Drinking a sugary drink increases the number of sugar-eating bacteria that break down the sugar in the mouth. Eating a fatty meal encourages the growth of bacteria that can break down the fat to get energy.

You will notice some fungi called yeasts living on the tongue. Fungi are another group of organisms, most of which are larger than bacteria. Many fungi are decomposers, and these fungi break down sugar in the mouth for energy. They like a habitat that is warm, dark, and has plenty of available food. Yeasts are often present in the mouths of healthy people. But illnesses, stress, or medicine can change conditions in the mouth. Then yeasts might grow out of control, causing mouth infections. Thank goodness we don't have to worry about that today!

Inside the Digestive System

This tour will spend a lot of time in the digestive system because there is so much to see. First we will enter the stomach. The stomach's environment is very sour, like lemon juice. This sourness is how the stomach protects itself from microscopic invaders. The sourness kills or disables most of the bacteria and viruses that a person might swallow. But occasionally, some of these make it through, and the bad ones can make you sick. Hold on tight—it is about to get bumpy. That is because the stomach is in constant motion as it churns and digests food. Whew, what a ride!

As you leave the stomach and enter the small and large intestines, the environment becomes much less sour. Many more organisms can live here in the intestinal habitat. They use partially digested food for energy. Warm temperatures and plenty of water also help them meet their needs.

Even worms and tiny animal-like organisms called *protozoans* can live in the intestines. They get inside the body through the skin or when a person eats undercooked meat or drinks water containing the eggs of these organisms. Pinworms and tapeworms are examples of worms that can live here. They latch onto the creased inside walls of the intestine, where they find shelter. Most intestinal worms get energy by eating nutrients found in digested food.

This tapeworm is living inside the human intestine. It gets energy by eating some of the partially digested food.

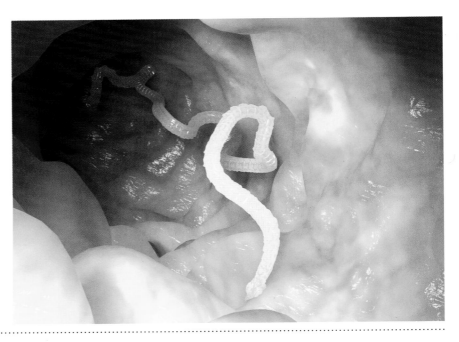

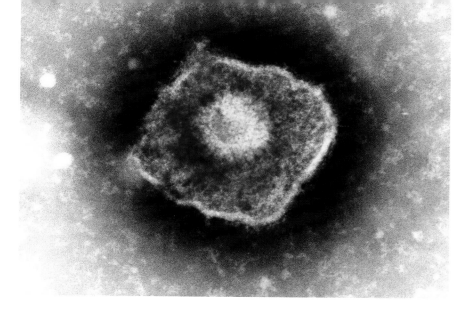

Scientists have taken photographs of the virus that causes chicken pox. It may be hard to believe, but these tiny structures harm the nerves in the skin and cause an itchy rash.

Side Trips Through the Body

I think that we have time to take a few side trips to other habitats in the body before you leave. How does that sound? First we will go to the nervous system to see if we can find anything. Surely, organisms and viruses can't reside inside nerves and the brain, can they? Actually, yes, they can!

Chicken pox is a contagious childhood disease that is caused by a virus. The virus gets into the nerves in the skin and causes an itchy rash. Once the rash heals, the virus may stay in the body for years.

Bacteria, fungi, and protozoans also can cause diseases of the nervous system. The organism that causes malaria is a protozoan. It lives in many parts of the body, including the brain. Malaria organisms get all the oxygen and food they need from their host's blood. No wonder they like to live *in* blood!

Let's make a final side trip to the habitat between the toes. There we will see the athlete's foot fungus that can fasten onto bare feet in showers. This fungus gets under the toenails and can invade other parts of the skin that are warm and moist.

You have now concluded your tour of the human body. You have visited habitats that have very different environmental conditions and different living things. If you take the tour on another day, you will see different organisms because the ecosystem within humans is always changing. Please watch your feet as you exit the feet. You have been great, folks—please come again!

How Do Ecosystems Change?

Science Vocabulary

disturbance

succession

Forest fires are one way that forest ecosystems can change. A forest fire is a very fast change. But ecosystems can also change slowly, as they do from season to season and from year to year. All ecosystems change over time. These ecosystem changes can affect what species are able to live there, and how they interact with each other and their environment.

NGSS

5-LS2-1. Develop a model to describe the movement of matter among plants, animals, decomposers, and the environment.

LS2.A. The food of almost any kind of animal can be traced back to plants. Organisms are related in food webs in which some animals eat plants for food and other animals eat the animals that eat plants. Some organisms, such as fungi and bacteria, break down dead organisms (both plants or plants parts and animals) and therefore operate as "decomposers." Decomposition eventually restores (recycles) some materials back to the soil. Organisms can survive only in environments in which their particular needs are met. A healthy ecosystem is one in which multiple species of different types are each able to meet their needs in a relatively stable web of life. Newly introduced species can damage the balance of an ecosystem.

Systems and System Models A system can be described in terms of its components and their interactions.

Developing and Using Models

1. Ecosystems Can Change

In the 1920s, parts of the American prairies changed dramatically. People plowed huge areas of thick, wild grass, tilling the soil to plant farm crops. Then a severe drought came in the 1930s and lasted many years. The bare, exposed soil crumbled to dust and blew away in huge dust storms. Many people had to leave the area. Fortunately, most of the prairie has since recovered.

Natural changes, ones that do not involve people, happen to ecosystems often. Even one year without rain can cause many plants to die. Animals that need the plants for food and shelter may die or leave as their food decreases and their needs are no longer met. The ecosystem may return to its former state if enough rain falls again.

All ecosystems change over time. Some changes happen very slowly. A drought such as the one during the 1930s may take many years to cause damage. Other changes happen quickly. For example, a flood can wash away soil and kill the plants that grow there. When a volcano erupts, changes occur in minutes or days.

People change ecosystems, too. They cut down trees in which birds build nests. The birds' need for shelter is no longer met. People build dams across rivers for power. River ecosystems change as a result of less water flow below the dam and the flooding of the area above the dam. Fewer species may be able to survive because the flow of water has changed. When people change ecosystems, they change the flows of matter and energy in the ecosystems as well.

All ecosystems change, with and without the involvement of people. In the 1930s, dust storms like this one covered the North American prairies. Dust storms can be caused by long droughts and bad farming practices.

Lichens are often the first producers to grow after soil is destroyed in an ecosystem.

This diagram shows how succession might happen in a forest after a fire. The first species to grow are grasses and wildflowers. Then shrubs and small trees might grow, followed by large trees.

2. Disturbance Leads to Succession

Sometimes ecosystems change rapidly, but the effects can last a long time. An event that changes an ecosystem for a long period of time is called a **disturbance**. These changes can be caused by humans or by natural processes.

When Mount St. Helens in Washington state erupted in 1980, the area around the mountain was covered with a thick layer of ash. Soil was buried and plant and animal life was destroyed. Years later, the area began to change back. Small plants were growing again, flowers were blooming, insects were feeding on the plants, and small animals had returned.

The changes that take place in an ecosystem after a disturbance are called **succession**. Succession is a slow process as species replace one another in the changing landscape. This occurs in one direction, from few species of small organisms to many organisms of all sizes.

Some Changes Destroy Soil

Some changes can cover or remove most of the soil in an ecosystem. For instance, some volcanic eruptions can cover everything around them in fresh lava. Glaciers scrape Earth's surface down to bare rock. When this happens, succession is very slow because new soil must be formed. The first species to grow after the disturbance are called *pioneer species*. Lichens are often pioneer species. They grow in tiny cracks in the rock and slowly help form new soil.

Ecosystem Succession

| Ecosystem disturbance | 1 week–3 years | Pioneer species | 3–50 years | Intermediate species | 50–1,000 years | Climax species |

Some Changes Do Not Destroy Soil

Not all changes to ecosystems destroy soil. Think about how a fire disturbs a forest. Many plants and animals are destroyed, but the soil is not. Floods, fires, logging, and even farming where a forest once grew leave most soil in place.

Succession after these changes is much faster than if the soil is destroyed. Seeds of pioneer plants that survived in the soil or are blown by the wind can begin to grow right away. The existing soil helps these pioneer plants, which are larger than lichens and mosses, to grow well. Soon, animals start moving in. First stage consumers like mice and rabbits come first. Animals that eat other animals quickly follow.

After a forest fire, new plants and those that were not burned will grow faster because the fire released nutrients into the soil. More species of producers grow until the ecosystem contains enough kinds of plants to support the needs of many animals. The kinds of living things gradually change. Over time, larger plants like shrubs and small trees grow. These are called *intermediate species*, and they might live in the ecosystem for many years.

Eventually, very long-lived plants called *climax species* come to rule the forest. Some types of animals, like certain owls, can only meet their needs in these very old forests. Now, hundreds of years after a disturbance, the ecosystem has reached the last stage of succession. The renewed forest may have the same species it had before the fire or new species. Eventually, another disturbance will come to the forest and start the cycle of renewal all over again.

The first plants to grow after a forest fire appear soon after the soil cools. They are followed by larger plants, and finally by trees.

In areas with temperate climates, many plants with wide leaves lose them as winter approaches. Changes like these happen with the seasons each year in a cycle.

3. Changes with the Seasons

How does a forest change with the seasons? During summer, many plants grow and produce flowers, cones, fruits, and nuts. Birds fly overhead and take care of their young in nests hidden in trees. Insects buzz, and the air is filled with sounds. As autumn approaches, squirrels bury nuts to eat during winter. Some animals start to leave the forest. In winter, the forest is quieter. Snow covers the ground. Many animals that are left may have trouble finding food. But spring brings new growth and new activity.

Many Changes Occur in Cycles

The changes with seasons in an ecosystem form a cycle. Each year, the changes repeat. The temperatures in some ecosystems change. Most areas of New England get warm in spring, hot in summer, cool in autumn, and cold in winter. Then the cycle repeats. Ecosystems in some other parts of the world have rainy and dry seasons. The Sonoran Desert, located in parts of Arizona and California, is dry most of the year. But it, and some other places in Africa, have two rainy seasons each year.

Plants Prepare for Winter

In temperate climates, many plants with wide leaves prepare for winter. They stop growing and making food when the days get shorter and colder. This period of *dormancy*, or rest, saves energy for a plant. The leaves of the plant fall off, which reduces the risk of damage from snow, ice, and wind and prevents water loss. Decomposers break down the fallen leaves and recycle their matter in the ecosystem. In spring, new leaves will grow to make the plant food again.

Many Animals Prepare for Winter

Animals also prepare for winter, when it is harder for most of them to stay warm and find food. Some animals move to warmer places when the weather begins to get cold. In the spring, they move back. Animals that move in a cycle to meet their needs are *migrating*. Monarch butterflies and caribou are examples of animals that migrate.

The kinds of animals in an ecosystem are often changing due to migration. Some species leave in winter but return in summer. Others leave in summer and return in winter. Some animals just pass through the ecosystem while traveling somewhere else.

Some animals *hibernate*, or go into a deep sleep, during winter. They hibernate because they cannot find enough food during the winter. When animals such as ground squirrels and bats hibernate, they can survive for a long time without eating food. Their life processes slow down, and they use little energy.

In many ecosystems, food for animals is not available year-round. Many trees and other plants only produce food animals can eat during summer. Many animals that do not migrate or hibernate to have enough food to survive the winter must store up food when it is plentiful. Squirrels bury nuts. Mice store seeds and nuts in underground nests. The stored food helps the animal survive until a new supply of food is available in a warmer season.

In autumn, large numbers of Alaskan caribou migrate to their wintering range before heavy snow arrives. Caribou eat lichens and grasses, which become covered with deep snow in their summer range.

This polar bear is on a melting ice floe. As the ice melts, the bear must swim farther to other ice floes, where it hunts for seals. Changes to Earth's climate affect ecosystems and the species in them, like polar bears.

4. Climate Change and Ecosystems

Polar bears living in the Arctic live on sea ice where they hunt for seals. When the ice melts in summer, the bears move to land, where they live on fat stored in their bodies. What would a polar bear do if the sea ice began melting earlier in the year? It would have to move to land sooner. It might run out of stored food before the ice froze again.

Scientists agree that Earth's climate is currently changing by rapidly warming over time. Climate change means that ecosystems are changing, too. Organisms in an ecosystem must change to survive. For example, the polar bear might have to find a food source on land. Or it might not survive.

Organisms live in specific climates that meet their needs. If the climate warms, the living things will be affected. Some animals might move to colder areas, disrupting food chains. The ecosystem's food web might change. Many animals that live in moderate climates in North America are moving farther north or to higher elevations, where they are finding more suitable places to live. When plants scatter their seeds, the seeds sprout and grow only in the cooler northern areas. These plants start disappearing from their original locations. The ecosystem is moving north.

Climate change also changes the life cycles of plants and animals. As temperatures get warmer, many plants start to grow and bloom earlier in the spring. They live longer into autumn. Animals that hibernate might come out of their dens sooner or migrate at different times of the year. But other species cannot adapt. As climate change continues, many species may disappear from Earth.

How Do Ecosystems Change?

1. Ecosystems Can Change   All ecosystems change over time. They can change slowly or quickly, and the changes affect what species can be found in those ecosystems. For example, periods of drought can cause plants to die. This can upset the ecosystem's food web. People are also able to change ecosystems, affecting both living and nonliving parts.

2. Disturbance Leads to Succession   A disturbance is an event or change to an ecosystem that has lasting effects. The changes that take place after an ecosystem has been disturbed are called succession. After a change that destroys or removes the soil, succession takes a long time. After a disturbance that leaves soil in place, succession can happen faster. Renewed ecosystems may or may not have the same kinds of species as before the disturbance.

3. Changes with the Seasons   Most ecosystems change with the seasons. These changes are cyclical and repeat every year. The changes cause different groups of organisms to live there at different times of the year. For example, some animals migrate during winter to warmer places. Other organisms stay and prepare for winter by going into dormancy, hibernating, or collecting food.

4. Climate Change and Ecosystems   Scientists around the world agree that Earth's climate is rapidly changing, warming over time. These changes are affecting ecosystems and the organisms that live in them. For example, food webs and life cycles have been altered. If the temperature or rainfall in an environment changes, some organisms will not be able to survive there anymore.

What a Dinosaur Needs

You see a lot of dinosaurs in books, movies, and video games. Of course, dinosaurs lived long before people ever invented such things. But what if scientists could bring back the dinosaurs?

One popular story idea is that scientists could find dinosaur genes preserved in an ancient bone or in an insect, like a fossilized mosquito. You may remember that genes are inherited information that tells offspring which traits to grow as they get older. The genes would then be used to clone the dinosaur. This means a new animal is grown from the genes. But, dinosaurs have been gone for many millions of years! Evidence suggests that the genes needed to clone an animal could not be used after one or two million years. And, even if scientists could recreate just one dinosaur, an even bigger problem must be solved. How would you keep the dinosaur alive?

It is not hard to imagine a scene from the age of dinosaurs. An enormous, long-necked dinosaur lowers its head to drink from a lake, while large flying reptiles glide through the foggy morning air. We know from fossils what dinosaurs may have looked like and some of the things they ate. Some fossils give clues about the environments that dinosaurs and other ancient animals lived in. But Earth has changed.

This illustration shows one artist's idea of what dinosaurs, flying reptiles, and some of the plants that lived in their world may have looked like.

Evidence from fossils and rock layers shows that the animals we think of as dinosaurs died out about 66 million years ago. As exciting as it would be to bring dinosaurs back to life, if scientists did, the dinosaurs would likely die out again. Different ecosystems exist on Earth today than 66 million years ago.

The presence of fossil ferns like this one gives a clue about the environment of the area where it lived. Scientists use these clues to determine what dinosaur ecosystems were like.

Ecosystem Clues

How do scientists know what the dinosaurs' ecosystems were like? Scientists can learn about the characteristics of past ecosystems in several ways.

Climate is one characteristic of an ecosystem that scientists can discover clues about. Some scientists study how rock layers form from sediments. They know that certain kinds of climate produce certain kinds of sediments. For example, a river in a flat area that gets lots of rain deposits layers of mud and sand in a particular way. When scientists see this, they know that the rock layer formed in a flat area with lots of rain. If it contains fossils, they can study the fossils to identify some of the animals that lived there.

Plant and insect fossils also provide clues about past ecosystems. For example, fossils of palms and ferns are found in dinosaur-age rocks from all over the world. Today, these types of plants are found in warm climates with a lot of water. These plant fossils are clues that many dinosaurs lived in warm climates with a lot of water.

Fossil evidence provides more clues about the dinosaurs' ecosystems. Dinosaurs were the dominant vertebrates on land from about 225 to 65 million years ago. During that time, the atmosphere contained different gases than it does today. For instance, there was more oxygen in the air. Dinosaurs were probably adapted to this higher level of oxygen. A dinosaur might not survive in today's environment because the amounts of gases in the air are different.

What a Dinosaur Ate

Another thing scientists know about dinosaur ecosystems is what dinosaurs ate. Scientists who study past life analyze fossils and compare them to plants and animals that exist now. They look for clues about what animals ate long ago.

The most obvious clues to what dinosaurs ate come from their teeth. For example, some dinosaurs, such as *Tyrannosaurus Rex*, were clearly meat eaters. They had long, knife-like teeth similar to the carnivores we know today, such as lions and hyenas. Other dinosaurs had flat teeth good for grinding plants. Still others had beak-like mouths similar to today's birds.

Some researchers have even been able to describe ancient food webs based on bite marks. They observed bite marks on shells of animals in a fossil field called the Burgess Shale. The marks match the tooth patterns of an animal found from that same field. Scientists have even learned what some dinosaurs ate by studying their waste. Fossilized dinosaur droppings sometimes preserve plants and animals that are not otherwise known from the fossil record.

Research suggests that food webs throughout Earth's history have been similar to modern ones. These food webs included plants, plant eaters, and meat eaters. Scientists expect they included bacteria and other decomposers, too. There would have been complex interactions between living and nonliving things. So, even if you could clone a dinosaur, you would also need to clone the many species it ate.

Scientists have found fossils of dinosaurs' teeth. This fossil of a Edmontosaurus's jaw shows flat, interlocking teeth to help it grind plants.

Approximately 65 million years ago, a worldwide event killed off many living things. Scientists estimate that 70 percent of all species died out and exist now only as fossils.

When Earth Changed

We know from fossils that many kinds of dinosaurs, insects, and other animals no longer exist. If a species entirely disappears, then at least one thing must have changed in its environment. The end of the age of dinosaurs was marked by worldwide changes for most living things.

Approximately 65 million years ago, nearly all species of dinosaurs died out. What happened to cause so much destruction? The strongest evidence suggests that at least one enormous meteorite or comet struck Earth. The impact would have been so great that it caused wide-reaching tsunamis and wildfires. These would have killed many living things directly.

The crash also would have thrown vast amounts of dust and ash into the atmosphere, which would affect climate worldwide. Enough ash and dust in the atmosphere would reduce the amount of sunlight that reaches Earth's surface. As a direct result, many plants would die. The plant eaters that depended on them would die. Following them would be the animals that ate the plant eaters. All other living things in the ecosystem would also be affected.

In spite of all this devastation, some living things survived this event. Earth eventually recovered, and new ecosystems developed over millions of years. It may disappoint some people to never get to meet an ancient dinosaur. But Earth's ecosystems today have changed so much that even if scientists could clone one, it might not survive.

How Do Humans Change Ecosystems?

Science Vocabulary

invasive species

Many human actions change ecosystems. Sometimes the changes can be positive, like setting up a wildlife preserve. Others can be negative, like cutting down all the trees in an entire forest. Sometimes, humans also introduce new species to an ecosystem, which can harm that ecosystem's native inhabitants.

NGSS

5-LS2-1. Develop a model to describe the movement of matter among plants, animals, decomposers, and the environment.

LS2.A. The food of almost any kind of animal can be traced back to plants. Organisms are related in food webs in which some animals eat plants for food and other animals eat the animals that eat plants. Some organisms, such as fungi and bacteria, break down dead organisms (both plants or plants parts and animals) and therefore operate as "decomposers." Decomposition eventually restores (recycles) some materials back to the soil. Organisms can survive only in environments in which their particular needs are met. A healthy ecosystem is one in which multiple species of different types are each able to meet their needs in a relatively stable web of life. Newly introduced species can damage the balance of an ecosystem.

Systems and System Models A system can be described in terms of its components and their interactions.

Developing and Using Models

1. Humans Can Change Ecosystems

When water from a heavy rain runs down a bare hillside, it can erode the soil. Sometimes, people plant bushes and trees on hills like these. The plant roots hold the soil in place and keep it from washing away. This is one of the things humans can do to change ecosystems for the better.

Humans are able to change ecosystems, and they often do. The changes can be either positive or negative. Planting new trees to replace those that have been cut down is a positive change. Setting aside land for the protection of plant and animal species is positive, too. But destroying the forest habitat of an endangered species to build human houses is a negative change.

Humans cause more negative changes than positive changes. When they clear a prairie to plant crops, wild animals and plants lose their homes. Some species leave the ecosystem, disrupting what is left of the food web. This is a negative change. When humans build a dam that changes the flow of a river, salmon are prevented from swimming to the place where they mate. This is a negative change. If salmon cannot mate, their species will die out in that river. When humans spill oil in oceans and rivers, oil coats water birds, often killing them. This, too, is a negative change. In each of these changes, food chains are disrupted because the organisms that form the links can no longer interact. Food webs are affected, and the flows of matter and energy in ecosystems change.

The land shown here once had trees and bushes that small mammals, birds, and insects used for food and shelter. Humans removed those plants to grow crops. The animals that lived here lost their homes.

The Kenai National Wildlife Refuge in Alaska was set aside to protect the lives and homes of moose, bears, mountain goats, Dall sheep, wolves, salmon, and other fish. Protecting an ecosystem is a positive action by humans.

Before these buildings could be built, the homes of plants and animals had to be destroyed. Human development often harms ecosystems.

 **Engineering Design**

2. Human Development and Ecosystems

Look around your town or city. How much land has remained in its natural state? Most likely, most of the land now holds buildings and roads. These changes were made because humans needed places to live, learn, and work. Changes like these affect ecosystems.

A Growing Human Population Causes Changes

Earth's human population is growing. There are now more than seven billion people on Earth. Humans build homes to live in. They build factories, offices, and stores that produce and sell things for making life easier. They build schools for teaching students. Power plants provide energy to light, heat, and cool all these buildings.

Buildings and roads take up space. Humans use large machines that change the shape of the land to make it more suitable for buildings and highways. To provide space, humans cut down forests. They fill in wetlands with soil and rocks. Then they build buildings on land that was once home to wetland birds, snakes, beavers, and ducks or to forest owls, songbirds, insects, and small mammals. To provide power and water for these buildings and to control floods, humans build dams. Dams flood ecosystems, drowning plants and displacing animals. Food chains and food webs are disrupted as human development affects ecosystem stability.

Humans Cause Pollution

One harmful change to an ecosystem is *pollution*. Pollution is anything people add to the environment that harms living things. When factories make products and dump their wastes into air and water, those nonliving parts of an ecosystem become polluted. Cars, trucks, and buses cause pollution because burning fuels sends harmful substances into the air. Air and water pollution can make plants and animals sick. Polluted air makes it hard to breathe. Polluted water can harm plants and animals that live in streams, ponds, and rivers. Land pollution, adding solid and liquid wastes to the land, disrupts ecosystems. Plants can no longer grow when the soil has trash on it and harmful substances in it. Without plants, animals lose their food sources. Pollution can kill living things, changing food chains and food webs.

Choosing the Best Solution

Humans often have to make a choice about what solution best solves a problem. Suppose the human population in a river valley ecosystem is growing rapidly. More space is needed for more houses and stores. Should a dam be built across the river? Damming a river and building homes will harm the river ecosystem, but maybe it would be less harmful to the ecosystem to change the course of the river. Both actions might solve the problem of space, but both will change the ecosystem. Engineers and ecologists must decide which solution would be less harmful and would best solve the problem.

Factories often release chemical wastes into the air, creating air pollution. Air pollution can make animals sick, which changes ecosystems.

Engineering Design

3. Taking Resources from Ecosystems

You wake up in the morning and get out of bed. Your bed may be made of wood and metal, both natural resources. You turn on a computer to check your homework. The computer uses electricity, which is generated using natural resources.

Humans Use Natural Resources

All the goods and services you need or want are either made of natural resources or produced using them. People use resources such as natural gas, coal, and oil to generate useful energy. Other resources, such as minerals and trees, are changed into products. Engineers are always inventing new or improved products that people want. So, over time, people use even more natural resources to make them.

When natural resources are removed from Earth's surface, the ecosystems in those places change. These changes may affect the ecosystem for a brief time or a very long time.

Long-Term Changes to Ecosystems

Strip mining is one common way to remove coal or rock containing metals from Earth's surface. Huge machines strip away soil, plants, and rock to reach the resource. Almost all of the organisms in the ecosystem are removed or move away. The ecosystem is disrupted for a long period of time.

Trees are also a resource. People sometimes cut down all the trees in a forest and use the wood for building and for making paper. Many forest organisms lose their homes when so many trees are cut down. The matter and energy flow of the ecosystem is disrupted for a long period of time.

Part of this forest ecosystem has been clear cut, meaning that all the trees have been cut down. Trucks took away the cut wood, leaving the branches and leaves behind.

In this strip mine, soil, rocks, plants, and animals have been removed. The ecosystem has been changed for a long period of time.

Sunken boats are good structures for building artificial reefs. Coral can find many surfaces to grow on, and fish like the dark hiding spots of the boat.

Other Ways to Take Resources

Resources can be removed in ways that do less harm to ecosystems. For example, people can cut only some of the trees in a forest instead of cutting all the trees. They can also replace the cut trees by planting new trees. However, this way of cutting down trees costs more money. Some kinds of forests recover better with this kind of logging, but not all. Engineers and ecologists have to weigh the pros and cons of each method of cutting trees. They test the different methods, finding out what each would cost, and determine how each would affect the forest ecosystem. Then they make a decision.

Aluminum is a metal that is found in certain rocks. The rocks are mined, and the metal is removed. Because removing the metal takes a lot of electricity, many people recycle beverage cans and other aluminum products. Engineers have determined that it is cheaper and better for the environment if this metal is recycled rather than mined.

Ecosystems Can Often Be Restored

An ecosystem can sometimes be restored after it has been damaged. Many coral reefs have been damaged or destroyed by people. If people fish too much or dump pollution into the water, those things can hurt coral reef ecosystems. But it is possible to restore coral reef ecosystems by stopping polluters and overfishing. Another way is by building a structure that coral can grow on and adding some coral. Over time, the coral will grow larger, and fish will move back. The coral reef ecosystem starts to recover.

4. Introducing Species to Ecosystems

Think about a plant growing uncontrollably and burying houses, trees, and cars with its leaves and stems. This is not science fiction. It has happened.

Ecosystems change when people bring in species that are not native to an area. An **invasive species** is a non-native organism that causes harm to the ecosystem. It often has no natural enemies in its new environment. Invasive species cause harm by crowding out native species. In doing so, they may take the place of food sources that native organisms need. Fewer species remain in the ecosystem.

Sometimes, people bring in new species to an area on purpose. Plant species may be brought in to prevent the loss of soil. The plant kudzu was brought into the southern United States for this reason. The problem is that kudzu vines grow more than 30 cm (1 ft) per day! They crowd out native plants by blocking sunlight. Kudzu has become an invasive species.

A nutria is a rat-like animal that was brought into the United States for its fur. These animals grow very fast. Nutria can eat all the tender plants in an area, leaving little behind. Fewer species can survive where these animals live.

Sometimes, invasive species are brought in by accident. Zebra mussels are small animals with a shell that live in the water. They were accidentally released by large ships into the Great Lakes. They have few predators, so they increase in numbers rapidly. They feed by filtering algae from water. Native fish have little left to eat. Native fish and other water animals have almost died out in some areas as a result. The matter and energy flow of the ecosystem has been damaged.

These three organisms are all invasive species. They have all caused damage to ecosystems after they were introduced into them.

Kudzu vines

Nutria

Zebra mussels

How Do Humans Change Ecosystems?

1. Humans Can Change Ecosystems   Many human activities can change ecosystems. These changes usually harm the ecosystem, but not always. When humans change ecosystems, food chains and food webs can be disrupted. For example, when farmers clear plants on a prairie for crops, animals lose their homes. The animals leave, disrupting the ecosystem's food web.

2. Human Development and Ecosystems   The human population is growing and needs places to live, learn, and work. Human development is often the reason that humans change ecosystems. For example, if humans want to build a new neighborhood, they change the existing ecosystem to make room. Pollution from human activities can also change ecosystems.

3. Taking Resources from Ecosystems   All human products use natural resources. Removing these resources from ecosystems can change the ecosystems. Sometimes, humans remove them in ways that do a lot of damage to ecosystems. Other times, the resources are removed in less destructive ways. People also work to restore unhealthy ecosystems.

4. Introducing Species to Ecosystems   Sometimes, new species introduced to an ecosystem become invasive species. Invasive species do damage to the ecosystem by displacing native organisms. This alters food webs, damaging an ecosystem's flow of matter and energy. Some invasive species were introduced on purpose by humans, and some were introduced by accident.

Unwanted Snakes

The Everglades cover a large, lush area of southern Florida. Many different species of plants and animals make their home in this warm, watery place. But a new, unwanted species is making its home here.

The first people to live in the Everglades called it Pa-Hay-Okee, which means Grassy Water. If you visit the Everglades, you may notice that it does look very grassy. Most of the Everglades are a large marsh that is up to 80 km (50 mi) wide in some places. This marsh ecosystem is full of grass-like plants.

There are also "islands" of drier land called *hammocks*. Many different species of trees and other land plants grow on them. Pine trees grow on some higher ridges of land that are completely dry. And where freshwater from the Everglades runs into the sea, swamps full of *mangroves* grow. Mangroves are trees that form thick tangles of roots and branches. The mangroves, saw-grass swamps, and hammocks of the Everglades supply shelter for many animals, including many endangered ones.

The tangled roots and branches of mangroves provide shelter for many animals that make their home in this ecosystem.

Mammals such as raccoons, skunks, and white-tailed deer live throughout the Everglades. So do many reptiles. The top native predators are Florida panthers and the American alligator. And all of these consumers depend on the hundreds of species of fish, mammals, and birds that live in the Everglades. Unfortunately, humans have introduced an invasive species that is affecting them all.

An Invasive Species

If you visited the Everglades, you might notice many different types of birds all around you wading in the water. Millions of birds live in the Everglades year-round. Millions more spend winter there or stop to eat during migration. The marsh has ideal places for birds to wade in the water and find food. Their young can hide among the roots and stems of reeds, grasses, and mangroves. At least 350 species of birds have been identified in the Everglades. But populations of all wading birds have decreased since the 1950s.

Why have so many birds disappeared so quickly? Scientists have evidence that at least 25 species of wading birds are eaten by a type of large snake known as the Burmese python. These pythons can grow up to 6 m (about 20 ft) long. However, these snakes are an introduced species. The Burmese python is native to India and Southeast Asia. In its native habitat, it is a top predator in the food web. Because of its very large size, it has few natural enemies. In the Everglades, far from its native habitat, it has even fewer enemies. The American alligator is the only predator that can fight a Burmese python. But when a Burmese python and an alligator fight, sometimes the python wins!

Without natural predators in the Everglades, the python population has grown. The Everglades food web was previously balanced between predators and prey. But now there is another major predator. As a result, there are fewer birds, deer, and other prey.

The Wood Stork is one of many bird species that live in the Everglades year-round. The Burmese python preys on Wood Storks and other birds.

Burmese pythons are an introduced species in the Everglades. These very large snakes are native to Southeast Asia. But they have made a new home in the Florida Everglades.

How Did They Get Here?

The invasive Burmese python was not introduced into the Everglades on purpose. Burmese pythons are beautiful animals, with smooth, dry, tan skin and many dark brown spots similar to those on a giraffe. They were brought to North America to be sold as unusual pets. However, wild animals do not like to be caged and will escape if they can. Some Burmese pythons escaped their human owners and found their way into the Florida wilderness.

In 1992, a hurricane caused a lot of destruction across southern Florida. Buildings were destroyed, including one business near the Everglades. Here, people were breeding reptiles from other countries. Experts believe that many more Burmese pythons escaped into the Everglades when this business was destroyed.

But not all of the Burmese pythons in the Everglades escaped from human owners. Some pythons were dumped into the wild by their owners. Some owners did not consider how difficult it is to care for a 3 m (10 ft) snake that can eat an entire deer! So, some people simply released their pets into the wild.

Releasing a pet into the wild can cause it to die. However, in the warm climate and wet habitats of southern Florida, many loose Burmese pythons have survived and reproduced. Enough pythons are now living in the Everglades to have a negative impact on native species. Burmese pythons are not only an introduced species, but have become an invasive species.

A new Burmese python hatches in the Everglades. Human activity has allowed these wild animals to become an invasive species far from where they naturally live.

Trained scientists may tag a captured Burmese python and release it. They then use the radio tag to follow its movements and learn about it.

Finding Solutions

Removing the Burmese python from the North American wilderness is a goal of many organizations, such as the Florida Fish and Wildlife Conservation Commission. Scientists sometimes catch an animal, attach a radio tag, and release it. They can then follow the snakes remotely and study how they live. They hope they can learn something that will help them control the python population. Some people think the pythons should simply be hunted. Others think the snakes should be caught.

The simplest solution to controlling invasive species is to prevent them from getting into the wild in the first place. While researchers look for ways to control their population, other people are working to keep any more pythons from entering the Everglades. They work to make sure people know what to do if they decide they cannot keep their pet python. Others have worked to pass laws preventing any more of these pythons from being brought to Florida.

Remember, pythons are wild animals. They do not choose to come to the Everglades and create problems. So, it is up to people to solve this problem. But do not try to handle one on your own! These snakes are very dangerous if you are not prepared to handle them. Instead, if you find yourself facing a Burmese python, call an organization trained in handling them.

Earth Systems

Suppose you live on an island. On a warm day, you and your family decide to go snorkeling. When you get to the beach, you breathe in the fresh ocean air. Underwater, you see fish swimming and crabs crawling across the sand. You also observe sea grass and coral reefs along the ocean floor. In this unit, you will learn how all of these things are part of systems that make up Earth, and how these systems interact in different ways.

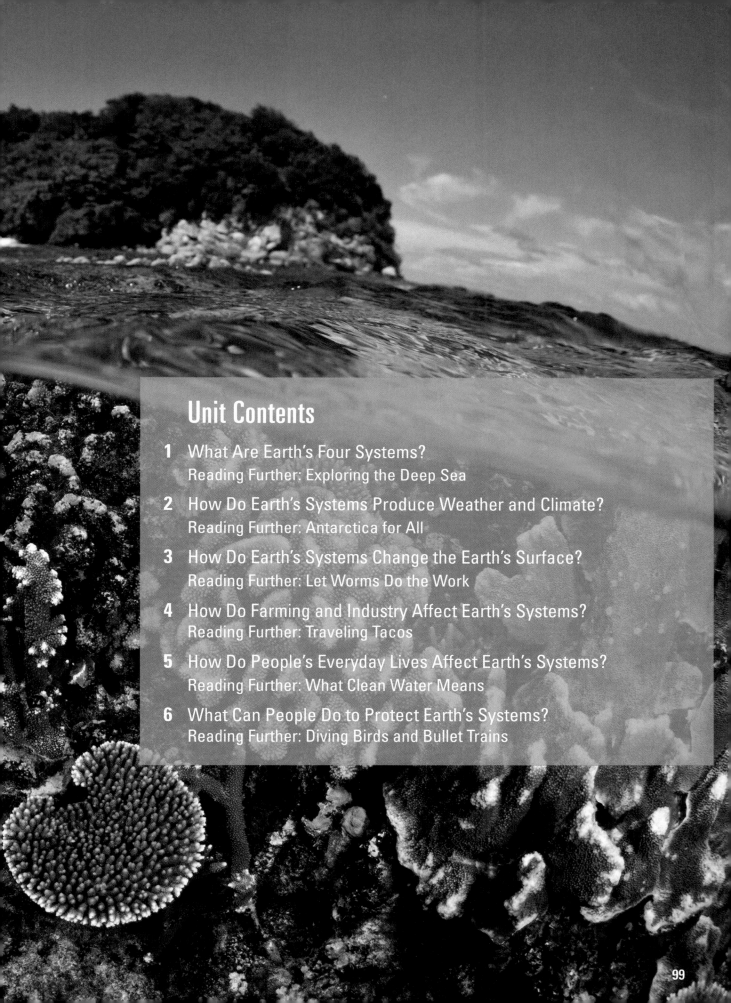

Unit Contents

Unit 2 Overview

Graphic Organizer: This unit is structured to present Earth as **four interacting systems**, describe important **interactions between the systems**, and finally investigate **humans' effects on the systems**.

1. What Are Earth's Four Systems?

2. How Do Earth's Systems Produce Weather And Climate?

3. How Do Earth's Systems Change the Earth's Surface?

4. How Do Farming and Industries Affect Earth's Systems?

5. How Do People's Everyday Lives Affect Earth's Systems?

6. What Can People Do to Protect Earth's Systems?

NGSS Next Generation Science Standards

Performance Expectations

5-ESS2-1. Develop a model using an example to describe ways the geosphere, biosphere, hydrosphere, and/or atmosphere interact.

5-ESS2-2. Describe and graph the amounts and percentages of water and fresh water in various reservoirs to provide evidence about the distribution of water on Earth.

5-ESS3-1. Obtain and combine information about ways individual communities use science ideas to protect the Earth's resources and environment.

Disciplinary Core Ideas

ESS2.A: Earth Materials and Systems

• Earth's major systems are the geosphere (solid and molten rock, soil, and sediments), the hydrosphere (water and ice), the atmosphere (air), and the biosphere (living things, including humans). These systems interact in multiple ways to affect Earth's surface materials and processes. The ocean supports a variety of ecosystems and organisms, shapes landforms, and influences climate. Winds and clouds in the atmosphere interact with the landforms to determine patterns of weather.

ESS2.C: The Roles of Water in Earth's Surface Processes

• Nearly all of Earth's available water is in the ocean. Most fresh water is in glaciers or underground; only a tiny fraction is in streams, lakes, wetlands, and the atmosphere.

ESS3.C: Human Impacts on Earth Systems

• Human activities in agriculture, industry, and everyday life have had major effects on the land, vegetation, streams, ocean, air, and even outer space. But individuals and communities are doing things to help protect Earth's resources and environments.

Crosscutting Concepts

Scale, Proportion, and Quantity

• Standard units are used to measure and describe physical quantities such as weight and volume.

Systems and System Models

• A system can be described in terms of its components and their interactions.

 Developing and Using Models

 Using Mathematics and Computational Thinking

 Obtaining, Evaluating, and Communicating Information

Have you ever wondered...

If you observe the weather where you live, you will notice that it changes. Some days it might be warm and sunny, and other days it might be cool and cloudy. This unit will help you answer these questions and many others you may ask.

How are the materials we use made?

How can I help protect the environment?

What causes the weather to be cold and snowy?

What Are Earth's Four Systems?

Science Vocabulary

atmosphere

biosphere

geosphere

hydrosphere

precipitation

sediments

water cycle

water vapor

Earth can be divided into four systems called the atmosphere, biosphere, hydrosphere, and geosphere. These four systems interact with each other and make up the Earth. Often you can see the four systems at the same time, such as when you visit a beach. The air, crabs or fishes, ocean water, and sand are part of different systems. These four systems interact to affect weather, shape landforms, and support living things.

NGSS

5-ESS2-1. Develop a model using an example to describe ways the geosphere, biosphere, hydrosphere, and/or atmosphere interact.
5-ESS2-2. Describe and graph the amounts and percentages of water and fresh water in various reservoirs to provide evidence about the distribution of water on Earth.

ESS2.A. Earth's major systems are the geosphere (solid and molten rock, soil, and sediments), the hydrosphere (water and ice), the atmosphere (air), and the biosphere (living things, including humans). These systems interact in multiple ways to affect Earth's surface materials and processes. The ocean supports a variety of ecosystems and organisms, shapes landforms, and influences climate. Winds and clouds in the atmosphere interact with the landforms to determine patterns of weather.
ESS2.C. Nearly all of Earth's available water is in the ocean. Most fresh water is in glaciers or underground; only a tiny fraction is in streams, lakes, wetlands, and the atmosphere.

Scale, Proportion, and Quantity
Standard units are used to measure and describe physical quantities such as weight and volume.
Systems and System Models
A system can be described in terms of its components and their interactions.

Developing and Using Models

Using Mathematics and Computational Thinking

1. Earth Has Four Systems

You may have planted bean seeds in a garden. When seeds sprout, roots grow into the soil to search for water that the new plant needs. Leaves form on the plant that take in carbon dioxide gas from the air and use it to make food.

You have just read about parts of Earth's four systems: the *atmosphere*, *hydrosphere*, *biosphere*, and *geosphere*. Above Earth's surface is the **atmosphere**, a mixture of gases that surrounds Earth. This mixture makes up the air that you breathe and that plants use to make food.

Earth's water makes up the **hydrosphere**. The hydrosphere includes all the liquid water in oceans, rivers, and lakes. It also includes the liquid water found in the ground. Earth's frozen water in glaciers and polar ice caps are part of the hydrosphere. There is even water in the atmosphere in the form of clouds and a gas.

The **biosphere** includes all the living things found on Earth. You are part of the biosphere. So are the plants in your garden, the bacteria that live on your skin, and the earthworms that live in the soil.

Earth's **geosphere** is made up of a thin surface layer of rock, soil, and sediments as well as the layers of hot molten, or liquid, rock that are inside Earth. Many objects you use every day, such as plastic or metal, come from the geosphere.

The four systems interact with each other to affect Earth. Plant roots growing into soil is an interaction between the biosphere and geosphere. Soil soaking up rainwater is an interaction between the geosphere and hydrosphere. You will learn more about each of Earth's systems in this lesson.

A plant is part of the Earth's biosphere. The soil is part of the geosphere, and the rainwater it absorbs with its roots is part of the hydrosphere. The plant is also using air from the atmosphere.

2. The Atmosphere

Suppose you are on a shuttle to outer space. You pass through Earth's atmosphere made of air. As you move away from the surface, the air's pressure and temperature change.

Air pressure is how much the air pushes on any surface. Air is made of tiny invisible pieces of matter. The closer together the pieces are, the higher the air pressure. The pieces are closest together near Earth's surface because Earth's gravity pulls air down. As you move away from Earth, the pieces of matter in the atmosphere are more spread out. The amount of air decreases as you move up into the atmosphere.

Temperature decreases as you move farther from Earth's surface. But air does not stay cool. It changes in layers.

Earth's atmosphere is the mixture of gases that surrounds Earth. It has five layers that vary in thickness and in temperature.

Earth's Atmosphere

Exosphere
(Temperature decreases)

500 km

Thermosphere
(Temperature increases)

87 km

Mesosphere
(Temperature decreases)

50 km

Stratosphere
(Temperature increases)

11 km

Troposphere
(Temperature decreases)

Layers of the Atmosphere

As you move upward through the atmosphere, the temperature changes. But it does not change in a constant pattern. Instead, it cools, warms, cools again, warms again, and then cools again as you go higher. Scientists divide the atmosphere into different layers depending on how the temperature changes.

The layer closest to Earth's surface is called the troposphere. You live in the warmest part of the troposphere. You live in the warmest part of the troposphere because the sun warms the Earth's surface, which then warms the air above it. As you move up in the troposphere, it grows colder.

Eventually you reach a point where the temperature begins to increase as you get farther from Earth's surface. This is a new layer called the stratosphere. When the sunlight hits the air at the top of the stratosphere, it forms a new substance called ozone that absorbs energy from the sunlight and heats up the air at the top of this layer.

Earth's atmosphere contains many different gases. Some of these gases, such as carbon dioxide, help keep Earth warm so life can exist on Earth.

There are several more layers above the stratosphere. There is another layer where the temperature decreases as you move away from the Earth. Above that is a layer where the temperature increases. The temperature decreases and increases in different layers until you reach outer space.

Gases in the Atmosphere

Air is a mixture of gases. The amount of each gas changes slightly from place to place. Nitrogen and oxygen make up almost all of the air in the lower layers of the atmosphere. The rest is made up of other gases such as argon, carbon dioxide, hydrogen, and ozone.

Many of the gases in the atmosphere are important to organisms in the biosphere. Plants use carbon dioxide as a building block to make food. Animals use oxygen to release energy from their food. Carbon dioxide also absorbs energy and warms the atmosphere.

The Atmosphere Heats Earth

Space is too cold for organisms to live in, but Earth is warm. How does life exist on Earth? Energy carried by light is absorbed by the Earth's surface. Earth then emits, or sends, energy outward. Most of that energy gets absorbed by gases in the atmosphere such as carbon dioxide. The atmosphere then emits some of that energy out into space. It also emits some of it toward the ground, making Earth's surface even warmer. This is called the greenhouse effect. Life can exist on Earth because the greenhouse effect warms the surface. But too much carbon dioxide in the atmosphere causes global warming, the overheating of the atmosphere.

This beaver is cutting the tree with its teeth.

3. The Biosphere

If you go to a park, you see many living things—trees, dogs, insects, grass, people. If you went under the sea, you would see other living things—fish, sponges, seaweed, maybe even a whale.

Parts of the Biosphere

The biosphere is made up of all the living things on Earth. Living things can be found in a layer that extends from the ocean floor upward several kilometers into the atmosphere. This may sound like a large space with a huge number of organisms. However, the biosphere has the least amount of matter of Earth's four systems.

Animals Affect Earth's Systems

Although the biosphere is small, it has a huge impact on Earth. Parts of the biosphere interact with other systems to change the Earth. Even a single animal can change how the Earth looks. A beaver is an animal that lives in and near streams and rivers. Beavers cut down trees to build a dam made of branches and mud. A dam blocks the flow of water in the river and creates a pond or small lake upstream. Beavers build their home in the center of this pond.

How does a beaver dam affect the environment? Cutting down trees causes soil to be washed away because tree roots no longer hold it in place, changing the geosphere. When the dam is built, water upstream floods fields and forests. The hydrosphere is changed as the river becomes a pond. Many animals lose their homes, but different animals move into the changed environment. The biosphere has also been changed.

A beaver dam changes a river or stream into a pond. Below the dam, little water flows.

Humans Affect Earth's Systems

Humans are part of the biosphere. Like beavers, humans build dams. These dams are much larger and have a much greater impact on the hydrosphere and geosphere. The large body of water that forms above the dam affects the atmosphere. Water evaporates and then condenses, forming clouds. If the body of water is large enough, it may change weather patterns and even the *climate* of the area.

Human activities affect the atmosphere and the hydrosphere. Cars, trucks, and buses send carbon dioxide and harmful chemicals into the atmosphere. You have read that carbon dioxide absorbs energy and raises the temperature of the air. Some of the chemicals that enter the atmosphere combine with water droplets to form acid rain. When acid rain falls to Earth, it can eat away rock, part of the geosphere. After long periods of time, the shape of the land changes. Other chemicals produce ozone, a gas in the atmosphere. Ozone is naturally found in the stratosphere, where it protects living things against harmful radiation from the sun. But ozone in the troposphere is harmful. It causes smog and makes breathing difficult.

Human activities affect the geosphere. When millions of trees are cut down or minerals are mined from the earth, the soil loosens and is easily washed away by rain. Removing oil and natural gas from Earth can even cause earthquakes, which can change Earth's surface within seconds.

This huge open-pit copper mine in Arizona has changed the shape of landforms in the area. Much of the exposed soil will be washed away by rain.

When astronauts first saw Earth from space, they thought it looked like a big blue marble.

4. The Hydrosphere

When humans first looked at Earth from space, they called the planet the "blue marble." It really looks like a marble with swirling white clouds, and it definitely is blue.

What makes Earth appear blue from space is its water. Earth is the only planet in its solar system that has water on its surface. About three-fourths of Earth's surface is covered with water. Nearly all of the Earth's water, about 97 out of 100 liters, or 97 percent, is salt water in the oceans. The rest, less than 3 out of 100 liters, or 3 percent, is fresh water.

Earth's Fresh Water

Many living things in the biosphere need fresh water to survive. But about 69 out of 100 liters of Earth's fresh water is frozen in ice caps at the North and South Poles and in *glaciers*, large bodies of slowly moving ice. Living things do not use this frozen water because it takes too much energy to melt the ice.

Surface water and groundwater provide most of the fresh water that living things need. About 30 out of 100 liters of fresh water is underground, or 30 percent. Only about 1 out of 100 liters, or 1 percent, of Earth's fresh water is surface water in rivers, streams, lakes, and ponds.

Streams are narrow bodies of flowing water. They collect water from rain or melting snow or ice. Streams usually flow into larger bodies of water such as rivers and lakes. Rivers are usually wider. Water in rivers eventually flows into seas or oceans. The water in lakes and ponds may have currents caused by wind, but it does not flow.

About three-fourths of Earth's surface is covered with water. Almost all of this water is found in oceans. Most of Earth's fresh water is frozen.

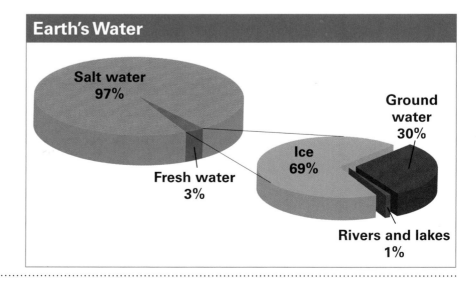

Earth's Water

Salt water 97%

Fresh water 3%

Ice 69%

Ground water 30%

Rivers and lakes 1%

Earth's Salt Water

The ocean holds almost all of Earth's available water. Although different parts of the ocean have different names, they are all connected to form one huge body of water. Ocean water is salty. Most of the salt in ocean water is the same kind of salt you sprinkle on your food. Many other kinds of salt are found in ocean water, too. A measure of the amount of salts in ocean water is called *salinity*.

The temperature and salinity of ocean water vary from place to place. The water is warmest at the surface. At the ocean floor, the water is very cold in most places. Some parts of the oceans are much saltier than other parts.

Oceans are home to thousands of different organisms in the biosphere. These marine organisms interact with the ocean. Some animals swim from place to place to catch food. Fish, whales, and turtles are some of the many animals that swim. Other animals such as sea stars crawl on the ocean floor. Sponges and clams stay in one place and filter tiny food organisms out of the water. Organisms that use photosynthesis to make their own food, such as seaweeds, can live only near the surface because they need sunlight.

The ocean interacts with the geosphere. Ocean waves beat against land, changing its shape and washing it away. You will learn in the next lesson about how water in the hydrosphere interacts with the atmosphere, affecting weather and climate.

Earth's oceans hold almost all of Earth's water. Even though the temperature and salinity of the water vary from place to place, they are all connected and cover most of Earth's surface.

Water is continuously flowing. Sometimes it is easy to see the movement of water, such as when this river flows into the ocean.

5. Earth's Water Cycle

Water on Earth does not remain fresh water or salt water. Water is always moving. Sometimes you can easily see the movement of water, such as when a river flows into a sea or when rain falls from the atmosphere. Other times it is harder to see the movement of water. Water is always moving on land and even in the air above.

Water Is Conserved

Water exists in three states: liquid, solid, and gas. The liquid state is usually just called water and solid water is called ice. The gas state of water is known as **water vapor**. Water can change from one state to another as it warms and cools. Putting water in the freezer changes liquid water to ice as the water freezes. A puddle of liquid water will evaporate, or turn into water vapor. Water vapor condenses in the atmosphere to form clouds made of droplets of liquid water.

All water is part of Earth's hydrosphere, and water is never lost from the hydrosphere. Rather, water changes state over and over again as it interacts with the geosphere and the atmosphere. This continuous movement of water over the land and above in the air is called the **water cycle**.

The Water Cycle

Water is continuously moving and changing states in a cycle, even when it appears to be still. It evaporates and then falls back to Earth's surface over and over. The energy in sunlight evaporates the water from oceans, rivers, and lakes, turning the liquid water to water vapor. Water vapor is also given off by plant leaves. Water evaporates as water vapor, which rises into the atmosphere.

As water vapor rises, the air cools and water vapor begins to condense into tiny water droplets. These water droplets form clouds. Within a cloud, the water droplets join and grow larger. When the droplets are large and heavy, they fall to Earth's surface. This is **precipitation**, water that falls to Earth's surface. Precipitation has many forms. Precipitation falls as rain where the air is warm and falls as snow where the air is cold.

Some precipitation soaks into the soil, and plant roots take up small amounts of the water. Some runs along the surface as runoff. Some precipitation, when the air is cold, remains frozen on the mountaintops and streets as ice and snow until it melts and joins the runoff. The runoff flows as surface water into freshwater streams and rivers. Eventually, these rivers flow into lakes and oceans.

When rivers run into the ocean, the fresh water mixes with the salt water. The *brackish* water that forms has more salt than fresh water, but less salt than ocean water. As the water continues to run towards the ocean, the water grows more salty until it becomes salt water.

The water in the soil, streams and rivers, lakes, and oceans evaporates. Water vapor is given off by plant leaves. The water vapor rises to the atmosphere again. The cycle continues and repeats again and again.

Water cycles from land to air and back again, but it is never lost from the hydrosphere. The continuous movement of water over the land and above in the air is called the water cycle.

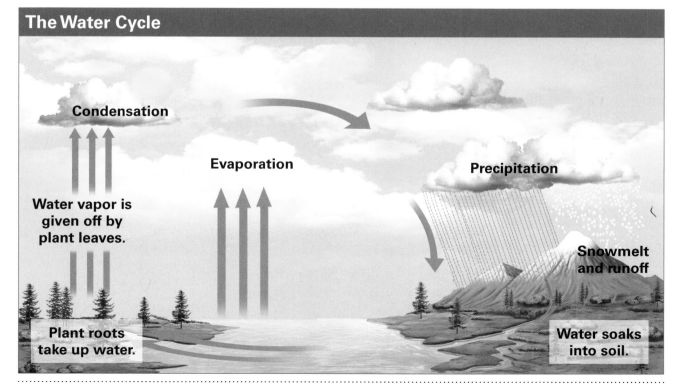

The Water Cycle

Condensation

Evaporation

Precipitation

Water vapor is given off by plant leaves.

Snowmelt and runoff

Plant roots take up water.

Water soaks into soil.

6. The Geosphere

You may eat a juicy peach. The skin of the peach is its thin outer surface, inside the skin is thick juicy flesh, and at the center of the peach is a hard seed made of two layers. You can think of Earth's geosphere as the parts of a peach.

Earth's Layers

The geosphere includes Earth's surface and its interior. It includes rocks and minerals, soils and sediments, and the processes that shape the surface. The geosphere has four layers: the crust, mantle, outer core, inner core.

The outside "skin" of Earth is the top layer of the geosphere, called the crust. You live on the crust. It varies in thickness from place to place but is generally from 8 to 40 km (5 to 25 mi) thick. The crust is made of solid rock and, near the surface, soil. As you move downward from the surface, the crust gets warmer.

Below the crust is the mantle, the second layer. The mantle is about 2,900 km (1,800 mi) thick. Most of it has a temperature of about 3,000°C (5,400°F) and is made of rock. But there are small parts near the surface made of melted, or molten rock. The mantle is like the thick juicy flesh of the peach.

Finally, beneath the mantle is Earth's metal core. You may have noticed a peach pit has two layers, a brown outer layer and a pale white inner layer. Just like a peach pit has two parts, Earth's metal core has two parts, an outer core and an inner core. The outer core is made of liquid metal. It is about 2,300 km (1,400 mi) thick and has a temperature of about 5,000°C (9,000°F). The inner core is a solid metal sphere with a radius of about 1,200 km (750 mi). It has a temperature of more than 6,000°C (11,000°F).

Earth's geosphere has four layers. Each layer has a different temperature and thickness and is made of different materials.

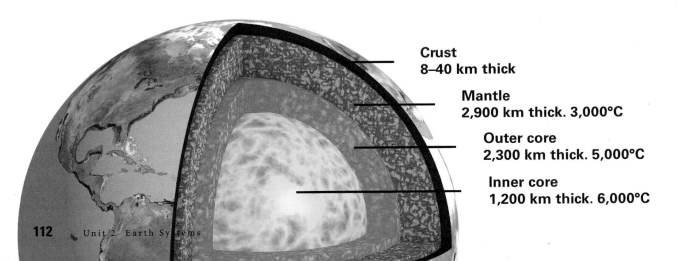

Crust
8–40 km thick

Mantle
2,900 km thick. 3,000°C

Outer core
2,300 km thick. 5,000°C

Inner core
1,200 km thick. 6,000°C

Rock is a part of the geosphere. Sedimentary rock often has colored layers because the rock forms from layers of sediments that are pressed together.

Rocks and Minerals

If you were to examine a rock with a magnifying glass, you would see that it is made up of tiny grains. Each grain is made up of a mineral. Rocks are mixtures of minerals. You are probably familiar with many of them. Table salt, the graphite in your pencils, chalk, metals, and diamond are minerals. Humans use many minerals from the geosphere to make things they need.

Many kinds of rock make up the geosphere. There are three main kinds of rock that form in different ways. *Igneous* rock forms when melted rock from Earth's mantle comes to the surface in a volcanic eruption. On the surface, the rock cools and hardens.

Sedimentary rock forms when tiny pieces of sand, rock, and shells settle and are buried and pressed together in layers. These tiny pieces are called **sediments**. Sediments form when larger rocks and shells are worn away. The sediments are carried by flowing water in a river or stream. When the water slows down, the sediments drop to the bottom. Over millions of years, the layers sediments form sedimentary rock. You can see these layers because each layer contains different minerals.

Metamorphic rock forms from existing rock. Heat and pressure inside Earth's crust change igneous or sedimentary rock into metamorphic rock by squeezing and heating it. Thus, one kind of rock can be changed into another kind.

7. Soil

Soil is the loose material that covers Earth's surface. It contains parts from all four of Earth's systems, such as tiny pieces of rock, minerals, and decayed plant and animal matter. Soil also contains water and air. The bits of rock and minerals came from larger rocks that were worn away. Decayed plant and animal material, called *humus*, came from organisms that died and were eventually covered by more material. It takes thousands of years for soil to form from these materials.

Different parts of Earth's surface have different kinds of soil. For example, forest soil has a lot of humus because many plants grew and died in the forest. Desert soil has a lot of minerals but little humus because few organisms lived in desert areas. Soil on mountains is very rocky, because rainwater washes away much of the humus from mountain soil.

Soil contains parts from all four Earth systems, from tiny pieces of rocks and minerals, to humus. A typical forest soil has four layers.

Soil is made of layers. A typical forest soil has an upper layer of humus and plant and animal material that is still decaying. Below this layer is topsoil. Topsoil is loose and contains a lot of humus and minerals. Topsoil holds water well. Most of the soil's organisms, such as fungi, earthworms, and insects, live in topsoil. Seeds and plant roots grow in topsoil.

Under the topsoil is a layer of subsoil, which contains minerals but little humus. Deep plant roots grow through the subsoil looking for minerals. Water carries clay and minerals down into the subsoil where it builds up. A layer with large pieces of broken rock is below the subsoil. These four layers rest on a layer of solid rock, called bedrock.

Soil's Layers

- Humus Layer
- Topsoil — Air
- Subsoil
- Broken rock fragments
- Solid Rock (no soil)

What Are Earth's Four Systems?

1. Earth Has Four Systems   Earth has four systems that interact with each other. They are called the atmosphere, biosphere, hydrosphere, and geosphere.

2. The Atmosphere   The air above the surface of the Earth is the atmosphere. There are many different gases in the air, and some of them make the Earth warmer as a result of the greenhouse effect.

3. The Biosphere   All living things are part of the biosphere. This may appear to be a very large amount, but the biosphere actually contains the least amount of material of Earth's four systems.

4. The Hydrosphere   All of the water on the Earth is part of the hydrosphere. About 75 percent of the Earth's surface is covered with water. Of this, 97 percent is salt water in the oceans. The rest, less than 3 percent, is fresh water.

5. Earth's Water Cycle   All of the water on Earth is moving, even when we cannot see it. Water evaporates into the air and then condenses to fall back to Earth's surface again and again in a water cycle.

6. The Geosphere   The geosphere is everything that includes the Earth's surface and its interior. Mountains, sand, rocks, and minerals are all part of the geosphere. The geosphere also includes the inner layers of the earth.

7. Soil   Soil contains parts of all four of Earth's systems. It is contains tiny pieces of rock, minerals, and decayed plant and animal matter. It also contains water and air.

Exploring the Deep Sea

The ocean floor is deep, dark, and under immense pressure. How do scientists overcome these obstacles to explore interactions between the hydrosphere, the geosphere, and the biosphere deep underwater?

A few days before setting sail, the person in charge of the science research ship *Okeanos Explorer* got an alarming email. The satellite antenna on the ship was not working. The ship was about to go on a voyage to discover new deep-sea vents in the Galápagos Rift, off the coast of South America. A rift is a large crack in the ocean floor. Deep-sea vents are openings in Earth's crust where heat from the geosphere warms the cold water of the deep sea. Substances from these vents make dark clouds in the water that look like smoke. The vents are extremely hot. They can reach around 400°C (750°F)! These areas are called "black smokers." Deep-sea vents and black smokers support whole communities of living things that use the heat and substances for energy.

The ship could still look for vents without the antenna. But the scientists on the ship would not be able to send photos and video to scientists who stayed on land. The whole team could not discuss the discoveries as they happened, or work together to decide where the ship should go next.

The research ship *Okeanos Explorer* was looking black smokers like this one when its antenna stopped working. Communities of living things live near these black smokers.

The news about the broken antenna arrived on a long holiday weekend. The people who could fix the antenna could not be reached. The ship's scientists and crew were already on their way to Costa Rica, where the ship was docked. Would it sail with or without a working antenna?

Scientists gather data before deciding on where to search for deep-sea vents. This piece of equipment can measure temperature and detect substances in the water. The scientist is attaching bottles for collecting water samples.

Sonar, Sniffing, and Sampling

When the antenna stopped working, scientists on the *Okeanos Explorer* were looking for clues about where deep-sea vents might be. They knew where deep-sea vents used to be. But scientists on earlier voyages found that vents often disappear, along with their organisms. New vents may appear somewhere else nearby. But they have to know where to look. To find these vents, the scientists first used a technique called sonar to map the ocean floor. Sonar uses sound to detect objects. The maps showed where the rifts were. But the maps did not show which rifts had active vents. Only active vents heat the water and put substances that support living things into it.

The next step to find vents was to "sniff" the water. Sniffing is a process that uses equipment to find warm water and certain dissolved substances. To sniff the water, the ship sails over a deep-sea rift towing a piece of equipment with sensors that can detect black smokers. Data from the sensors are graphed to show where the water is warm and full of the right substances. Those places are where living things are likely to be.

Scientists also look for vents with water samples. The equipment that carries the sensors also carries water sampling bottles. This allows scientists to collect water samples for testing.

Sonar, sniffing, and water samples from the first part of the *Okeanos Explorer's* voyage suggested that there were new places to explore for ocean vents and the organisms they supported. Scientists discussed the data they had gathered and decided where to look on the second part of the voyage.

Equipment for exploring the deep sea must be strong enough to hold up under the crushing weight of tons of water. *Little Hercules* is an ROV that takes photos and video of the ocean floor.

Seeing in the Deep

With their new data, the scientists had planned to go back to the Galápagos Rift to look for vents. Looking at the ocean floor is not easy. The Galápagos Rift is more than 2 km (1.2 mi) below the ocean surface. Any equipment that goes that deep has to withstand the weight of all that water without collapsing on itself. It also needs light because sunlight only reaches about 200 m (650 feet) below the ocean surface.

Even though the equipment must go deep underwater, people do not in order to explore the ocean floor. Research ships carry equipment that lets scientists see photos and live video while staying on board the ship. Scientists on land can see the ocean floor, too—if the satellite antenna is working.

On this expedition, *Okeanos Explorer* had some brand-new equipment for exploring the ocean floor. The equipment was in two parts: a camera sled and a remotely operated vehicle (ROV). The sled, *Seirios*, carried high-definition cameras, lights, sonar, and sensors for sniffing. It also carried an ROV named *Little Hercules*. A team of scientists would control the equipment from the ship. *Seirios* would hover in the water, shining lights down on the ocean floor. *Little Hercules* would separate from *Seirios* and travel close to the floor, taking close-up photos and video of the organisms living there. But unless the antenna was fixed, very few people would see the amazing live video feed from the bottom of the ocean.

Sharing Data and Discoveries

The *Okeanos Explorer* left port four days behind schedule. The satellite antenna had been partially fixed, but it still could not send video. Then, an hour into the voyage, one of the engineers found a way to make the antenna work. Data, photos, video, and voice would all be available to the scientists on shore and to anyone who wanted to watch and listen over the Internet.

The scientists discovered some deep-sea vents surrounded by living things. Videos showed giant tubeworms swaying in the currents. They live in tubes made of special material that protects them from the vent's substances. Instead of eating, tubeworms get nutrients from bacteria that live inside of them. These bacteria get energy from substances that come out of the vents and thrive in this environment.

Videos captured other organisms that near the vents. Pink crabs crawled over unusual pink corals. Yellow "dandelions," which are a group of smaller animals that cluster together, swarmed at one vent. The crabs and dandelions near vents are scavengers. So, they feed on dead animals and bacteria.

Every year, research ships like the *Okeanos Explorer* take scientists out to sea to investigate interactions between the geosphere, the hydrosphere, and the biosphere. You can share in these voyages of discovery. Just look up *Okeanos Explorer* online and hope that their satellite antenna is working!

Giant tubeworms live only at deep sea rifts. A small crab is crawling between the tubeworms.

Scientists have nicknamed this cluster of sea creatures a "dandelion."

How Do Earth's Systems Produce Weather and Climate?

Science Vocabulary

air mass

air pressure

climate

prevailing wind

weather

As long as you are living on Earth, you are experiencing the weather and climate. Sometimes the weather is sunny, sometimes it is rainy, and sometimes it is even foggy. Earth's systems interact with each other to produce the weather you are familiar with. You will learn more about how Earth's systems interact to produce different weather patterns.

NGSS

5-ESS2-1. Develop a model using an example to describe ways the geosphere, biosphere, hydrosphere, and/or atmosphere interact.

ESS2.A. Earth's major systems are the geosphere (solid and molten rock, soil, and sediments), the hydrosphere (water and ice), the atmosphere (air), and the biosphere (living things, including humans). These systems interact in multiple ways to affect Earth's surface materials and processes. The ocean supports a variety of ecosystems and organisms, shapes landforms, and influences climate. Winds and clouds in the atmosphere interact with the landforms to determine patterns of weather.

Systems and System Models A system can be described in terms of its components and their interactions.

Developing and Using Models

1. Earth's Systems Interact

Your baseball game is postponed because of a summer storm of dense black clouds, rain, streaks of lightning, and loud thunder. A thunderstorm can result when Earth's atmosphere and hydrosphere interact.

Earth's four systems interact with each other. They can even interact with each other to produce the weather that you experience. For example, water vapor is part of both the hydrosphere and atmosphere. When the water vapor high in the atmosphere cools and changes to water droplets, clouds form. Wind results when heat from Earth's surface, the geosphere, warms the air in the atmosphere unevenly. Moving water in a river wears away soil and rock to change the shape of the surface of the Earth. Plants and animals in the biosphere exchange gases with the atmosphere when they make food or breathe.

All of the weather and climate you experience are produced by interactions of Earth's systems. **Weather** is the condition of the atmosphere at a place for a short period of time, such as a few hours or days. **Climate** is the general weather of a place over a long period of time, such as many years. A thunderstorm is a kind of weather that resulted from an interaction between parts of the hydrosphere and parts of the atmosphere. Warm summers and cold winters may be the climate in your area. Climate is affected by many things, such as how close an area is to oceans and mountain ranges.

A thunderstorm is a kind of severe weather. It results from interactions between parts of Earth's hydrosphere and its atmosphere.

2. Air Pressure and Temperature

The weather is always changing. Many factors in the atmosphere affect the weather, such as the air pressure and temperature in that area.

Air Pressure

You have learned that air is made of tiny invisible pieces of matter. The matter in air pushes down on the surface of Earth. **Air pressure,** or how much air pushes on any surface, affects the weather. So, air pressure is affected by the amount of water vapor in the air. Water vapor makes air moist and lowers the air pressure. When the air pressure changes, the weather usually does too. Rising air pressure usually means dry weather is nearing while falling air pressure usually means wet weather is approaching.

Temperature

Temperature also affects the weather. The particles of matter in cold air are packed more tightly together. So, cold air weighs more than the same volume of warm air. The cold air then sinks down and pushes the warm air up. Earth's surface, its hydrosphere and geosphere, affects the temperature of the air. During the day, the sun warms the land and oceans. Energy transfers from the land and water, and heats the atmosphere. At night, the air cools.

The amount of change in air temperature also affects an area's climate. Land areas near a warm ocean tend to be warmer than inland areas, and land near cold oceans tends to be colder. Even the color of a land area affects air temperature. Dark rocks absorb more of the sun's energy. White snow and ice reflect most of the energy off Earth's surface. Some of the reflected energy is absorbed by gases in the atmosphere.

During the day, the sun warms the land and oceans. Heat is transferred to the atmosphere and warms the air.

Organisms in the biosphere can affect air and land temperatures. You may have noticed that the air in a room warms up when it is crowded with people. Some of the body heat of animals is transferred to air.

Air Masses, Fronts, and Weather Maps

An **air mass** is a large quantity of air that has similar temperature and moisture all through it. A single air mass may be large enough to cover several states.

Air in the atmosphere is always moving. As it moves, energy and water vapor are transferred from the land and water to the air, or from the air back down to the land or oceans. The place where one air mass meets another air mass is called a *front*. Weather changes at fronts. Suppose a cold air mass is moving toward a warm air mass. This is called a cold front. Cold air cannot contain as much water vapor as warm air can. So there might be rain or thunderstorms at the front. This can be followed by cool dry weather as the cold dry air mass replaces the warm air mass in the area.

What happens when a moving warm air mass meets a cold air mass? This is called a warm front. The incoming moist air pushes over the top of the cold air mass. The rising warm air cools off, often producing rain. After the warm front passes by, the weather gets warmer and clearer.

Air masses and fronts can be shown on a weather map. The numbers and symbols on a weather map identify the air masses. Blue triangles identify cold fronts and red semicircles identify warm fronts.

A cold front forms when a moving cold air mass runs into a warm air mass, pushing the warm air upward. A warm front forms when a moving warm air mass runs into a cold air mass. The warm air slides over the cold air. A cold front is shown by blue triangles while a warm front is shown by red semicircles.

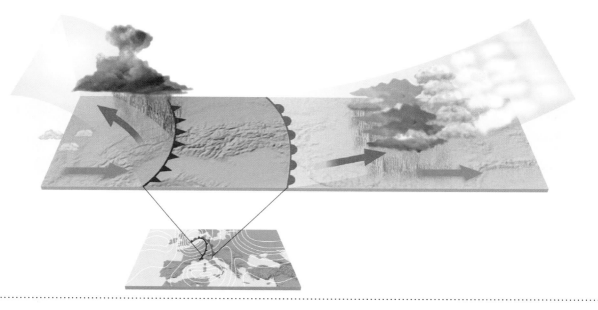

Clouds form when Earth's hydrosphere interacts with the atmosphere. Cirrus clouds are made of ice crystals that form high in the atmosphere.

3. Clouds and Precipitation

When you look up at the sky, you might see white puffy clouds or black storm clouds in the atmosphere. Can you make predictions about the weather by observing the different shapes and colors of clouds?

Formation of Clouds

Clouds form when Earth's hydrosphere interacts with the atmosphere. The air cools and water vapor condenses, turning into liquid water droplets. These droplets are a cloud. If the air is cold enough, as it is high in the upper atmosphere, the droplets freeze to form ice crystals.

One way clouds can form is when a warm, moist air mass meets a mountain and rises. Mountains located near oceans often have clouds over them because the air picks up moisture over the ocean. Clouds also form when warm, moist air is pushed upward by a front.

Kinds of Clouds

The kind of clouds in the sky can tell you what the weather is going to be. *Cirrus clouds* are feathery clouds that form high in the atmosphere and are made of ice crystals. Cirrus clouds usually mean good weather. *Cumulus clouds* are fluffy and white with flat bottoms that form lower in the atmosphere than cirrus clouds do. Cumulus clouds mean good weather. *Stratus clouds* are flat, gray, and layered. They are the lowest clouds in the sky and usually cover the whole sky. They might bring rain and drizzle. *Cumulonimbus clouds* are storm clouds. They are dark and heavy and usually mean that a strong storm is approaching.

Cumulonimbus clouds are dark and heavy in the atmosphere. When you see cumulonimbus clouds you know that a strong storm is coming.

These hailstones are the same size as blueberries. Hailstones can be as large as baseballs.

Formation of Precipitation

Remember that precipitation is water that lands on the Earth's surface, in other words, an interaction between the hydrosphere and the geosphere. After clouds have formed, the water droplets in the clouds grow larger and heavier as water vapor continues to condense. When the droplets get too large and heavy, they fall to Earth.

Kinds of Precipitation

There are several kinds of precipitation. They vary according to the size of the droplet and the state of water. Rain is liquid water drops that fall from clouds. Some raindrops are quite large, whereas others are small. Small raindrops are sometimes called *drizzle*. *Snow* is frozen water that is made of ice crystals called snowflakes. Each snowflake has six sides or points and has a different shape. Sleet is small drops of ice that are formed when falling snow melts and then freezes again. *Hail* is made of pellets or chunks of ice. A hailstone forms when a frozen raindrop is pushed upward in rising warm air. More water freezes on it, and makes it a larger pellet of ice. When the hailstone gets too heavy to be suspended, it falls to the ground.

Fog

Fog is small liquid water drops that lie close to the ground. You can think of fog as being a cloud that forms at ground level. Fog and clouds are made of water droplets. However, clouds form from rising and cooling moist air. Fog forms when air moves over a cool surface. Thus, fog forms when the atmosphere and geosphere interact. Clouds form when the atmosphere and hydrosphere interact.

4. Ocean Currents

In 1992, 12 boxes of bathtub toys were washed overboard into the hydrosphere from a ship in the Pacific Ocean during a storm. Within 10 months, colorful blue turtles, yellow ducks, red beavers, and green frogs began to appear on beaches throughout the geosphere. Some of these toys were washed up in Australia and Alaska. Others landed in western South America. Scientists think the last of the toys will wash up in England.

The Ocean in Motion

The water in Earth's ocean is constantly moving. Ocean water that flows from one place to another is called an ocean *current*. An ocean current is like a river of water within an ocean. Different currents have different properties and effects. Some flow near the ocean's surface. Others are much deeper. Some currents consist of cold water, but others are warm. The floating bathtub toys traveled around the world on surface ocean currents. Earth's ocean currents can be mapped. Maps show that huge systems of surface currents move water in a circular pattern. Each system is made up of several main currents.

How Surface Currents Form

Surface currents result from interactions between the hydrosphere and the atmosphere. Wind is moving air. It pushes on the ocean's surface and moves the water in a horizontal direction. Some surface currents last for only a short time in a small area. Many, however, are long lasting. They cover large parts of the ocean.

Earth's ocean current systems move and mix water in a circular pattern. Within each circle are several currents.

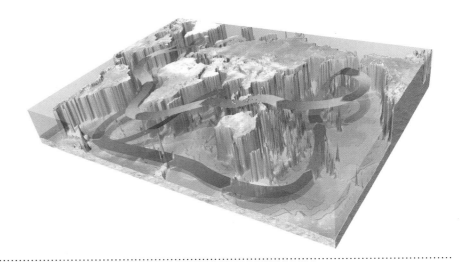

Palm trees grow in southern England because warm ocean currents warm the climate. Southern England is almost as far north as Alaska, which is not warmed by ocean currents.

How Deep Water Currents Form

Deep water currents are caused partly by temperature differences in the ocean. Cold water is usually heavier than warm water. When the cold water meets warmer water, the cold water sinks. This causes a vertical current.

The Effects of Ocean Currents

Surface currents have an important effect on climates. The Gulf Stream, one of the best known warm currents, flows along the East Coast of the United States. Then it turns east and crosses the Atlantic Ocean, when it is called the North Atlantic Current. The Gulf Stream carries warm water north from the Gulf of Mexico. As it flows, it transfers heat from warmer areas of Earth to cooler areas. England and much of northwestern Europe would be much colder in winter if it were not for this current.

Cold currents start near the poles. They carry cold water toward the equator. California would be warmer if not for the cold current from the Arctic. Western Africa would be warmer if not for the cold current from the Antarctic. Thus, ocean currents play an important role in determining the climate of an area.

Ocean water contains tiny organisms that are food for fish and other ocean animals. Ocean currents carry this food from one part of the ocean to another. This interaction of the hydrosphere and the biosphere provides food for marine animals so they can live in different areas of the ocean.

Orange growers sometimes lose their crop when the jet stream dips south and brings freezing weather to Florida.

5. Prevailing Winds

Why does a plane trip from New York to London take less time than a similar plane trip from London to New York? Winds moving from west to east through the atmosphere help push the plane east.

Wind is moving air. Air moves because Earth's surface is heated unevenly. Land heats up faster than water does so the air above a beach becomes warmer than the air above the water. The warm air rises and is replaced by cooler air that moves in from above the water. This is a sea breeze.

Winds also form high in the atmosphere. When the wind blows more often from one direction than from any other, it is called a **prevailing wind**. In the United States, prevailing winds generally blow from west to east. The winds carry clouds and air masses with them. Weather seen in the west on Monday will usually be seen in the east later in the week.

The pattern and direction of wind currents in the lower atmosphere is very similar to that of the surface ocean currents in the hydrosphere. You may have heard of a jet stream. Jet streams are fast flowing worldwide air currents similar to ocean currents. Most blow from west to east. A jet stream usually flows through the middle of the United States, separating the cooler air in the north from the warmer air in the south, but it can move. In winter, it may dip to the south. Then it brings cold air to the southern part of the country. If it moves north in summer, it can bring a heat wave north. A jet stream can produce low-pressure areas and stormy weather in the air underneath it.

How Do Earth's Systems Produce Weather and Climate?

1. Earth's Systems Interact   Earth's systems interact with each other to produce weather and climate. Weather is the condition of the atmosphere at a place for a short period of time, while climate is the general weather of place over a long period of time.

2. Air Pressure and Temperature   Air in the atmosphere is always moving. Air pressure is affected by the amount of water vapor in the air. The Earth's surface affects the temperature of the air. Air pressure and temperature affect the weather and climate of an area.

3. Clouds and Precipitation   Clouds form when water vapor in the air cools and condenses to turn into liquid water droplets. When the water droplets in the clouds grow too large and heavy, they fall to earth as precipitation. You can make different predictions on the weather from what the clouds and precipitation look like.

4. Ocean Currents   The water in Earth's ocean is constantly moving. Ocean water that flows from one place to another is called an ocean current. Ocean currents affect many things, including the climate of areas and the organisms that live in the ocean.

5. Prevailing Winds   Wind is moving air. Winds can form just above the Earth's surface or high in the atmosphere. Wind can carry clouds and air masses with them to affect the weather and climate of an area. When the wind blows more often from one direction than another, it is called a prevailing wind.

Antarctica for All

For more than fifty years, scientists of many nations have set aside Antarctica for research. How do scientists live and work together in Antarctica? And what are they learning about climate and how Earth's systems interact in this frozen continent?

Ah, springtime! The sun rose last week, and it will not set again for six months. The temperature is below freezing, but it is warm for October—a toasty −13°C (8°F). But it is springtime because seasons are reversed in the southern hemisphere, where Antarctica is located. It is now time to get the research stations ready for the arrival of the scientists and others who work at or near the South Pole.

Staying in Antarctica is not easy, but scientists from all over the world do it. Some scientists study the plants, animals, and other organisms in Antarctica. Other scientists study the weather there. Glaciers and snow are other topics that scientists visit Antarctica to study. No matter what scientists in Antarctica study, it is important for them to know more than one language. This is because people come to Antarctica from all over the world.

Many nations have signed a treaty called the Antarctic Treaty, which forbids military bases and encourages scientific research. This treaty was signed on December 1, 1959 by twelve nations. Since then, more nations have agreed to the treaty to set aside Antarctica for research. Once a year, representatives from each country that has signed the treaty gather to make decisions about the continent. The group discusses any changes that might affect Antarctica, from drilling a hole to choosing a fuel source for electricity.

By international treaty, Antarctica is set aside for peaceful scientific research. These scientists are using a robot to study sea ice.

The atmosphere in Antarctica behaves very differently than the atmosphere in other places. Scientists discovered that the ice does not warm up the air above it, so the air does not rise.

The Weather Down South

Antarctica is unlike any other continent. Nearly all of Antarctica is covered with an ice sheet that is more than 1.8 km (about 1 mi) thick. This ice has a huge effect on the interactions among the geosphere, hydrosphere, and atmosphere.

On continents without ice, the sun first heats the ground. Then, the heated ground heats the air directly above it. The air that is heated by the ground rises, which causes it to mix with cooler air. Scientists discovered that this mixing process does not happen in Antarctica. The sun shines on the ice, but the ice stays colder than the air above it. The ice does not warm the air, so the air does not rise. So, there is always a cold layer of air above the ice.

The effects of the cold ice on the air get stronger in winter because there is no sun. In parts of Antarctica, the sun stays in the sky 24 hours a day for six months. Then, the sun sets and does not rise again for the next six months. There is no sun heating the ground. As a result, the ground gets even colder. The air still does not rise and mix. The winds in this layer of air can be very strong and steady. Some gusts of wind reach 200 kilometers per hour (124 miles per hour)!

Wind is not the only extreme weather in Antarctica. It can be cold with no rain and very little snow. There can also be ground blizzards. These blizzards happen when old snow is blown by the wind. The top of the ice sheet is very flat, with nothing to block the wind, so the blowing snow buries research stations and equipment.

Drilling into the Past

Antarctica's ice sheet not only affects the weather and climate. It also keeps a record of it. This record in the ice forms through interactions between the atmosphere and the hydrosphere. How does this record form?

First, snow falls or gets blown onto the ice sheet. The snow traps some air. As time goes by, more and more layers of snow build up and each layer traps more air. As the snow piles up, it turns to ice with bubbles of air inside. These bubbles are the record kept of the weather and climate in Antarctica.

Scientists study the history of the atmosphere by drilling out ice cores. Then they analyze the air bubbles in them. Data from ice cores show how much of each gas was in the air at different times in the past. These gases are clues about the temperature.

The ice cores tell scientists a lot about climate—even the climate hundreds or thousands of years ago. For example, a group of scientists from ten countries in Europe drilled all the way through the Antarctic ice sheet to the rock below. They took an ice core sample that dates back 800,000 years. Data from the core shows eight time periods with *ice ages*. An ice age is a long period of time in which Earth's atmosphere is cooling so that there is more ice. There is much more to learn from this ice core. As the layers are analyzed, the European group is making the data available online to other scientists worldwide.

The ice sheet holds hundreds of thousands of years of data about Antarctica's climate history. These two scientists from the British Antarctic Survey are dressed in clean suits so they do not contaminate the ice core sample.

Antarctica is a difficult place to live. Here, a cargo ship brings supplies for the research season. Everything that the scientists use must be brought in by ship or by plane.

Living in Antarctica

Studying the atmosphere is just one field of research in Antarctica. Biologists go there to study the biosphere, from microorganisms to whales. Geologists go to investigate the interactions between the ice sheet (hydrosphere) and the mountains (geosphere) that lie underneath it. Astronomers enjoy six months of night sky and the dry air that gives telescopes a clear view.

But although the science in Antarctica is great, the living is difficult. Everything that scientists need must be brought in by boat or plane. This includes food, clothes, shelter, and fuel sources of electricity. There are no clothing stores, farms, or power plants in Antarctica. The only thing that is plentiful is ice, and even that takes fuel to melt it into water. But scientists often use snow caves as freezers for their food.

Of course, another reason Antarctica is difficult to live is that it is cold. In the winter, temperatures can dip below −73°C (−100°F). That's so cold that plastic bags and rubber bands freeze and break when bent! Touching metal with your bare skin can cause burns, and just breathing the air without covering your mouth can burn your lungs.

Even though living in Antarctica is difficult, scientists continue to come together to study there. So, Antarctica has been a model of international cooperation. As more scientists become more involved in research there, our understanding of how Earth's systems interact grows. Perhaps someday you be a scientist who spends time "on the ice" working with scientists from all over the world on a continent-sized research lab. But if you go, remember to bundle up!

How Do Earth's Systems Change Earth's Surface?

Science Vocabulary

deposition

erosion

landform

weathering

Earth's surface looks very different now from how it looked thousands of years ago. Earth's systems are constantly interacting with each other and the Earth's surface changes as a result. Canyons in the geosphere, like the Grand Canyon in Arizona, are formed when rivers in the hydrosphere wear away rock.

NGSS | **5-ESS2-1.** Develop a model using an example to describe ways the geosphere, biosphere, hydrosphere, and/or atmosphere interact. | **ESS2.A.** Earth's major systems are the geosphere (solid and molten rock, soil, and sediments), the hydrosphere (water and ice), the atmosphere (air), and the biosphere (living things, including humans). These systems interact in multiple ways to affect Earth's surface materials and processes. The ocean supports a variety of ecosystems and organisms, shapes landforms, and influences climate. Winds and clouds in the atmosphere interact with the landforms to determine patterns of weather. | **Systems and System Models** A system can be described in terms of its components and their interactions. | **Developing and Using Models**

1. Earth's Surface Changes

What changes occur to Earth's surface when systems interact? Millions of years ago, a glacier dug out a deep valley in the area where Yosemite National Park is today. A river flowing nearby met a steep wall of the valley and plunged over it. Bridalveil Falls was created in the river from an interaction between the hydrosphere and the geosphere.

Earth's surface is always changing. Many of these changes occur because Earth's systems interact. Mountains are worn down by water and wind, changing their shape and forming new soil over time. Glaciers in the hydrosphere pick up rocks and soil in the geosphere and carry them far away. The rock and soil forms hills when they stop moving. The hydrosphere's flowing water carries away soil from river banks and beaches in the geosphere. The water and wind deposits the soil in new places to build new beaches, sand dunes, and other natural structures. These natural structures on Earth's surface are called **landforms**.

Plants and animals in the biosphere change Earth's surface in many ways. Plant roots break up rock, part of the geosphere. Decaying plant matter in the biosphere helps to form new soil for the geosphere. People remove soil when they mine minerals. They build dams, creating new bodies of water where forests and hills once stood.

As Earth's surface changes, the other systems change. Weather and climate may change if a new mountain range in the geosphere causes more or fewer clouds to form. Animals may leave an area if weather patterns change.

Bridalveil Falls in Yosemite National Park was created when a glacier gouged out the valley and changed the landscape.

2. How Islands Form

When you think of an island, you may picture a sandy area with a palm tree surrounded by water. Islands are surrounded by water, but they are not always sandy nor have palm trees. Manhattan is an island covered with tall buildings. There are four kinds of islands and they form in different ways.

Continental Islands

A continental island forms when a chunk of land breaks off from a continent, a major land mass. This piece becomes an island. Continental islands form when the hydrosphere and geosphere interact. Greenland, Earth's largest island, formed in this way millions of years ago.

Continental islands can also form when changes in sea level occur. Thousands of years ago, the northern part of Earth was covered with glaciers. Sea level was much lower than it is today. As the Earth warmed, the glaciers began to melt and the sea level rose. The ocean covered some of the low-lying land, creating continental islands. Great Britain was formed in this way. It was once part of mainland Europe.

Volcanic Islands

There are volcanoes on the ocean floor that erupt to release lava that hardens on the ocean's floor. When a volcano erupts over and over again, layers of lava build up until it appears above water and an island is formed. Lava is molten rock from the Earth's mantle that reaches the Earth's surface. Thus, volcanic islands form when the hydrosphere and geosphere interact. Volcanic islands are made of igneous rock. The islands of Hawaii are volcanic islands.

The Hawaiian Islands were formed when underwater volcanos erupted. Layers of lava stacked on top of each other until they formed the islands you see today.

Barrier Islands

Barrier islands also form by the interaction of the hydrosphere and the geosphere. They are narrow islands that form near coastlines when ocean currents deposit piles of sand and other sediments. Eventually the piles rise above the water's surface and become islands. Barrier islands act to protect the coast from ocean waves and wind during storms. Barrier islands can also form in rivers when sediments are deposited.

Barrier islands can also form when glaciers melt. The sea level rises and floods areas around sand dunes, creating sandy islands. The Outer Banks along the southeastern coast of the United States formed this way. Glaciers pick up rock, soil, and gravel as they move over land. This material piles up when a glacier melts. The piles are surrounded by water as sea level rises.

Coral Islands

Coral islands form when the biosphere and hydrosphere interact. Tiny sea animals called corals live in warm ocean water. Corals produce hard skeletons made of limestone outside their bodies that are similar to the shells of clams. Corals live in large colonies that contain thousands of organisms. A coral colony forms a huge limestone reef on the ocean floor. As corals reproduce, the reef grows larger. It grows upward in layers until it breaks through the water's surface. A coral island is formed. Coral islands are made mostly of limestone but sand and other kinds of rock may be included. The islands of the Bahamas and the Florida Keys in the Atlantic Ocean are coral islands.

The Florida Keys are coral islands. You can see much of the submerged coral reef through the clear water.

This sea cave was formed by weathering of the rock cliff by ocean waves.

3. Weathering, Erosion, and Deposition

What would happen if you hit two rocks against each other above a table? You might find crumbs of rock on the table. If you hit the rocks hard and long enough, you might even break off a large piece. Rock on the Earth's surface can also crumble and change shape.

Weathering

Earth's surface and its landforms are always changing. Many changes take millions of years. Weathering is one of these slow changes. **Weathering** is the breaking down of rock by interactions with Earth's systems. Wind carries tiny pieces of sand. They hit and rub against rock and wear it away. This is an atmosphere-geosphere interaction. Rain, rivers, and ocean waves also carry tiny pieces of sand. They beat against rock and weather it. Water also seeps into cracks in rock. The cracks expand when the water freezes. Eventually, pieces of rock break off and are carried away. Glaciers gouge out rock when they move over it. These are examples of hydrosphere-geosphere interactions. Plant roots grow into cracks in rocks when the roots search for water. As roots grow larger, they expand the cracks and push apart the rock. This is a biosphere-geosphere interaction.

Weathering changes the shape of landforms. Water moving through the geosphere can slowly hollow out a large area of rock. Some caves form underground when water trickles through soil and rock. Sea caves form when waves weather rock at the base of cliffs. Wind weathered rock in the Sahara Desert in North Africa to create strange rock shapes.

These rock formations were created when wind weathered the soft sandstone rock in the Sahara Desert.

Erosion occurs on the outside of a river bend because water is flowing faster there and rubs harder against the river bank. Deposition occurs on the inside of the bend where water flow is slower and sediments are dropped.

Erosion

Sediments form from weathered rock. What happens to the sediments? **Erosion** is the loosening and carrying away of weathered material from one place to another. Wind in the atmosphere, and water and glaciers in the hydrosphere cause erosion. They pick up the sediments and carry them away. The amount of erosion is greatest when the wind or water moves fast for long periods of time. It took millions of years for water in the Colorado River to weather and erode enough rock to form the Grand Canyon.

Deposition

When moving wind, water, and glaciers in the atmosphere and hydrosphere slow down, they drop the sediments they carry. This process is called deposition. New landforms are created by **deposition**. For example, rivers slow when they approach the ocean. They drop their load of sediments to the river bottom. Eventually, a *river delta* forms. A river delta is a large flat area of land at the mouth of a river. Soil in a river delta is often very rich because the river erodes nutrient-rich soil and deposits the soil at the river delta.

New beaches form where sediments in ocean water are deposited. The shape of a river may change as soil is eroded from the outside of a bend and deposited on the inside of the bend, where water flow is slower and does not push as had on the river bank. Glaciers deposit gravel and rocks at their front and sides before and as they melt and shrink. Ridges of rocks form. The geosphere is shaped by the different Earth systems.

4. How Soil Forms

Imagine that a volcano erupts and covers the soil with lava that hardens into a thick layer of rock. Within a few years, tiny plants begin to grow in cracks in the rock. Plants need soil to grow. How did this soil appear?

Soil contains parts from all four of Earth's systems. It has pieces of rock and minerals, bits of decaying plant and animal matter, water, and air pockets. The pieces of rock and minerals in soil come from sediments, or weathered rock. It is mixed with bits of decaying plant and animal matter from organisms that have died. Water comes from recycled precipitation and runoff from the water cycle. Air comes from the atmosphere. The parts mix together to form soil. Worms and other living things in soil help to mix together the parts of soil. Worms and plant roots make channels in soil. Air enters the soil through these channels.

It can take more than a thousand years for new soil to form. Climate plays a role in soil formation. Warm temperatures and a lot of rain cause soil to form faster because weathering is faster. Soil forms more slowly in cold dry climates where less weathering occurs. Soil accumulates faster on flat land because newly formed topsoil is not carried away quickly. On steep slopes such as mountainsides, new soil may be eroded almost as soon as it forms.

Soil is carried by wind and water to new places, where it is deposited. Small amounts may be deposited in the crack of a rock. If a seed falls into this tiny bit of soil, it begins to grow. The developing roots help to break down the rock. The broken-down rock is added to the soil to make more soil.

This plant has begun to grow in the crack of a rock. A tiny bit of soil has blown into the crack. The plant roots will help make more soil.

How Do Earth's Systems Change Earth's Surface?

1. Earth's Surface Changes   Earth systems are constantly interacting. Glaciers and rivers in the hydrosphere, the wind in the atmosphere, and plants and animals in the biosphere all shape the natural structures on Earth's surface. These natural structures are called landforms.

2. How Islands Form   Islands are landforms surrounded by water. There are four different types of islands. The different types of islands are formed in different ways and from different interactions. Some are formed as the hydrosphere and geosphere interact, and some are formed as the biosphere and geosphere interact.

3. Weathering, Erosion, and Deposition   Wind, water, glaciers, and plants and animals weather, erode, and deposit rock in the geosphere. The Earth's surface changes as rocks in the geosphere are weathered, eroded, and deposited by the atmosphere, hydrosphere, and biosphere. Different Earth systems interact to result in weathering, erosion, and deposition.

4. How Soil Forms   Soil is formed from parts of all four of Earth's systems. It contains pieces of rocks and minerals, decaying plant and animal matter, water, and air. Soil can take more than a thousand years to form. The wind and water carry soil to new places where it is deposited.

Let Worms Do the Work

Worms are important actors in the interactions between the biosphere and geosphere. How do some farmers use worms to turn cow manure and other waste into high-value compost?

The farmer checked on her livestock before going indoors for the night. Her barns were filled with healthy, contented animals quietly munching their dinner. The cows had done a good job that day, turning feed and hay into milk that would nourish people. The cows also produced *manure*, or droppings that can be used as fertilizer. The farmer used to have trouble finding something to do with all the cow manure. Now, her new neighbor was helping out.

Next door, the neighboring farmer also checked on his "livestock." His barns were also filled with healthy animals quietly munching their dinner. The worms had done a good job that day, turning cow manure from the neighbor's farm into worm compost that would nourish plants.

Vermiculture is the practice of farming worms. Worms turn plant and animal waste from the biosphere into compost for soil, which is an important part of the geosphere.

The worm farmer next door practices vermiculture, which is a fancy name for worm farming. Vermiculture is growing due to the demand for worm compost. Crop farmers love worm compost because it does an excellent job nourishing plants and protecting them from disease.

Why do worms produce such great compost? Whether they are living in a worm barn or living outdoors, worms turn waste from the biosphere into important ingredients of soil, which is part of the geosphere. But getting worms to help change cow manure into good worm compost takes more than simply dumping worms into manure.

From Cow Barn to Worm Farm

In the early days of vermiculture, some farmers fed their worms fresh cow manure. But doing this led to problems. First, manure contains disease-causing bacteria such as *E.coli*. Second, cow manure can carry undigested seeds from weeds. Worms do not digest seeds, either. So, any seeds in the worm compost would sprout and grow in the farm fields where the compost was used.

To prevent these problems, many worm farmers pre-compost the manure. Pre-composting is done like any other composting that does not rely on worms. The manure is stacked in large heaps and left to decompose through the action of *microbes*, which are organisms that are too small to see. As the microbes work, the temperature of the manure rises. The manure gets hot enough to kill off *E.coli* and weed seeds before the manure is fed to worms.

Worm farmers use various systems to feed and care for their worms. Some systems are as simple as shallow beds framed in railroad ties. Dark fabric that covers the beds is pulled back to shovel in manure and to harvest compost. Others systems use special metal containers. Manure is added at the top and worm compost is harvested at the bottom. The whole process, from pre-composting to finished product, takes from two to six months.

Regardless of the system used, the worms do the same thing: eat manure or other biosphere waste and produce castings, or the technical name for worm droppings. Worm castings are the high-value compost that farmers use to enrich the soil of the geosphere.

Many worm farmers feed their worms with dairy cow manure.

Pre-composting manure for a few weeks raises its temperature high enough to kill disease-causing bacteria and break down weed seeds. The pre-composted manure is then fed to the worms.

Worm compost costs more than other fertilizers, but some farmers say it is worth it. Scientists and farmers are working together to find out whether worm compost really does have all the benefits that farmers say it does.

Worm Your Way to Bigger Vegetables

Worm compost is more expensive than most other fertilizers. But it is in high demand by fruit, vegetable, and nut farmers. This is because farmers have discovered that worm compost seems to have extra advantages over regular compost.

Farmers find that plants fertilized with worm compost are stronger and healthier than plants grown with other forms of fertilizer. The plants are less likely to get diseases and be damaged from pests. New trees are less likely to die before bearing fruit. The plants produce more fruits and vegetables, and those fruits and vegetables are bigger. So, many farmers are happy to pay more for worm compost.

The advantages of worm farming are being explored. So, worm farmers are working with scientists to test the effect of worm compost on crops. Some experiments compare the size and health of crops grown with and without worm compost. Other experiments study the properties of worm compost that make plants less likely to get diseases. So far, results show that worms add microbes to the manure. The worms' microbes protect certain plants against disease-causing microbes. But for other plants, something other than microbes seems to be protecting them. Many more experiments are needed to know for sure.

Make Your Own Worm Compost

Worm compost is helpful for house plants and home gardens, as well as full-size farms. You can have your own worms working for you to make compost, even if you live in an apartment.

Start by making a worm bin for your worms to live in. A simple worm bin is a dark container with a lid, with holes drilled in the sides, bottom, and lid. A dark container keeps out light, which worms do not like. Holes in the top and sides let air in, while holes in the bottom let extra water drain out. Use bricks to prop your worm bin up on a tray or in another container. The tray will catch any water that leaks out.

Next, fill your worm bin with bedding. Torn newspaper and brown cardboard are great bedding. Do not use colored paper or magazines, which may have poisonous chemicals. Spray the bedding with water until it is as wet as a wrung-out sponge. For food, add vegetable peelings, banana peels, used tea bags, and similar scraps. Do not add meat, dairy, or anything greasy.

Let your bin sit for a week, and then add worms. The best worms for composting are red wigglers. Some worm farmers sell worms online. Or, if you know someone who already has a worm bin, he or she may be willing to share. Healthy worms reproduce all the time. After adding the worms, you'll need to add food and bedding every week. Keep everything moist but not wet. Your first worm compost should be ready in a couple of months. And, thankfully, you can have it without using any cow manure!

You can drill holes in a container for your worm bin.

To make a worm bin, drill holes in a large plastic bin. Then fill it with wet cardboard or paper, food, and worms.

How Do Farming and Industry Affect Earth's Systems?

Science Vocabulary

pollution

toxic

Humans have a huge impact on Earth's systems. The food you eat is grown and raised in farms. The electricity you use is generated in a power plant. Objects are manufactured in industries like the one pictured here. Most of these activities produce pollution that affects Earth's systems.

NGSS

5-ESS3-1. Obtain and combine information about ways individual communities use science ideas to protect the Earth's resources and environment.

ESS3-C. Human activities in agriculture, industry, and everyday life have had major effects on the land, vegetation, streams, ocean, air, and even outer space. But individuals and communities are doing things to help protect Earth's resources and environments.

Systems and System Models A system can be described in terms of its components and their interactions.

Obtaining, Evaluating, and Communicating Information

1. Humans Affect Earth's Systems

Coal, crude oil, and natural gas are fossil fuels. You have probably heard that Earth's fossil fuels are being used up. People use them much faster than nature can make them. Why are people using so many fossil fuels? What are people doing to prevent them from being used up?

Humans are part of Earth's biosphere. Although the biosphere contains the least amount of matter of Earth's four systems, and humans make up only a small part of it, human activities have a huge effect on Earth's systems.

Most fossil fuels are used in power plants to make electricity. You might use electricity to keep your home warm in winter and cool in summer. People also use electricity to run machinery in factories. People use fossil fuels in cars, buses, and trucks to move people and things from place to place. As more people use fossil fuels to meet their many needs, the supply is being used up. Scientists have estimated that the world's supply of crude oil will be gone between 2050 and 2075 if we continue to use it as quickly as we do now.

Scientists and engineers are working to develop other energy sources. If people use solar, wind, and water power to make some of the electricity people need, then less fossil fuels will be used. If people build cars that run on batteries, they will save more fossil fuels.

There are many ways humans have an impact on Earth's systems. Two ways are through farming and industry.

Humans affect Earth systems whenever they use electricity. More than two-thirds of all fossil fuels, a part of the geosphere, are used to make electricity.

Large-scale chicken farms can produce thousands of eggs in a small space, but they produce a lot of waste. Wastes often pollute water.

2. Farming Affects Earth's Systems

Humans on Earth need food to survive. Most food comes from large commercial farms that raise fruit, vegetables, and animals used for meat. You may not notice, but farming actually affects Earth's systems.

Farming Affects the Hydrosphere

Most farmers add fertilizers to the soil. Fertilizers provide crops with nutrients. Farmers also spray their crops with *toxic* chemicals that kill weeds and harmful insects. **Toxic** materials are materials that cause injury or death to an organism. But fertilizers and toxic chemicals can also cause *pollution*. **Pollution** is the presence of anything in the environment that can harm living things or damage natural resources.

Fertilizers and toxic chemicals cause water pollution when rain washes them from soil. Animal wastes also pollute water. All of these materials seep into streams, rivers, and ground water that provide our drinking water. They may flow into ponds, lakes, and the ocean and harm life there. Fertilizers can also cause huge numbers of green, plantlike organisms called algae to grow. After the algae die, they decay. The decaying process uses up oxygen that is dissolved in the water, causing many fish that need oxygen to die. Sometimes living things that need less oxygen move into the pond or lake. Other times, there is no oxygen, so the pond or lake becomes "dead." A body of water is "dead" when nothing can live there. Parts of the Gulf of Mexico are dead because there is so little oxygen in the water.

Fields of crop plants and the thousands of animals that large-scale farms raise need a lot of water. Farmers must irrigate their fields and provide water for animals. Using this fresh water can cause water shortages for people.

Farming Affects the Atmosphere

Livestock, especially cows, produce a large amount of methane gas in their intestines. This gas is released into the air and affects the composition of the atmosphere. Recall that carbon dioxide and water vapor absorb energy from the warm surface of Earth. Methane does, too. Millions of cows are raised on large-scale farms. The large quantities of methane they produce contribute to global warming.

Farmers that work large farms spray toxic chemicals onto their crops by plane to kill weeds and insects. Occasionally, these chemicals mix with the air and pollute it. The chemicals may spread onto living things that will be harmed by them. Farmers must be very careful not to spray in windy weather or when rain is predicted.

Farming can create pollution in the atmosphere. Crop duster planes spread chemicals and may pollute the atmosphere.

Farming Affects the Geosphere

Rich topsoil is often blown away by wind when it is plowed. Running water can wash away topsoil when crops are planted on sloping land. Some farmers avoid this by contour plowing. They plow the soil in curved bands that follow the shape of the land. By doing this, running water does not wash away topsoil as easily. Contour plowing reduces soil erosion. It helps the soil hold moisture and nutrients. Tree farmers also prevent soil erosion when they cut only a few trees in a forest instead of clear-cutting the entire forest. This method is time-consuming and expensive, but it leaves tree roots that hold soil.

Farmers are developing different methods to reduce farming's effect on Earth's systems. Contour plowing reduces soil erosion and helps the soil hold moisture.

Industries sometimes release chemicals and other wastes into rivers. The materials pollute the water and harm fish that live there.

3. Industry Affects Earth's Systems

Humans have built factories to produce the many things they need. Plants and animals lose their homes when factories are built. Earth's systems are also affected in other ways.

Industries Affect the Hydrosphere

For a long time, engineers have found different ways to change the way a river flows to help industries. They have straightened a river, made it deeper, or blocked it with a dam. People might dig out a river to make it straighter and deeper. Large ships can navigate a straight, deep river more easily than a shallow, curved river. Making a river deeper can also prevent flooding. Building a dam produces water power that is used to make needed electricity. Humans also straighten rivers so roads, houses, and factories can be more easily built.

But changing a river causes problems. River water flows faster when curves are straightened. This increases erosion. Removing plants from a river bank also increases erosion. It also affects the animals that live in and near the river. When dams are built, the environment changes. So does the wildlife. Engineers are beginning to remove some dams that are no longer needed. The rivers will slowly recover.

Nuclear power plants produce electricity. They also produce toxic waste and a lot of heat. The plants are usually built near a body of water such as a river or ocean so engineers can use its water to get rid of the heat. This causes the body of water to warm up, killing fish and other animals. Warming up water can be a form of water pollution. Industries also pollute water when they pour toxic chemicals into a body of water.

Industries Affect the Atmosphere

Industries release harmful chemicals into the air. These chemicals react with sunlight to form smog, a kind of air pollution. Chemicals formed from burning gasoline in vehicles can also form smog. Smog makes breathing difficult. Some chemicals in the air combine to form acids that dissolve in raindrops. This acid rain kills forest trees and creates dead lakes where fish cannot survive. Governments have tried to prevent acid rain by limiting the amount of toxic chemicals released into the air. They have had some success. But acid rain is still a problem.

You may not have thought of space debris as pollution of the atmosphere, but it is. Discarded and old satellite parts and burned-out rocket stages orbit Earth. This space garbage is dangerous because it may collide with working spacecraft.

Industries Affect the Geosphere

Factories need raw materials. These materials are often mined from the geosphere. Mining destroys landforms. It creates land, water, and air pollution. It leaves the soil contaminated with harmful chemicals. Factories also cause land pollution because they generate large amounts of wastes and trash. Some are dumped illegally, and others are added to landfills. Many places are running out of space for landfills. Garbage often contains toxic chemicals. Even newspaper ink can be harmful. These chemicals can seep into soil and harm plants and animals.

Industries produce chemicals that can react with sunlight to form smog. This layer of smog over Los Angeles, California, makes breathing difficult. Smog alerts are issued that warn people to stay indoors.

Nature of Science

4. Scientists Study Pollution

Suppose a community's river has become polluted with a toxic chemical. Fish are dying. Scientists need to find out where the chemical comes from. They need to find out how the chemical harms fish. And they need to find out how the river water can be made safe again.

Scientists collect information by asking questions. Scientific questions can be answered with data that come from doing experiments. For example, scientists may ask and answer "Does the chemical in the river come from the new shoe factory in town?" and "How does the chemical harm fish?" A question that scientists cannot answer scientifically is "Do you believe this factory should be moved to a different location?" This question asks for an opinion and cannot be answered with data from experiments.

When scientists study pollution, they also learn how people can use science to protect the environment. Some of this information comes from books or science journals. Some comes from doing experiments. And some comes from observations in field studies. The information often helps the engineers design a solution to a problem. They may find out that a pipe at the shoe factory has broken and is leaking toxic chemicals. They may just fix the pipe. They may want to design a pipe made of a different material that will not break. They may find out that factory workers are dumping the toxic chemicals into the river on purpose. If so, they may turn the problem over to the police or government officials.

Scientists study the effect of pollution on fish when they learn that harmful chemicals have entered the water. They ask questions that can be answered with data that come from experiments.

How Do Farming and Industry Affect Earth's Systems?

1. Humans Affect Earth's Systems   Humans are only a small part of the biosphere, but they can have a huge effect on Earth's systems. One impact humans have on Earth's systems is through producing electricity. The energy you use is generated by fossil fuels, which are slowing running out.

2. Farming Affects Earth's Systems   Farming produces pollution, something in the environment that can harm living things or damage natural resources. The fertilizers and chemicals that kill weeds and harmful insects can seep into streams and rivers, or mix into the air. Animal waste can also pollute the water you drink. Farming affects many different Earth systems.

3. Industry Affects Earth's Systems   Humans have built many factories to produce the many things they need. These industries affect Earth's systems in many different ways. They can change the environment to make it hard for plants and animals to live. They can also release harmful chemicals that pollute the Earth.

4. Scientists Study Pollution   Scientists collect information by asking scientific questions that can be answered with data from doing experiments. They read books or science journals, perform experiments, and conduct field studies to find information to help engineers design solutions to problems.

Traveling Tacos

Ordering in a restaurant is easy, but the foods in just one meal may travel long distances before you eat them. How does food get to a restaurant, and how does its journey affect Earth's systems?

Suppose you are at a Mexican restaurant. Your family is seated around a table, looking at menus. So much to choose from! Should you get fajitas, a burrito, a quesadilla, or something else? You make your decision and order fish tacos. While you wait, watching the servers go by with plates of food, you start wondering. How did the food get to the kitchen? The fish must have come from the water somewhere. But how did the fish get here? How did any of the food get here?

Most restaurants serve food that has traveled great distances. Food in the United States is produced, processed, and shipped in large quantities. One benefit of this production is that food is plentiful, good quality, and less expensive. Another benefit is that a wide variety of food is available across the United States, all year long. Where you live or what season it is does not matter.

Food travels a short distance from a restaurant's kitchen to your table. But the ingredients traveled much farther to reach the kitchen.

But these benefits have costs. Energy is needed to raise food, to process and package it, and to ship it to a restaurant or grocery store where the consumer buys it. Whether the food is shipped by airplane, by rail, or by truck, emissions from the burning fuel affect the atmosphere.

Believe it or not: the ingredients in your fish tacos most likely traveled from all over the country to get to you. Maybe even from all over the world!

Making a corn tortilla starts with growing and harvesting corn before it is shipped to a mill for processing. Once it is processed, it goes to a bakery and then is shipped to a warehouse or restaurant. All these steps affect Earth's systems.

Tortilla Travels

The wrappers of your tacos are soft, corn tortillas. Corn is the main ingredient in corn tortillas. The United States grows more corn than any other country. So, your tortilla probably started in Iowa, Illinois, Nebraska, or another corn-producing state.

Growing corn involves interactions between all of Earth's systems. Corn grows in the soil of the geosphere. It uses gases from the atmosphere and water from the hydrosphere. Corn plants use up nutrients in the soil, so farmers add fertilizers to replace them. Organic fertilizers are made from biosphere materials, such as manure. Chemical fertilizers are made from minerals in the geosphere and gases in the atmosphere. Farmers have to be careful with fertilizer. It could run off fields and into ponds and rivers where it can pollute the hydrosphere.

Before corn becomes a tortilla, it has to be harvested with a tractor, which uses fuel. Then, the corn is shipped to a mill, which uses more fuel. At the mill, the corn goes through several steps to remove its hard outer coating. Next, the corn is cooked in a liquid, and then ground into corn meal and corn flour.

The mill then ships the corn products to a bakery, which can be almost anywhere in the country. The bakery produces and packages the tortillas. Finally, the bakery ships the tortillas to restaurants. Your corn tortillas went through many steps and traveled hundreds of miles using plenty of fuel before it reached you. And the tortilla is just one part of a fish taco.

Cabbage is often shipped from the field to a factory to be shredded before it travels to restaurants.

Vagabond Vegetables

Most fish tacos contain cabbage and salsa. Salsa is made from tomatoes, onions, peppers, and some spices. How do all these vegetables end up inside that corn tortilla?

Shredded cabbage is less processed than most other fish taco ingredients. The cabbage is grown and harvested, like the corn was. Then, it has to be cleaned, shredded, and served fresh. Often, cabbage is shredded before it reaches a restaurant. So, after the cabbage is grown, it is shipped from the field to a factory. The factory washes, shreds, and packages the cabbage in plastic bags. The bags are then shipped to restaurants. That's a lot of traveling for a product that is served fresh!

Salsa is made in factories all over the country and in Mexico. Many salsa factories are close to their customers but far away from where the ingredients grow. So, the vegetables travel from the farms to the factories. The factories cook the salsa, seal it in jars, and send it out to restaurants. Some restaurants choose to make their own salsa, but they still have to get ingredients from other places. Each time an ingredient is shipped or salsa is made, it uses fuel.

A lime wedge served on the side of your tacos could have traveled very far to get to your plate. Lime trees need a warm, sunny climate to grow. Many limes used in the United States are grown in California. Many limes come from Mexico and Guatemala, which are in North America. But your lime may have traveled from as far away as Spain or South Africa. Think about that when you squeeze a little juice on your fish!

Limes served in the United States may have been grown in this country. But some limes come from as far away as Spain or South Africa.

Far-Flung Fish

The fish in your tacos may have traveled the farthest of all the ingredients. Fish tacos usually contain a white fish that has a mild flavor, like cod or tilapia. The fish's voyage to your plate can be very different, depending on the kind of fish. However it reaches your plate, the hydrosphere is involved.

Cod is often caught in the wild. Almost all cod eaten in the United States is fished from the Atlantic Ocean or the Pacific Ocean. If cod is in your taco, it might have been caught off the coast of Alaska, Oregon, or New England. But it may have easily come from Russia, Norway, or Iceland, too. After the fish are caught, they are either put on ice whole or cut into filets. Fishing ships are equipped to freeze fish and keep them frozen for months. The freezers need fuel to run, just as the ship needs fuel to move.

Much of the fish eaten in the United States is farm-raised tilapia. Some tilapia farms raise the fish in ponds or in cages set into a lake. Other farms use giant tanks filled with water. Some tilapia farms have machines that automatically feed the fish and clean the tanks. Like the other ingredients in your taco, this fish is shipped. Both farming the fish and shipping it also uses fuel.

So, when the server walks the short distance from the kitchen to your table, be thankful that he didn't have to travel all over the world to gather the ingredients for your tacos. You would have to wait a long time for you dinner if he did!

Some fish are caught in the ocean and are then shipped to factories that clean and filet them. This fisherman is holding a cod, a fish that has mild-tasting, white meat.

How Do People's Everyday Lives Affect Earth's Systems?

Science Vocabulary

recycling

decompose

Every day you interact with the Earth's systems. When you are at home, when you are at school, and even when you are just walking around on the street. The food you eat and the objects you use all come from Earth's systems! Think back on your day. Can you think of how you have affected Earth's systems?

NGSS

5-ESS3-1. Obtain and combine information about ways individual communities use science ideas to protect the Earth's resources and environment.

ESS3-C. Human activities in agriculture, industry, and everyday life have had major effects on the land, vegetation, streams, ocean, air, and even outer space. But individuals and communities are doing things to help protect Earth's resources and environments.

Systems and System Models A system can be described in terms of its components and their interactions.

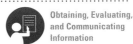

Obtaining, Evaluating, and Communicating Information

1. Affecting Earth's Systems in the Morning

Your alarm clock goes off. Still sleepy, you climb out of bed and head for the shower. It's a new day, one in which you will interact with Earth's four systems.

The shower helps to wake you up. Shower water is part of the hydrosphere. As you dry yourself, you notice the label on the towel which says the towel is made of cotton, a plant that is part of the biosphere. You brush your teeth, remembering to turn off the water while you brush. As you know, Earth's supply of fresh water is limited because most of it is trapped in ice. It is important to keep this small amount of usable water clean.

You get dressed and notice that your T-shirt is made of cotton and polyester. Polyester and many other fabrics are made from materials in crude oil, part of the geosphere.

You go downstairs for breakfast, and you smell toast as you walk into the kitchen. The smell of toast is caused by substances in the toast that float from the toast to your nose through air, part of the atmosphere. Toast is made from wheat, another plant in the biosphere. The toaster gets its power from electricity, which is produced by burning fossil fuels from the geosphere. The glass that holds your milk was made from sand. So many of the products you use are from the geosphere. You throw your trash in a trash can so it will be taken to a landfill to decompose. When a material **decomposes** it is broken down into smaller pieces.

You grab your books and run to catch the bus. You have hardly left your house, but you have already interacted many times with Earth's four systems.

Cotton fabric is made from plants in the biosphere. Cotton is a natural product that you might use every day.

Think of the many school buses that each school needs. Almost all of these buses use fuel from the geosphere and produce air pollution.

2. Affecting Earth's Systems at School

As you travel and spend your day in school, you continue to interact with Earth's systems.

In the School Bus

The bus you take to school is made mostly of steel. Steel is a mixture of several metals, such as iron, all of which are mined from Earth's crust. The plastic steering wheel and seats, rubber tires, and glass windows—in fact, most of the bus—are made from parts of the geosphere. The bus is powered by gasoline, a fossil fuel. You know that exhaust gases from buses can pollute the atmosphere and cause smog.

In the Classroom

Books are made of paper which comes from trees. You think about the forest and hope some of the trees remain. You also hope that new trees were planted to replace those that were cut down. Pencils are made from trees, too. The black inside core of a pencil is made of graphite, a mineral from Earth's crust. Ball-point pens are made of plastic, a material made from crude oil. The ink in your pen is a complex mixture of many chemicals, and the color in ink often comes from ground-up minerals.

In the Cafeteria

It is lunchtime and you head for the cafeteria. All of the food you eat comes from the biosphere, either plants or animals. As you learned, farming can deplete soil and pollute the atmosphere, hydrosphere, and biosphere. Animal wastes can pollute our water sources.

The Obstacle Course in Gym Class

In gym class, you run through an obstacle course made of cones. The cones are made of rubber manufactured from fossil fuels. The wood floor is made from trees. You breathe faster as you run. Breathing takes oxygen from the air and releases carbon dioxide and water vapor. You do not have to worry about using up all the oxygen in the atmosphere because plants produce oxygen when they make food.

As you run, you begin to sweat. Sweat is mostly water which evaporates from your skin and enters the air as water vapor. Your sweat may someday become part of a cloud. Remember that water is cycled among Earth's systems in the water cycle.

The Playground

After school, you and your friends go to a playground. Some of the equipment is made of metal, which comes from Earth's crust, part of the geosphere. Other equipment is made of wood, which comes from trees, part of the biosphere. Plastic parts are often made in factories from oil from the geosphere. If the park has a fountain, the fresh water is part of the hydrosphere.

Some of your friends use chalk to draw on the sidewalk. Chalk is a sedimentary rock that is taken from Earth's crust, part of the geosphere. Other friends start a baseball game, using a wood bat and a leather ball. Both are part of the biosphere. The wood is from trees and the leather is from animals.

Some of the equipment from a playground comes from Earth's systems. Climbing bars are made of metal. Metal comes from Earth's crust, part of the geosphere.

3. Affecting Earth's Systems at Home

When you get home from school, you relax before starting your homework. You may watch television for a while, call friends, or play a game on the Internet.

A friend may call you before dinner about going for a bike ride. Bikes are made in factories. The raw materials in a bike are mined from Earth's crust. Factories that manufacture the millions of bikes that are sold every year can affect the environment if they cause pollution.

Electronic devices such as television sets, cell phones, and computers are made in factories. They contain hundreds of materials that are taken from Earth's crust. Some metals, such as the cadmium found in computer batteries, are rare. Mercury and lead are toxic. Mercury is found in some light bulbs and flat screen monitors. Plastic cases made from fossil fuels can also be harmful. Factories that make these electronic devices must be careful not to cause pollution.

Old computers and other electronic devices can pollute land, water, and the atmosphere when they are not disposed of properly.

When electronic devices are discarded, they end up in landfills. The plastic cases do not decompose easily, so they become land pollution. Cathode ray tubes in old television sets and computer monitors contain lead. These devices should not be thrown out with trash. They must be discarded properly so they do not pollute the land and water. Some of their parts can also be recycled. **Recycling** is taking materials from old discarded objects and making new objects from them. You will read about recycling in the next lesson.

How Do People's Everyday Lives Affect Earth's Systems?

1. Affecting Earth's Systems in the Morning When you take a shower, you use water from the hydrosphere. When you get dressed, the clothes come from the biosphere or geosphere. The smell of breakfast is carried through air, part of the atmosphere. You can interact with all four Earth's systems even before you leave the house!

2. Affecting Earth's Systems at School Whether you're in the school bus, classroom, cafeteria, gym, or playground, you are affecting Earth's systems. The objects you interact with come from Earth's systems. Objects such as wood, metal, cloth, and plastic come from different Earth systems. The sweat and trash you produce affect Earth's systems. Everything you interact with, consume, or produce is a part of one or more Earth systems.

3. Affecting Earth's Systems at Home When you get home, you may use electronics. These electronics are made with materials from the geosphere. They must be discarded properly so they do not pollute the land and water. Some electronics and other objects can be recycled. Recycling, or taking materials from old discarded objects and making new objects from them, keeps objects out of landfills.

What Clean Water Means

Millions of people around the world either do not have enough water or do not have water that is safe to use. Many people must walk an hour or more each day to get water. How do engineers provide access to safe, clean water to improve people's lives?

In many parts of the world, children must fetch water for their families. Often, this means a long walk to bring a small amount of water that may not be clean.

Louise starts her day like any other girl in her class at school. As soon as the sun is up, she rises, gets dressed, and fetches water for her family. She walks half an hour on an uneven dirt road to a swampy stream. For months, that stream has been the closest water source available. At the stream, she has to wait in line behind the other people who also depend on the stream for water. When her turn comes, she wades in and fills her bucket with brownish, gritty water. She balances the bucket on top of her head and heads back home. She walks more slowly on the way back. Otherwise, she might trip, spill the water, and have to go back for more.

Forty-five minutes later, Louise sets down her bucket. Her mother will make the water last as long as she can. But she will make the trip herself at noon to refill the bucket for the afternoon. Then, Louise will make the trip again after school to refill the bucket for the evening.

Louise cleans up, grabs a bite to eat, and hurries to school. It is just a five-minute walk, but Louise is late again. Her teacher scolds her. Louise is looking forward to next month when the school will have a new well. The well will provide water for the whole village. Louise will be able to carry home three buckets of fresh, clean water in half the time it takes her to carry one bucket now. And she will get to school on time.

Clean Water Means Good Health

Drilling a well for Louise's village is an engineering solution to a very basic problem. Worldwide, nearly 800 million people do not have a convenient, reliable source of safe, clean water. Not having access to water affects people's health in more than one way.

When people have to haul water long distances, they collect less water than they need. They may have enough to drink and cook with, but they often do not have enough to wash their hands. Dirty hands spread germs that lead to illness, especially among children.

Dirty water sickens people after they drink it. Water from open sources, such as rivers, is often contaminated with disease-causing bacteria from the biosphere. The water becomes contaminated when waste from animals or people gets into the water.

On the other hand, water from a deep, closed well can be easier to keep clean. But even germ-free well water can be contaminated by the geosphere. In some places, the ground has high levels of minerals that contain dangerous elements such as arsenic and fluorine. The elements get into the well water. People who drink this water can get cancer or suffer from nerve damage.

Fortunately, engineers have come up with solutions for many of these challenges. The solutions vary depending on what the main challenge is.

Open water sources are often contaminated with disease-causing bacteria. Engineering a closed source of water, such as a well, helps reduce illness.

Providing clean water means creating a new water source, finding a way to use a source that is unavailable, or cleaning unsafe water. Here, men in Burkina Faso, a country in West Africa, are building a new water well.

Making Clean Water Happen

Providing clean water starts with figuring out what needs to be done. Generally, one of three engineering problems must be solved: A new water source is needed, an existing water source needs to be made available for use, or water that is already available needs to be made safe.

Drilling a well is a common way to create a new water source. This solution works in places that have enough groundwater, or water that is below Earth's surface, stored in the geosphere.

Like any machine, a well can break down. If no one knows how to fix it, the water is not available for use. Some engineers add water meters that charge a small fee when people draw water from the well. Someone in the village keeps part of the fee in exchange for fixing the well if it ever breaks.

Some places have water available for use, but only during a brief rainy season. Building a dam lets people collect the rainwater and save it for later use.

Making water safe is important for preventing illness. Engineers have come up with many ways to remove disease-causing germs and minerals from water. One way is to add chemicals that kill germs. Some engineers are working on containers that use sunlight to kill germs in water. Another way to clean water is to pass it through a filter. Some filters use simple materials, such as clean sand or charred bone. Other filters use ceramics coated with metals.

Part of engineering a solution is making sure that it works for the people and the place where it is used. Once a working solution is found, people's lives change for the better.

Clean Water Means Opportunity

The benefits of safe, clean water are so great that the United Nations passed a resolution in 2010 that recognized water as a basic human right. The resolution set goals for providing water to people who still need it. Much progress has been made already. It is a lot of work, but providing water is worth the effort.

When people have clean water to drink and enough water to wash with, they are stronger and healthier. They are better able to take care of themselves and their families. These results are the immediate benefits of having a reliable source of clean water nearby. Other benefits quickly follow. When people do not have to spend hours each day getting water, they use that time to do other things.

Adults have more time to farm and more water to use for farming. They can raise more crops and livestock for their own families. They may even have extra food to sell. Adults may choose to work or start a business, which also brings in money. Money pays for necessities such as medical care, clothing, and housing.

When the well at Louise's school is ready to use, the whole village gathers to watch the first buckets of water come up. The well will change Louise's life and the lives of her friends at school. They will now arrive to school on time, rested, and ready to learn. They will miss fewer school days because the clean water will not make them sick. Louise knows that getting an education is important. She hopes to learn enough to be able to help her family when she grows up. The new well means so much more than water to her!

Access to reliable water helps improve cleanliness and health.

Less time hauling water means more time for school. Getting an education is key to having a better standard of living.

What Can People Do to Protect Earth's Systems?

Science Vocabulary

conservation

scrubbers

wildlife refuge

All of Earth's systems are connected. When one system changes, the rest of the systems change as well. It is important to protect Earth's systems so you can continue to live on Earth. There are many different ways individuals, engineers, communities, and governments can protect Earth's systems.

NGSS **5-ESS2-3.** Obtain and combine information about ways individual communities use science ideas to protect the Earth's resources and environment.

ESS3-C. Human activities in agriculture, industry, and everyday life have had major effects on the land, vegetation, streams, ocean, air, and even outer space. But individuals and communities are doing things to help protect Earth's resources and environments.

Systems and System Models A system can be described in terms of its components and their interactions.

Obtaining, Evaluating, and Communicating Information

1. Protecting Earth's Systems Is Important

The dinosaur species *Tyrannosaurus rex* (*T. rex*) disappeared because Earth's systems changed. Many people think the systems changed because an asteroid hit the earth. Whatever happened 65 million years ago, *T. rex* could no longer meet its needs and went extinct. Can changes in Earth's systems today cause species to become extinct?

Changes to the environment occur all the time, and species naturally become extinct from these changes. Many scientists worry that unbalancing Earth's systems more will lead to many more species becoming extinct. It is important to keep Earth's systems relatively stable so that organisms in the biosphere, such as humans, can meet their needs.

Systems interact with each other, and changes in one system usually cause changes in other systems. If the climate in an area gets colder and drier, less water may evaporate. Fewer clouds may form in the atmosphere, and the amount of rainfall may decrease further. A land area that was once a forest may become a desert.

If the atmosphere warms, glaciers and polar ice may melt and raise the sea level. Low-lying land may be flooded with sea water. The fresh water may become too salty for plants and animals. Some of these organisms may become extinct.

Burning fossil fuels pollutes the atmosphere with carbon dioxide that warms Earth. Polar bears live near the North Pole and hunt for seals from floating pieces of ice, called ice floes. As the Arctic ice warms and melts, fewer ice floes are left. Fewer polar bears can leave land to hunt for seals, and some may starve. Polar bears may soon become extinct.

The fate of polar bears in the Arctic depends on how much the atmosphere warms Earth. More carbon dioxide leads to the earth warming faster.

Some objects in a landfill do not decompose easily, and the landfill fills up with pollution. You can conserve resources by reducing the amount of pollution you produce.

Soapy water is a form of water pollution. You can help conserve water resources by washing the family car in a self-service lot, where the soapy water will be collected to be cleaned in a water treatment plant.

2. Individuals Can Protect Earth's Systems

The increase in carbon dioxide in the atmosphere is the result of millions of actions. Every time you turn on a light, you use electricity. Generating electricity with fossil fuels produces carbon dioxide. Every time you ride in a car or bus to the library instead of riding your bike or walking, the car or bus's engine produces carbon dioxide. Every day you make choices that affect Earth's systems.

One part of protecting Earth's systems is **conservation**. Conservation is the wise use of material and energy resources so we do not run out of them. You can help conserve these resources by reducing the amount of pollution you produce. When you help wash the family car, what do you do with the soapy water? If you pour it into a storm drain in the street, it will end up polluting a nearby stream or river in the hydrosphere. Instead, your family can take the car to a self-service car wash where the runoff water is collected to be cleaned for reuse at the community's water treatment plant. This keeps the soapy water from polluting a stream or river.

You can also reduce the amount of air pollution you produce by making choices that do not produce air pollution. Riding your bike instead of a car is a healthy choice that produces less air pollution.

What happens to an object after you throw it in the trash? Trash is taken to a landfill to decompose. A landfill is a large area where trash is piled up and buried. Some materials such as plastic do not decompose easily. When they are taken to a landfill, they stay on the ground and produce pollution.

You can help conserve material and energy resources to protect Earth systems by reducing, reusing, and recycling. These aluminum cans have been crushed and baled at a recycling center. The cans will be shipped to an aluminum foundry to be made into new cans.

Many of the materials that you use in daily life, such as plastics and metals, do not decompose easily. You can help conserve material and energy resources to protect Earth systems by following the three Rs: reduce, reuse, and recycle.

You can reduce how much materials you use in many different ways. When you walk or ride your bike instead of taking a car or bus, you reduce the amount of fossil fuels you are using. Turning off water when you brush your teeth and taking shorter showers reduce your use of fresh water. Buying fruits and vegetables that are not pre-wrapped saves the resources that made the wrapping. Bringing your own grocery bags to a store instead of getting new bags with each visit saves paper and plastic.

Reusing items conserves resources and decreases the amount of trash. Paper plates and cups are thrown in the trash after one use, but plastic or porcelain dishes and glass cups can be used and washed again and again. You can reuse a water bottle many times to conserve the energy resources and the plastic needed to make a new plastic bottle.

Glass jars, plastic bottles, aluminum cans, and newspaper can be recycled. Aluminum cans are melted down and can be made into new objects. Plastic bottles can be melted down to make new plastic bottles. When you recycle materials that came from the geosphere or biosphere, you help prevent these systems from being mined for more resources. A compost pile made with your yard waste and kitchen scraps can be recycled into fertilizer to make the soil richer. This reduces the amount of trash you are putting in a landfill.

These tall smokestacks from power plants send smoke into the atmosphere. Scientists and engineers worked together to design solutions to the pollution problem such as designing better smokestacks.

 Engineering Design

3. Engineers Can Protect Earth's Systems

Many years ago, scientists suspected that power plants were a major source of air pollution. They tested the smoke from the smokestacks of power plants and found that it contained many harmful chemicals.

Identifying the Problem

Scientists first worked to identify the problem. They found that harmful chemicals are produced when high-sulfur coal is burned. Much of the coal that is mined in the eastern United States is high-sulfur coal. Coal that comes from the western part of the country has less sulfur. There are many minerals in coal that contain sulfur, and some of these minerals contain more sulfur and some contain less. Some minerals produce gases that cause acid rain when they are released into the atmosphere. Other forms cause smog.

Designing a Solution

Scientists found that some sulfur-containing minerals could be removed from coal. Other minerals could not. Scientists and engineers worked together to design solutions to the pollution problem. Some solutions they tested were designing better smokestacks, using only low-sulfur coal, and reducing the rate at which the coal burned. They also studied the effect of scrubbing the smoke. **Scrubbers** are devices that remove dirt and harmful pollutants from smoke. This smoke is produced by burning high-sulfur coal. The engineers tested the solutions to find places where they could improve. They compared all the solutions against each other. They also tested the solutions against previously used solutions. In this way, they decided the best way to approach the problem.

Balancing the Options

Engineers had to balance the best solution with many other factors. They had to think about the locations of power plants and coal mines. They had to look at the cost of shipping low-sulfur coal to eastern plants. They had to learn about government rules for how much sulfur can be allowed in the atmosphere. They also had to think about how much electricity would be produced with each solution. Some solutions lowered the rate at which electricity was produced so much that the solution would not be effective.

Applying the Solution

Engineers decided that low-sulfur coal should be burned in power plants in the western part of the country. For eastern power plants, a different solution was needed. The engineers chose burning of high-sulfur coal combined with scrubbing as the best solution.

They set to work designing new scrubbers that remove pollution more effectively. Research in scrubber technology is still going on. Today, several different kinds of scrubbers are used. Some clean harmful chemicals and gases from smoke. Some also remove dirt and other large particles. Others even clean coal before it is burned. Scientists and engineers are working on more ways to reduce air pollution.

Engineers worked to determine the best solution among many other factors. One of their solutions involves a device called a scrubber. Scrubbers remove dirt and dust, harmful chemicals, and gases that would pollute the air if they weren't removed.

4. Communities Can Protect Earth's Systems

Suppose you want to start recycling newspapers and plastic bottles. If your community doesn't have a recycling program, you could try starting one in your school. You could help your community protect Earth's resources and environments.

Protecting the Geosphere

Recycling helps the geosphere because less metal has to be mined from Earth's crust and less trash builds up to pollute the land. Many communities have recycling programs. Some have recycle centers where people bring materials to be recycled. Other towns have curbside pickup of materials to be recycled. Hazardous waste centers collect batteries and paint so they do not pollute the environment.

Protecting the Biosphere

Many communities have tree-planting programs. They plant trees along sidewalks and streets. The more trees that grow in a town, the more carbon dioxide they will take up to make food. Less carbon dioxide will build up in the air. Some cities have been named Tree Cities USA because of their tree-planting programs. To be named a Tree City USA, a city must plant and take care of its trees.

Communities also pass laws protecting the environment. Some laws forbid people from digging up rare plants in parklands. Other laws regulate hunting wildlife to prevent overhunting or overpopulation. There are many zoning laws that determine where companies can build factories and office buildings.

Communities can create recycling centers to protect Earth's systems. If your community has a recycling center, you may be responsible for separating and sorting items to be recycled.

Protecting the Atmosphere

Many community programs protect the atmosphere. These programs aim to conserve fossil fuels and prevent the air pollution they cause. Have you ever visited a farmer's market? Many towns and cities have outdoor markets where local farmers can sell their fruits and vegetables. By buying locally-grown food products, less gasoline is needed to transport food from farther away.

Some towns and cities build bike paths and bike lanes. They encourage people to ride bikes to work and to school on safe pathways. A new bike program that some towns are adopting is called bike sharing. Bike sharing is a transportation program that provides city-owned bikes for moving short distances within the city. Users pay a small fee to pick up a bike at a bike station and return it to any other bike station. Fewer trips in cars are needed within the city.

Protecting the Hydrosphere

Often, communities have water and wastewater treatment plants. They protect water resources and ensure that citizens have safe water. Water treatment plants take water from a water source and treat it to be sure it is safe to drink. Scientists are always researching better ways to treat water. After water has been used by people, it is returned to a wastewater treatment plant. There it is treated to remove waste products. When the water is safe, it is released back into the environment.

Local farmers sell their fruits and vegetables at farmers' markets that communities create to protect Earth's systems. Less transportation is needed when people buy local products.

Countries can pass laws to protect Earth's systems. One law provides money to create wildlife refuges. These bison in Yellowstone National Park are protected because they cannot be hunted or captured.

5. Countries Can Protect Earth's Systems

One of the best ways a country can protect Earth's systems is to pass national laws. Laws can protect wildlife from extinction. For example, the U.S. government passed the Endangered Species Act in 1973 . This law identifies species that might become extinct, and forbids killing or catching these species. It also provides money to create wildlife sanctuaries and refuges. A **wildlife refuge** is an area of land or water that is set aside to protect wildlife. Hunting and farming are restricted in refuges.

The Clean Air Acts of 1970 and 1990 set dates for reducing the amounts of certain air pollutants. Vehicles and factories are tested to make sure they do not pass their limits. Companies are fined if they do.

Countries can also work together to protect Earth's systems. In 1997, the United Nations called a meeting of countries to find ways to prevent climate change on Earth. The result of the meeting was the Kyoto Protocol. This agreement became effective in 2005. It sets limits to the amounts of greenhouse gases each country can produce. Remember that carbon dioxide and methane are two greenhouse gases. They absorb radiation emitted by the surface of the Earth and make the Earth warmer. Climate change occurs if the atmosphere warms too much. Each country agreed to reduce air pollution by a certain amount. The United States has not agreed to these limits.

What Can People Do to Protect Earth's Systems?

1. Protecting Earth's Systems Is Important   Systems interact with each other, so when one Earth system changes, the others will also change. It is important to keep Earth's systems relatively stable so the organisms in the biosphere, such as humans, can meet their needs.

2. Individuals Can Protect Earth's Systems   One part of protecting Earth's systems involves conservation, the wise use of material and energy resources. There are many ways that you can protect Earth's systems. Some of these ways are reducing, reusing, and recycling.

3. Engineers Can Protect Earth's Systems   Engineers discovered that toxic chemicals are produced with high-sulfur coal is burned. Engineers identified the problem, designed scrubbers to help remove the toxic chemicals, weighed the options, and then applied the solution. Now many power plants use coal with less sulfur and also have scrubbers to clean the air.

4. Communities Can Protect Earth's Systems   Communities can protect Earth's systems by organizing programs, passing laws, or building infrastructure to encourage reduced use of material and energy resources.

5. Countries Can Protect Earth's Systems   Countries can pass laws to protect Earth's systems. They can create wildlife refuges where an area of land is set aside to protect wildlife. Countries can also work together to protect Earth's systems. They can make agreements to conserve resources and prevent pollution.

Diving Birds and Bullet Trains

Nature has been designing living things for millions of years. This is one reason it is important to conserve Earth's systems. What have human engineers learned from animals and plants?

Nature has inspired some of the best scientific inventions. One example of this is a myth that is part of the history of the Inupiat people, who live in what is now Alaska. Ekeuhnick, an Inupiat hunter, knew that his people needed new ways to get food. One day, on a walk in the woods, he watched a spider catching flies in its web and eating them. He thought that he could make a web out of strips of animal hide and that might work to catch fish. So, he made a web, and it worked as he had hoped.

Ekeuhnick showed others his invention so that they could make webs, too. They tried different materials, different knots, and different sizes of nets to catch various kinds of fish. Observing the spider web led to an important human invention—the fishing net.

The story of Ekeuhnick's invention of the fishing net is a very old account of *biomimicry*. Biomimicry means looking to nature for design solutions that address human needs. Other examples of biomimicry are the machines inspired by bird wings that Leonardo da Vinci studied. The airplanes you see today were designed after observing different birds while they were flying!

Today's engineers continue to find amazing solutions by looking to nature. So, it is important to protect Earth's systems so that engineers can continue to study organisms for ideas.

The fishing net is an example of biomimicry. It was designed by Ekeuhnick, an Inupiat hunter, to mimic a spider web.

Speeding trains make noise when they move through air. The faster the trains go, the more noise they make. Owls move silently through air. Although you cannot see it, engineers made fast trains quieter by mimicking the edges of owl wing feathers.

Noisy, Booming Bullet Trains

One amazing example of engineering imitating nature is the design of the Japanese bullet trains. The trains are called "bullet trains" because they move much faster than regular trains at about 320 kilometers per hour (200 miles per hour). Every day, hundreds of thousands of people in Japan ride the trains. Making the trains move as quickly as they do is an example of a successful engineering design. But as good as the trains are, engineers constantly look for ways to improve them.

Noise is a problem for fast-moving trains. The faster a train moves, the noisier it is. At one time, people who lived near certain train tracks in Japan could not sleep because of the train's noise. The noise was even worse near tunnels. The shape of the train and the shape of the tunnel combined to cause sonic booms. Sonic booms sound like thunder and can shake everything around them. Sometimes sonic booms even break glass. So, the Japanese government set very strict standards for noise. The bullet trains had to be quieter, and the sonic booms definitely had to stop.

A Japanese design engineer wanted to make trains go faster, but the trains were already too noisy. What could he do? This particular engineer was a bird watcher. From another bird watcher, he learned that owls fly silently. The feathers on an owl's wing have many fine, thin, fluffy strands laid out like the teeth on a comb. The engineer had his team try adding structures similar to those strands to part of the high-speed train. The strands worked! The train was quieter than it had been before, even when it moved faster. This reduced the noise from the moving train but not the sonic booms.

A kingfisher plunges beak-first into water to catch fish. Its beak allows it to enter the water with very little splash.

Enter the Kingfisher

The owl wing idea worked so well that the engineer went back to the biosphere for more ideas. He knew that when a high-speed train entered a tunnel, there was a sudden change in how much the air resisted the movement of the train. That sudden change in resistance built up air pressure, which caused the sonic booms. He asked himself, is there an animal that, in its everyday life, moved quickly through a sudden change in resistance?

Yes, there is such an animal. It is another bird, the kingfisher. Kingfishers live near lakes, ponds, and streams. They dive beak-first into the water to catch fish. When the bird goes from the air into the water, it experiences a sudden change in the resistance of what it is moving through. What is more amazing is that the kingfisher can go through this change in resistance without a splash. It just plunges into the water and catches its fish.

The engineer wondered if the shape of the kingfisher's beak helped it enter the water without splashing. He and his co-workers made and tested models using many different shapes for the nose of the bullet train. The tests showed that the best shape for the front of a new bullet train was based on the shape of a kingfisher's beak. Success!

When the new trains were built, the sonic booms stopped. And even when the trains were not going through tunnels, they could move faster without going over the strict noise limits. An added benefit was that the new trains used less energy than the older trains did. Nature had come up with an excellent design!

Copying the shape of the kingfisher's beak resulted in a train that can travel through tunnels without causing sonic booms.

Biomimicry Everywhere

More and more, engineers are looking to the biosphere to inspire design solutions. For example, some engineers are analyzing videos of mammals shaking off after being drenched with water. From tiny mice to full-grown tigers, the mammals' motions provide insights that could improve washing machines.

Observing animals is an obvious approach, but plants inspire inventions, too. The lotus plant stays clean even though it lives in muddy water. Its leaves look smooth, but they are actually covered in tiny bumps. The spaces between the bumps form a layer of air that sheds dirt and water. Engineers developed self-cleaning paint based on lotus leaves. The paint looks smooth, but its tiny bumps keep it clean.

As human technology advances, engineers are better able to mimic design solutions from the biosphere. But too often, human technology comes with a price—the loss of species from the biosphere. When species get destroyed or become extinct, engineers cannot study them. Lots of plants and animals have already become extinct that engineers could have maybe used to get design ideas from. But conservation and other practices can prevent future species from being destroyed. With effort, nature's designs will be around to inspire engineers of the future.

Engineers are observing the biosphere to find solutions to a wide range of engineering challenges. Appliance engineers watch videos of mammals shaking themselves dry to get ideas for improving the spin cycle of washing machines.

UNIT 3
Changes in Matter

Look around you. Perhaps you are sitting on a plastic chair in front of a wooden desk. You may have pencils and paper in front of you, or even a book. All of this is made of matter. Matter is all around you. The ground you walk on, the water you drink, and the air you breathe are all matter. In this unit you will read about what matter is made of. You will learn how different materials can be identified, and how different materials can change to become new materials.

Unit Contents

Unit 3 Overview

Graphic Organizer: This unit is structured to introduce matter in terms of **particles** of matter, its **properties**, and the **changes** matter undergoes.

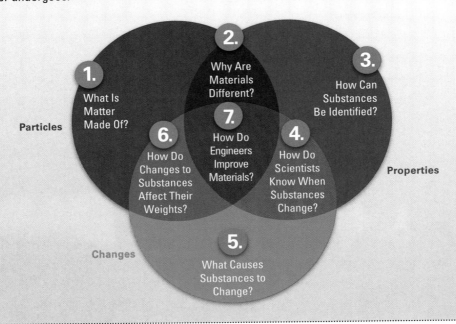

Particles

1. What Is Matter Made Of?

2. Why Are Materials Different?

3. How Can Substances Be Identified?

6. How Do Changes to Substances Affect Their Weights?

7. How Do Engineers Improve Materials?

4. How Do Scientists Know When Substances Change?

Properties

Changes

5. What Causes Substances to Change?

NGSS Next Generation Science Standards

Performance Expectations

5-PS1-1. Develop a model to describe that matter is made of particles too small to be seen.

5-PS1-2. Measure and graph quantities to provide evidence that regardless of the type of change that occurs when heating, cooling, or mixing substances, the total weight of matter is conserved.

5-PS1-3. Make observations and measurements to identify materials based on their properties.

5-PS1-4. Conduct an investigation to determine whether the mixing of two or more substances results in new substances.

Disciplinary Core Ideas

PS1.A: Structure and Properties of Matter

• Matter of any type can be subdivided into particles that are too small to see, but even then the matter still exists and can be detected by other means. A model showing that gases are made from matter particles that are too small to see and are moving freely around in space can explain many observations, including the inflation and shape of a balloon and the effects of air on larger particles or objects.

• The amount (weight) of matter is conserved when it changes form, even in transitions in which it seems to vanish.

• Measurements of a variety of properties can be used to identify materials.

PS1.B: Chemical Reactions

• When two or more different substances are mixed, a new substance with different properties may be formed.

• No matter what reaction or change in properties occurs, the total weight of the substances does not change.

Crosscutting Concepts

Cause and Effect

• Cause and effect relationships are routinely identified, tested, and used to explain change.

Scale, Proportion, and Quantity

• Natural objects exist from the very small to the immensely large.

• Standard units are used to measure and describe physical quantities such as weight, time, temperature, and volume.

 Developing and Using Models

 Planning and Carrying Out Investigations

 Using Mathematics and Computational Thinking

Have you ever wondered...

Matter is all around you, even if you cannot see it. Matter is always changing from one material to another. This unit will help you answer these questions and many others you may ask.

What can you observe to identify materials?

What causes materials to change when you mix them together?

Why does refrigerating food keep it from spoiling?

What Is Matter Made Of?

Science Vocabulary

dissolve

matter

particles

solution

state of matter

Look at the objects around you. All of these objects are made of matter. Matter is made up of tiny particles that are too small to see. Some objects are made of smaller pieces, just like matter is made up of smaller particles. Particle board is a type of wood which is made of smaller pieces of wood pressed together.

NGSS

5-PS1-1. Develop a model to describe that matter is made of particles too small to be seen.

PS1.A. Matter of any type can be subdivided into particles that are too small to see, but even then the matter still exists and can be detected by other means. A model showing that gases are made from matter particles that are too small to see and are moving freely around in space can explain many observations, including the inflation and shape of a balloon, and the effects of air on larger particles or objects.

Scale, Proportion, and Quantity Natural objects exist from the very small to the immensely large.

Developing and Using Models

1. Matter Is Made of Particles

Look around you and name the objects that you can see and touch. Perhaps you see a pencil and a pair of scissors, or water in a water bottle. What do all these objects have in common? They are all made of matter.

Everything around you is made of matter. **Matter** is anything that takes up space. A pencil and scissors take up space, so you cannot put them in the same location. You can place the pencil on top of the scissors or the scissors on top of the pencil, but you cannot put one inside the other. Water and a plastic bottle are also made of matter. When you pour water in the bottle, they both appear to be in the same place, but they are not. The matter that makes up the bottle surrounds the water, so the bottle and the water take up different spaces.

All matter has weight. You can feel the weight of a glass of water because the glass and water are made of matter. If you pour more water in the glass, it will be heavier because the glass is holding more matter.

All objects are made of matter, but what makes up matter? All matter is made up of smaller pieces of matter called **particles**. You cannot see these tiny particles without certain tools, such as very powerful microscopes, but they still take up space and have weight.

Particles are always moving. When you look at a pencil or a pair of scissors, they appear to be still. But the particles that make up the pencil and pair of scissors are actually vibrating back and forth. The particles in water are always flowing over, under, and around each other, even when it appears motionless. Particles of matter are always moving.

Everything you see in this photo is made of matter. Each of these objects is made of tiny particles, too small to see without very powerful tools. The particles are always moving.

Ice, water, and vapor are the different states of matter of water. Water vapor is usually invisible, but here you can see it carrying small droplets of water. Each state is made of the same kind of particles, moving differently.

2. States of Matter

Particles are always moving, but they do not always move in the same way! Particles can vibrate in place, flow over each other, or spread apart.

Look at some matter around you. Its **state of matter** is the way the particles in that piece of matter are moving. In each state of matter, the particles are arranged differently. How particles are arranged and how they move changes the volume and shape of the matter. Ice cubes from the freezer are hard, water can flow out of a faucet, and water vapor rises from a pot of boiling water and mixes with the air around it. Ice, water, and water vapor are all different states of the same material—water. Three common states of matter are solid, liquid, and gas.

Solids

Ice is water in a solid state. The particles in a solid are close together and locked in position, so they cannot move around each other and can only vibrate in place. The particles in a solid are like marbles packed tightly in a jar. The marbles cannot move around, but they can wiggle slightly.

Unlike marbles in a jar, the particles in a solid are attached to one another. If you moved a solid from one container, it would stay the same shape because the particles do not move around each other. Solids have a fixed volume and shape. The word *fixed* means "not changing," so, the size and shape of a solid object does not change. A book is a solid, so the amount of space it takes up does not change and it always stays in the shape of a book.

Liquids

Water from a faucet is a liquid. The particles in a liquid are close together but they are able to move about. Liquid particles are always sliding past one another like marbles in a bowl. If you tilt the bowl back and forth, the marbles roll over one another and change position. Although the marbles move, they always stay near each other. Liquid particles flow over each other, but stay close together like the particles in a solid.

A liquid has a fixed volume but does not have a fixed shape. The amount of space a liquid takes up cannot change, but the liquid's shape can change. If you pour water from a tall glass into a shallow bowl, the water in the bowl takes up as much space as it did when it was in the glass. But the water in the bowl now has a bowl shape instead of a glass shape.

Gases

The water vapor coming from boiling water is a gas. The particles in a gas spread apart and move freely in all directions. Gas particles bounce off one another and the sides of their container. Although the particles run into each other, they do not stay near one another. They are always moving throughout their container.

A gas does not have a fixed volume or shape. The amount of space that a gas takes up and the shape of a gas can change. A gas gets bigger or smaller depending on the container it is in. A gas always takes the shape of its container. Air is a mixture of different gasses. When you blow into a round balloon, the air fills the balloon and takes the round shape of the balloon.

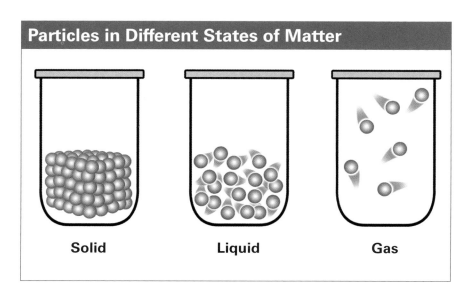

Particles in Different States of Matter

Solid   Liquid   Gas

The particles in different states of matter move differently. In a solid, they vibrate back and forth. In a liquid, they remain close but flow around and over each other. In a gas, they spread throughout the entire container and move in all directions.

3. Matter Seems to Appear and Disappear

You have learned that everything around you is matter, and all matter is made of tiny particles. A scientist observed small pieces of dust as they floated on water. The dust seemed to jiggle even if the water did not seem to move. Scientists studied this observation and realized that the dust was being moved by the water particles as they flowed over and around each other.

However, not every material will float in water. Some materials seem to disappear if they are mixed with water. Where do the particles that make up matter go when a material seems to disappear?

Matter Seems to Disappear

If you put a spoonful of sugar into a glass of water, you will see the sugar sink to the bottom of the glass. If you then stir the water with a spoon, you will see the pile of sugar get smaller and smaller. Eventually, the sugar will seem to disappear completely. The sugar *dissolved* in the water.

When a material **dissolves**, it mixes completely with another material and appears as just one material. When sugar is dissolved in water, the resulting sugar water looks just like water and you do not see sugar floating around. The particles of sugar mixed completely with the water.

When the particles of one material are dissolved with the particles of a different material, the mixture is called a **solution**. Each part of a solution is the same as all other parts of the solution. Sugar water is a solution, so a drop of sugar water from the top of a glass has the same amount of sugar as a drop of water from the bottom of the same glass.

Sugar and water are both materials. When sugar dissolves in water, it forms a solution of sugar water.

Matter Seems to Appear

Although sugar seems to disappear when you dissolve it in a pot of water, it is not gone. The sugar is still inside the water. If you boil the sugar water until all the water is gone, there will be grains of sugar left behind. The sugar seems to appear out of nowhere. In fact, this sugar is the same sugar that you mixed in the water.

You can see the sugar again because, as the water turned into vapor and left the pot, the sugar particles got closer and closer together. Eventually, the particles were close enough that they started to stick together. As more and more particles stuck together, larger and larger grains of sugar formed until they became large enough to see.

Often people will make different colored sugar crystals with food coloring. Sugar and food coloring are dissolved in hot water. The sugar appears to disappear, but the food coloring mixes and spreads throughout the water to give the liquid an even color. The sugar, food coloring, and water form a solution.

A string is placed in the solution. As the solution cools, more and more sugar particles stick to the string and particles of food coloring get trapped in amongst the sugar particles. Eventually, big "rocks" or crystals of colored sugar appear on the string. These crystals are made up of the sugar and food coloring that were dissolved in the water.

To make sugar crystals like these, sugar and food coloring are dissolved in hot water. Over time, the water cools down and the sugar forms large crystals.

Though you cannot see air, you can detect it by how air affects other objects. The air inside the bounce house takes up space to create a sturdy surface to play on.

4. Some Matter You Cannot See

When you look around, you can see many things made of matter. But did you know that you are surrounded by matter that you cannot see?

You cannot always feel or see matter. You cannot see the air around you, but air is made of matter. Like all matter, air takes up space, has weight, and is made up of particles.

Air Takes Up Space

A balloon can show that air takes up space. Before you inflate a balloon, the balloon is flat. You can easily fold and crumple an empty balloon. But as you blow into the balloon, it gets bigger and bigger. The air you put into the balloon fills the balloon because the air takes up space.

When you tie off the balloon, the air is trapped inside the balloon. You can no longer fold the balloon easily or crumple it into a small ball because of the air inside. The air in the balloon takes up space and stretches the balloon so that it cannot be crumpled.

Often you do not even realize that air is taking up space in objects all around you. Basketballs, footballs, and soccer balls are all filled with air. If air did not take up space, these objects would always be flat, even if you tried to pump them full of air. Car tires and bicycle tires are filled with air to allow the tires to keep their shape. This makes it easier to drive and bike to different places. Bounce houses are filled with air to make a surface strong enough to stand and jump on. When air is pumped into a bounce house, it takes up space and helps the bounce house to keep its shape.

Air Has Weight

You may think that air is weightless, but because air is matter, it has weight. When you hold an object in your hand, you can feel its weight. But when you hold your hand out, you do not feel the weight of the air above your hand. You do not feel the weight because you are always surrounded by air. You are used to the weight of the air pushing on all parts of your body.

However, if you weigh an empty balloon and then weigh the same balloon after it is blown up, you will find that the balloon weighs more when it is filled. The inflated balloon weighs more because of the air inside of it.

Air Is Made Up of Particles

Like vapor, air is also made of gases. And those gases are made of particles that move around freely. The rubber that makes up the balloon is also made of particles. The particles in the rubber are very close together. The air particles are trapped by the rubber. Instead, the air particles move around inside the balloon in all directions. The air particles often hit the sides of the balloon. When they hit, they push on the balloon and give the balloon its shape.

Just as air particles push on a balloon to stretch it, air particles can push on other objects. If you blow on a feather, the air particles in your breath will push the feather away. Similarly, wind is moving air particles. These particles push on leaves and make them shake and flutter. If air were not made of particles, nothing would push on the leaves and the leaves would not move.

This palm tree is being pushed by the wind. Wind is moving air particles. Like other matter, air particles can push against things.

Odors from baking food spread through the air. Tiny particles of the food float through the air, slowly spreading out.

5. Odors Come from Matter

If you walked by a bakery with your eyes closed, you would probably still know that you were near a bakery. You could smell the delicious odors of baking bread, cookies, and cakes. These odors would reach your nose and tell you where you are. How do those odors reach your nose?

Odors, such as the scent of baking food, reach your nose through the air. Particles of food that are too small to see float through the air. When these particles reach your nose, you smell the food.

Because odors travel through the air, they cannot be smelled at all parts of a room at once. Suppose your teacher opens a bottle of perfume in one corner of your classroom. The students closest to the bottle will smell the perfume first. Slowly, students farther and farther away from the bottle will start to smell the perfume. The particles from the perfume need time to travel across the room.

The movement of the odor particles is similar to your movement when you walk across a crowded room. As you make your way across the room, you cannot go in a straight line. You bump into people and change directions. Similarly, the odor particles bump into air particles and change direction. There are so many odor particles in the air from the perfume that even though they are bumped in random directions, they eventually spread throughout the room. The odor particles slowly make their way across the room by chance.

What Is Matter Made Of?

1. Matter Is Made of Particles   Matter is anything that takes up space. All matter has weight and all matter is made up of particles that are too small to see without powerful tools. The particles of matter are always moving.

2. States of Matter   All matter has a state of matter, which is the way the particles in that matter move and are arranged. Solid, liquid, and gas are three states of matter. Solids have fixed shapes and volumes. Liquids can change shape but have fixed volumes. Gases can change shape and volume.

3. Matter Seems to Appear and Disappear   When a material dissolves it mixes evenly with a different material forming a solution. When water in a solution turns to water vapor, the matter that was dissolved seems to appear out of nowhere. This matter was simply left when the water goes from a liquid to gas state.

4. Some Matter You Cannot See   The air around you is invisible, but it is matter. Air takes up space, has weight, and is made up of particles. The particles in air move about and can cause objects to move. Wind is moving air particles.

5. Odors Come from Matter   Particles of matter that are too small to see can travel through the air. Odors are made of particles of a material that travel through the air. When these particles reach your nose, you can smell the material. Particles need time to travel through air.

A Fourth State of Matter

You walk on solid ground. You drink liquid water. And you breathe gases in the air. Yet, solids, liquids, and gases are rare in the universe. What type of matter is most common throughout the entire universe?

Most of the matter that scientists have found in the universe is made of plasmas. Plasmas are found in all the stars that you see in the sky, including the sun.

At the electronics store, you feel dizzy watching the colorful images flash across the screens covering the wall. The televisions showing the crisp, bright videos are only a little thicker than a picture frame. But the televisions are not all the same. Yes, some are bigger than others. But if you look closely, you will notice another difference. Some televisions are LCD televisions, while others are plasma televisions. The televisions may look the same on the outside, but plasma televisions have matter on the inside that is not a solid, a liquid, or a gas.

Plasma televisions are named after *plasma*, a fourth state of matter. Plasmas are similar to gases in that their particles race around in space. Like gases, plasmas spread out to fill the space they are in and do not have a fixed volume or shape. Yet, a plasma is not a gas. The particles in a gas are neutral, which means that they do not have an electric charge. The particles in plasma do have electric charges, so electric currents can flow through plasmas.

Plasmas make up most of the matter that can be observed in the universe. All the stars in the universe, including the sun, are made mostly of plasma. However, plasmas are rare on Earth. To make the charged particles that make up plasmas, gases need to be heated to very high temperatures. Earth is usually too cold for gases to become plasmas, but that does not mean that plasmas do not exist on Earth. After all, there's plasma in a plasma television.

Auroras are glowing gases high above Earth. The gases glow when they are hit by plasma particles from the sun.

A Different Kind of Plasma Light Show

When you turn on a plasma TV, an electric current flows through a mixture of gases and turns the gases into plasmas. The particles of plasma then hit tiny containers of substances, which causes the substances to glow either red, blue, or green. This plasma light show is similar to a plasma light show that happens in nature.

The sun, like all stars, is mostly made up of plasma. Some of the plasma particles on the outside of the sun are moving so fast that they escape and go hurtling through space. The stream of plasma coming from the sun is called the *solar wind*. You cannot see the solar wind, but you can see the natural light shows produced by it. These natural light shows are called *auroras*.

Auroras happen when the charged particles of the solar wind smash into gas particles in the atmosphere that surrounds Earth. The collisions make the gas particles glow. Different kinds of gas glow different colors, making brilliant green, red, or blue light. The brightness of the aurora can change. When the sun gives off more plasma, the solar wind is stronger. And, the glow of the aurora is brighter.

Although auroras light up in a similar way to plasma televisions, you cannot flip a switch to see an aurora. Most of the plasma from the solar wind flows around Earth. It usually reaches the air above Earth only around the North Pole and the South Pole. So, you might have to take a trip to see auroras. Just remember to dress warmly!

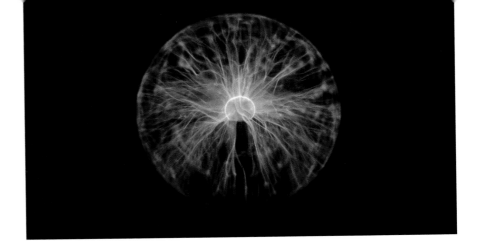

The glowing streaks inside the ball are plasma. They are made using electricity.

Making Plasmas on Earth

Auroras are only one example of a spectacular, natural plasma light show. Another natural plasma show is much easier to see. You just have to wait for the next thunderstorm. Lightning streaks across the sky when there is enough energy to change the gases in air into plasma. Electric current flows through the plasma, making the gigantic spark you see as lightning. Lightning is different from auroras because, in lightning, the plasma itself glows.

Each lightning strike lasts for less than a second. If you want to see plasma glow for a longer time, you could get a plasma ball. The glowing streaks of light inside a plasma ball are glowing plasma. They last as long as the machine is turned on. The streaks look like lightning magically enclosed inside a glass orb. Although the streams might seem magical, no magic is needed to make them.

Like the lightning, the plasma inside a plasma ball forms because of electricity. When the ball is turned on, the metal sphere inside the ball becomes loaded with electric charges. These charges leap into the gas inside the ball. They cause the particles in the gas to become charged, forming the dancing strands of plasma.

Electricity is also used to make plasmas inside plasma televisions, fluorescent lights, and neon signs. The plasmas exist as electric current flows through them. When the electricity is turned off, the plasma changes back into a gas. These plasmas are contained in glass. Yet, the glass does not melt. Although these plasmas are very hot, they are not nearly as hot as the plasmas in the sun.

Plasma Power

Plasma is hard to study because its particles race around like a gas. You cannot hold a piece of plasma in your hand, because its particles will spread out and take the shape of the room. Plasmas are also hard to study because they form when temperatures are very high. Unlike the plasmas in a television, the temperature of the plasmas scientists study can be so high that glass will melt! Scientists believe that understanding plasma will help engineers design better machines.

Engineers have designed rocket engines that run off of plasma. These engines are used for exploring parts of space that are very far because they turn a small amount of solid into a lot of plasma. The plasma is then used to propel the spaceship to faraway places in outer space.

Scientists also are studying plasma to help design machines that generate electricity without making pollution. Most power plants generate energy by burning fuels that release carbon dioxide and other pollution into the air. The fuels are also in limited supply and will run out. Scientists are looking for new ways to generate electricity, including studying the sun. The sun produces large amounts of energy. This energy produces plasma that helps the sun continue to produce more energy. Scientists hope that by understanding plasma, they can copy the way the sun produces energy on Earth.

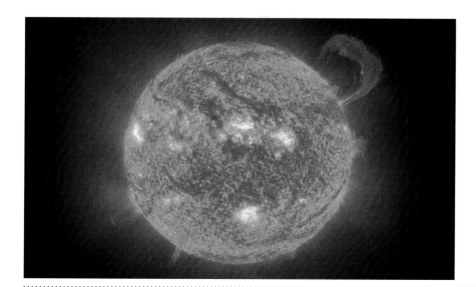

Plasmas are very hard to study, but scientists believe that understanding plasmas will help engineers design and build better machines. Engineers are also trying to copy how the sun produces energy to generate electricity on Earth.

Why Are Materials Different?

Science Vocabulary

mixture

property

substance

There are millions of different materials all around you. The truck in the image has glass in the windshield, has rubber on the tires, and is made of steel. Materials are a form of matter, and so they are made of particles. However these particles can be very different. The types of particles that a material is made of determine many of the properties of that material!

NGSS

5-PS1-1. Develop a model to describe that matter is made of particles too small to be seen.
5-PS1-3. Make observations and measurements to identify materials based on their properties.

PS1.A. • Matter of any type can be subdivided into particles that are too small to see, but even then the matter still exists and can be detected by other means. A model showing that gases are made from matter particles that are too small to see and are moving freely around in space can explain many observations, including the inflation and shape of a balloon, and the effects of air on larger particles or objects.
• Measurements of a variety of properties can be used to identify materials.

Scale, Proportion, and Quantity
• Natural objects exist from the very small to the immensely large. • Standard units are used to measure and describe physical quantities such as weight, time, temperature, and volume.

Developing and Using Models

Planning and Carrying Out Investigations

1. There Are Many Different Materials

When you bake, you might use three different white powders—salt, sugar, and baking soda. The three powders seem similar, but if you study them more closely, you will see that they are different. The powders are not the same shade of white. The pieces of baking soda are smaller than the grains of sugar and salt. If you taste each powder, you will find that sugar is sweet, salt is salty, and baking soda does not taste like anything you want to eat. Why are salt, sugar, and baking soda different? The three powders are different materials.

Scientists know of millions of different materials and think that millions more can be made. Some of these materials you see and use every day. For example, the air you breathe contains about 15 different materials. Other materials are so rare that most people will never observe them. Some materials, such as water and sugar, are found in nature. Other materials, such as plastic and nylon, are made by people.

All materials are similar in some ways. For example, all materials are matter, so they take up space and have mass. Also, because materials are matter, each material is made up of particles that are too small to be seen.

But materials can differ from each other in many ways. Materials may look or taste different. Salt, sugar, and baking powder differ in the way they look and taste. Other materials may differ in their color or their ability to dissolve in water. This is because different materials are made of different types of particles.

Salt, sugar, and baking soda are all white powders that are used in baking. But each powder is a different material that looks and tastes different.

Salt

Sugar

Baking soda

Table salt is a substance, so it is made of the same type of particle throughout. Each salt particle has certain properties that can be measured. The properties of the particles in table salt are all the same because the particles are all the same type.

2. Different Types of Materials

Some materials are made of only one type of particle. Suppose that you could take a grain of sugar and divide it in half with a powerful machine to get two smaller grains of sugar. Then you divide the new piece in half again. If you could keep dividing the sugar into smaller and smaller pieces, you would end up with a piece of sugar that you cannot cut into smaller pieces of sugar. That piece would be a particle of sugar.

Sugar is a material that is also a *substance*. A **substance** is a material where each part of it is made of the same type of particle. Each particle of a substance has certain characteristics that can be measured called **properties**. No two substances have exactly the same properties.

Substances

Many of the materials you encounter in your daily life are substances. Sugar, water, and table salt are all substances. Sugar is made of one type of particle that is sweet and white. Water is made of water particles that are all liquid at room temperature. Table salt is made of salt particles that are all salty.

Could you take a single particle of a pure substance and break it into smaller pieces? You could, but the smaller pieces would not be the same particle and would have different characteristics. If you took a particle of sugar and broke it into smaller pieces, the pieces would no longer be sweet and white. A substance has the same properties throughout all of it.

Mixtures

You have learned that sugar is a substance and water is a substance. But what do you get when you dissolve sugar into water? It looks clear like water, but it contains sugar and water particles so it cannot be a substance. Instead, it is a type of material called a *mixture*.

A **mixture** is a combination of two or more substances whose particles are not joined together. You may remember the example of sugar dissolved in water from the last lesson. Sugar water is a solution because the sugar particles spread out evenly in the water, but they did not join together with the water particles. That means that sugar water is not only a solution, but also a mixture.

All solutions are mixtures, but not all mixtures are solutions. There are mixtures that are not solutions. When you mix salt and sugar together, you create a solid mixture that is not a solution. The salt and sugar particles are not spread out and are, instead, clumped into tiny grains. A salad is also a mixture that is not a solution.

Some materials that appear to be one substance are actually mixtures. For example, metal spoons and forks are often made of stainless steel. This steel looks like one substance. But it is actually a mixture of several substances including iron and a substance called carbon. Wood is a mixture of different substances, including a substance called cellulose. Air is also a mixture of different substances in their gas form, including oxygen and nitrogen.

Stainless steel is a solid mixture that may appear to be one substance. It is actually made of several substances, including iron and carbon.

3. Separating Mixtures into Substances

There are many materials in the world that are substances, and many more that are mixtures. How do you know if a material is a substance or a mixture? The different substances in a mixture can also always be separated again. For example, if you boil a pot of sugar water, the water will evaporate until you are left with just sugar. The sugar and water particles have separated. When water evaporates, it changes from its liquid state to its gas state. When water is in the gas state, its particles spread out and around into the air above the pot. The water particles are now separated from the sugar particles. You can also boil saltwater until water and salt separate to leave you salt.

You can also separate mixtures of solid substances. For example, if you have a pile of salt and sugar, you can separate the pile into two piles, one of salt and one of sugar. The salt particles and sugar particles did not join together, and you could separate them out eventually.

It is also possible to separate mixtures that appear to be one substance. Wood is a material that is made of many different substances, including a substance called cellulose. When people make paper from wood, they separate the cellulose out from the other substances. The cellulose is used to make paper, which is another material that appears to be one substance. A material that can be separated into two or more pure substances is a mixture.

Wood is a mixture of different substances, including a substance called cellulose. People separate cellulose from wood to make paper.

Why Are Materials Different?

1. There Are Many Different Materials   Millions of different materials exist. All materials are matter, so they take up space and have mass. They are made of particles that are too small to be seen. But materials differ from each other in various ways. Materials may look or taste different. Other materials may differ in color and their ability to dissolve in water.

2. Different Types of Materials   A substance is matter that is made up of one type of particle with unique properties. Thus, all particles of a given substances are the same. Particles of different substances differ from each other. A material made of two distinct substances is called a mixture. A solution is a mixture, but not all mixtures are solutions.

3. Separating Mixtures into Substances   A mixture is a combination of two or more substances. Many materials are mixtures including materials that appear to be one substance. However, the particles of the substances in a mixture are not joined together and can always be separated again. Sugar water, saltwater, and wood are examples of materials that are mixtures.

Marie Curie

"All my life through, the new sights of nature made me rejoice like a child," wrote Marie Curie. Her lifelong fascination with nature and love of new discoveries helped her become a famous scientist. What struggles did Marie Curie go through on her path to greatness?

Marie Curie was a famous scientist who won two Nobel Prizes for her discoveries. One of the prizes was for discovering two new substances, radium and polonium.

Searching for a needle in haystack seems like an impossible task. But if you are as creative and persistent as Marie Curie was, you would find that needle. For Curie, the needle was a substance called *radium*. The haystack was the complex mineral that contained many substances called *pitchblende*. Toiling in an old shed that was too hot in the summer and too cold in the winter, she tried to separate radium from other substances in pitchblende. She spent three years separating more than a ton of the mixture. She got barely a pinch of a powder for all her efforts. This tiny bit of powder contained the radium that she was searching for.

Marie Curie is one of the most famous scientists of all time. She was the first woman to win a Nobel Prize, which is one of the highest honors in science. She won this honor for her work on radioactive substances. *Radioactive* substances are substances that give off energy or tiny particles.

Her careful studies of radioactivity led her to the discovery of two new substances: polonium and radium, which are both radioactive. Radium even glows in the dark because of the energy it gives off. She won a second Nobel Prize for discovering these substances. She was the first person to win two Nobel Prizes. While many people know about Marie Curie's great success as a scientist, they may not know about the challenges she overcame during her life.

Marie Curie grew up in Warsaw with her brothers and sisters as the youngest of five children. Her family experienced many hardships as she grew up, but she never gave up on her dream to go to college and become a scientist.

Early Hardships

Marie's early life was not easy. She was born Maria Skłodowska in 1867 in Warsaw, Poland as the youngest of five children. At that time, the part of Poland where Maria lived was part of the Russian Empire and people who wanted Poland to be independent faced discrimination. Maria's father was one of these people. He was a teacher, but he was fired because of his opinions about Poland. He had difficulty finding a good teaching job that paid enough money for him to support his family.

Young Maria faced tragic losses. Her oldest sister died when Maria was only eight years old, and her mother died two years later. The loss of her mother was heartbreaking for Maria, but she still managed to excel in school, especially in math and science.

Although Maria graduated at the top of her class, she could not go to college in Warsaw because women were not allowed to attend. Instead, she and one of her other older sisters went to secret classes at night. They also made a promise. Maria would help pay for her sister to study medicine in Paris, France, where women could go to college. When her sister finished school, she would help Maria go to college.

Maria took this promise very seriously. She became a live-in governess, teaching the children of a wealthy family and sending money to her sister in France. She continued to teach herself math and science because she still dreamed of going to college one day. Although few women were scientists at the time, Maria hoped to become one.

Marie Curie was a working mother with two daughters, Irene and Eve. She continued to work as a scientist even after she started a family.

Reaching Her Dreams

At the age of 24, Maria Skłodowska achieved her dream of going to college when she was able to join her sister in Paris. Skłodowska was excited to finally be able to study science, but classes were not easy for her. Although she had tried to learn as much as possible on her own, she was not as well prepared as other students. Instead of giving up, Skłodowska spent hours studying late into the night in her small Paris apartment. Sometimes, she would even forget to eat.

With her hard work, Skłodowska became an outstanding student. She was on her way to becoming a great scientist. She would begin her career studying steel. Her search for a place to do her research led her to the lab of scientist Pierre Curie. Pierre and Maria (Marie in French) shared a passion for science and married a year after meeting. They would devote their lives to their scientific work and to raising their two daughters, Irene and Eve.

At first, the Curies did not work together. Then, Marie began investigating the newly discovered uranium rays. Uranium is a substance, and the rays it gives off are now known to be from radioactivity. Another scientist had discovered uranium's mysterious rays, but he did not know what they were. Marie studied different mixtures that contained uranium, including pitchblende, and learned that radioactivity was a property of certain substances. Pierre was excited by Marie's work and joined in the research. Together, they discovered the radioactive substances radium and polonium.

Marie Curie met her husband, Pierre, at a university in Paris. They were both scientists and worked together. They won the Nobel Prize for their work on radioactive substances.

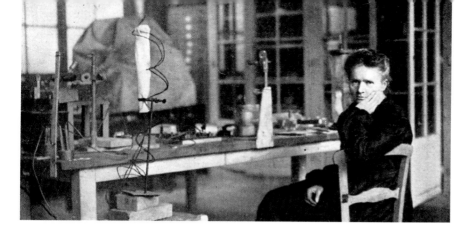

Marie Curie continued her research after the death of her husband. She proved radium was a substance and promoted its use to treat diseases.

Final Challenges

Marie and Pierre Curie would share the Nobel Prize for their work on radioactivity with the scientist who discovered the uranium rays. However, their research was hurting their health. Scientists now know that radioactive substances are dangerous to the human body. But no one knew this fact back then, and the Curies carried vials of radioactive substances in their pockets.

Pierre died a few years after they received the Nobel Prize. However, it was not radioactivity that killed him, but instead he was run over by a carriage on a rainy afternoon. Marie was devastated by the death of the man who was her husband, her best friend, and her co-worker. But she found comfort in her work and in taking care of her daughters. After Pierre's death, she took over his job at the university and became the first woman professor there.

Marie Curie faced a particular challenge in her research. Some scientists questioned whether radium was a substance. They thought that what she called radium might be a solid mixture made of other substances. Through more years of work, Curie proved that radium was a substance and won her second Nobel Prize. Her discoveries forever changed scientists' understanding of matter.

Marie Curie continued her work on radioactive substances throughout her life. She was interested in using radium to treat diseases. She did not know it could cause diseases. She died of leukemia, which was caused by her life's work. The needle in the haystack that Marie Curie worked so hard to find turned out to be a poisoned needle.

Marie Curie became famous around the world for her discoveries. Coins and stamps have been made in her honor.

How Can Substances Be Identified?

Science Vocabulary

electrical conductivity

solubility

thermal conductivity

Substances have different properties that you can observe and measure to identify those substances. Some properties like color, size, or shape can be seen just by looking at the substance. Others are harder to see. And some properties may eventually cause the substance to change into a new substance.

NGSS **5-PS1-3.** Make observations and measurements to identify materials based on their properties.
5-PS1-4. Conduct an investigation to determine whether the mixing of two or more substances results in new substances.

PS1.A. Measurements of a variety of properties can be used to identify materials.
PS1.B. When two or more different substances are mixed, a new substance with different properties may be formed.

Cause and Effect Cause and effect relations are routinely identified, tested, and used to explain change.
Scale, Proportion, and Quantity Standard units are used to measure and describe physical quantities such as weight, time, temperature, and volume.

Planning and Carrying Out Investigations

1. Substances Have Identifiable Properties

Sugar and salt are both white, grainy solids, but they have very different flavors. You do not want to get them confused when you are cooking. So, if you switched their containers by accident, how could you tell them apart? One way is to taste them. Scientists do not usually taste substances to tell them apart because some substances are poisonous. Instead, scientists might use a magnifying glass to look at the shape of each grain, or crystal. Salt crystals look like tiny cubes. Sugar crystals are not cubes. Instead, they have slanted sides.

When you compare the crystal shape of sugar and salt, you are studying a property. When you observe properties, you see things like color, size, or shape. You can observe the crystal shape of sugar or salt just by looking at it closely.

When you measure properties, you are seeing a clear result from a test. For example, you can test how hard chalk or iron is by scratching it with different materials and seeing if it gets scratched or not. Substances have many different properties that can be observed or measured.

Many properties can be studied just by looking at matter. By looking at an object, you can see many of its properties, such as its shape, color, and shininess. A sheet of paper and a sheet of aluminum foil are both shaped like flat rectangles. Paper is white and dull. Aluminum foil, on the other hand, is gray and shiny. You can use the difference in properties to tell paper and foil apart. In a similar way, scientists use properties to identify different substances.

Sheets of aluminum foil and paper can both be identified from their properties. Even though both are the same shape, they are different colors and one is much shinier than the other. Scientists observe and measure properties like these to identify different materials.

You can observe and measure different properties of gold and iron pyrite to tell them apart. Even though they have some properties in common, they have many more that are different.

Gold

Iron pyrite

2. Properties You Can See

Gold is a valuable metal. A piece of gold is yellow and shiny. Iron pyrite is a rock that looks like gold, but it is not very valuable. How can you tell these two substances apart? If you have the right tools, you can study their particles. Tools that are powerful enough to study particles are expensive, so you might compare different properties that you can see. Hardness, color, brittleness, and reflectivity are four different properties you can see.

Hardness

One way that gold is different from iron pyrite is hardness. Hardness is how easily a material is scratched or dented. Wood is soft, so it scratches and dents easily. Diamond, on the other hand, is very hard. It is almost impossible to scratch diamond.

You can compare the hardness of different materials by scratching them. Gold is much softer than iron pyrite. If you have a steel knife, you could scratch gold with it but you could not scratch iron pyrite.

Color

Another way that you can tell substances apart is by their color. Gold and iron pyrite are both yellow. But gold is a very bright yellow, while iron pyrite is very pale.

Matter can be found in a wide range of colors, and some of it is even colorless, such as water. Other matter is black or white. Coal is black and salt is white. Still other matter has colors like those you find in a box of crayons. The substances in flowers give them their bright colors.

Brittleness

Another property is whether a substance can be shaped or not. Some substances are very brittle and hard to shape, while other substances are not brittle and can be easily shaped. If you hit a piece of gold with a hammer, the gold will flatten. If you flatten the gold enough, you will be able to bend it with your hands. There are many other metals that are not very brittle. You can crumple a sheet of aluminum foil and crush an aluminum can. You can even bend a copper wire to spell your name.

However, if you hit a piece of iron pyrite with a hammer, it will break into thin pieces. Iron pyrite is very brittle and does not have the ability to be shaped. Chalk is also brittle. If you try to bend a piece of chalk to form a curve, it will break into two pieces.

Reflectivity

Reflectivity is another property. Reflectivity describes how much light bounces off a material. Pale materials tend to bounce back more light than dark materials. Chalk, which is white, is more reflective than iron, which is almost black. Metals tend to be more reflective than objects that are not made of metal. For example, aluminum foil is more reflective than paper. Shiny objects are usually reflective.

However, whether an object is shiny is not always useful for identifying substances. A piece of gold is very shiny, but if you scratch up the surface it will not be as shiny. It will still be more reflective than iron, because the pale yellow color will bounce back more light than the dark iron.

Copper wire can be bent into new shapes, so it is not very brittle. Copper has many properties that are different from other substances.

Cooking pots are made of metal because most metal has a high thermal conductivity, so it transfers heat well. The handle on the pot is plastic, which has a low thermal conductivity, so it does not burn your hand when you grasp it.

3. Some Properties Are Harder to See

Some properties are easy to see. Other properties, such as solubility, electrical conductivity, thermal conductivity, or the ability to change, are harder to see.

Solubility

Solubility is a property that describes whether a substance can dissolve in another substance. For example, sugar dissolves in water. Sugar mixed in water seems to disappear. Flour, on the other hand, does not dissolve in water. Flour mixed with water does not disappear.

Solubility depends on the substance being dissolved and the substance it is being dissolved in. Salt dissolves easily in water. But only a little salt will dissolve in alcohol. Salt has a high solubility in water and a low solubility in alcohol.

Electrical Conductivity

Electrical conductivity describes how well a substance allows electric current to pass through it. Electrical conductivity is measured by running electric current through a substance. In general, electricity travels well through metals such as copper, so the wires in your home are made of copper.

Thermal Conductivity

Thermal conductivity describes how well a substance allows heat to pass through it. Many metals have high thermal conductivity. Kitchens pots are made of metal, which transfers heat from the stove to the food. Other substances, such as plastic and glass, do not transfer electricity or heat well. Plastic has both low electrical conductivity and low thermal conductivity, which is why electric cords are covered in plastic.

Ability to Change into New Substances

Substances have the ability to change into new ones. Scientists study the ability for a substance to change into new substances, whether it is by burning, bubbling, or rusting.

When a substance burns, it changes into a new substance. Wood contains substances that can burn. When these substances burn, the substances change into ash, water vapor, and a gas called carbon dioxide. You have to test whether a substance can burn to know if it has that chemical property. For example, you learn that iron does not burn when an adult puts an iron fireplace poker into a fire. The poker will get very hot, but it will not burn.

Substances are also changing if they bubble when mixed with vinegar. If you put a few drops of vinegar on baking soda, you will see bubbles form where the two substances touch. The bubbles tell you that a gas formed when the baking soda and vinegar mixed. But if you put vinegar on sugar, the sugar will get wet, but no bubbles will form. This is a property that must be tested. You cannot see whether a substance will bubble when mixed with vinegar without testing it.

Rusting is also a change that can occur. Iron can rust. When iron rusts, it changes from a shapeable, gray substance to a brittle, orange substance. Mixtures that contain iron can also rust. If you test a material and find that it rusts, you know that the material contains iron.

The ability to burn and the ability to rust are two properties that are hard to see. Wood has the ability to burn. Iron has the ability to rust, but wood does not.

This scientist is testing different properties of the rock he is holding to identify the substances it is made of. Each substance has its own unique set of properties that can help identify it.

 Nature of Science

4. Scientists Use Properties to Identify Substances

Iron pyrite is called fool's gold because it can be mistaken for gold. Some properties of iron pyrite and gold are similar. They are shiny and are shades of yellow. But, as you have learned, other properties of iron pyrite and gold are different.

Each substance has its own set of properties. No substance has the exact same properties as any other substance. Two substances may share many properties, but at least one property will be different. Thus, scientists use properties to identify substances.

Which properties scientists use to identify a substance depends partly on what they think the substance is. If a scientist thinks that a powder is salt, the scientist may see if it dissolves in water. If a scientist thinks that a metal contains iron, the scientist may test if it rusts. If a scientist is trying to decide if something is one of two substances, the scientist may test only a property that is different between those substances.

The properties a scientist uses may depend on the tools the scientist has. Some scientists work outdoors to identify minerals. Minerals are solids that are found in nature. When scientists work outside, they have only the tools that they carry with them. Such scientists may carry a small kit that contains things that test various properties. The kit may have a nail, a penny, and a glass plate to test hardness. It may also contain vinegar to test if a mineral causes bubbles to form. After the properties of a mineral have been checked and tested, the results are used to identify it.

How Can Substances Be Identified?

1. Substances Have Identifiable Properties   A property is a characteristic of matter that can be observed or measured. Properties can be used to identify substances. Properties may include a substance's color, shape, size, shininess, and hardness. For example, both paper and aluminum can be folded. But paper is white and dull. Aluminum foil is gray and shiny. They have similar and different properties.

2. Properties You Can See   Some properties are easy to study by touching or looking at a substance. Hardness, color, brittleness, and reflectivity are a few properties you can see. Hardness is how easily a material is scratched. Brittleness is whether a substance can be shaped or not. Reflectivity describes how much light bounces off the material. Copper is shiny and can be bent into shapes.

3. Some Properties Are Harder to See   Some properties of matter are harder to see. Solubility, electrical conductivity, thermal conductivity, and the ability to change are all properties of matter that are hard to see. The ability to burn, bubble, or rust are ways some substances can change. For example, iron will rust. Wood does not rust, but it will burn.

4. Scientists Use Properties to Identify Substances   Each substance has its own set of properties. Two substances may share many properties, but at least one property will be different. Scientists observe and measure different properties to identify unknown substances. The properties a scientist uses for identification may depend on the tools the scientist has or depend partly on what the scientist thinks the substance is.

Substances That Glow

"Oh! Look at that one!" Glittering red lights explode across the sky and slowly fizzle out as they fall to the ground. Boom! Now green and yellow fireworks light up the sky. What property causes fireworks to glow in so many different colors?

The bright colors of fireworks come from glowing substances. Each color comes from a different substance.

If you ever see a fireworks display, you can see the different colors lighting up the night sky. But where do these colors come from? There are substances in a firework that have a special property. These substances can glow!

Substances can glow when they release energy that they have absorbed when a firework is lit. As a firework shoots into the sky, substances inside of it explode and release energy. Boom! Other substances inside the firework absorb the energy. Then these substances release energy that is carried by brightly colored light as they fall. Once they lose most of their energy, you no longer can see the substances glow.

But what causes different colored fireworks? Each color is made by a different substance. Each substance glows a certain color when it releases energy. Calcium chloride glows orange. Barium chloride glows blue. The color a substance glows is a unique property that scientists can use to identify the substance.

The next time you see fireworks, observe all the different colors you can see. Each unique color is another unique substance!

Going up in Flames

Because a substance always glows the same color, scientists can identify substances by making them glow. One test scientists do is called a *flame test*. Flame tests help scientists identify substances from the color that they glow when they are put in a flame.

A flame test is like a mini firework, but without the explosion. To test a substance, a scientist dips the tip of a clean wire in a powder of the substance. The powder-coated tip then goes into a flame. If heat makes the substance glow, the flame will change color. Similar to fireworks, the color of the flame depends on the substance. For example, potassium is a substance that glows a light purple color when it is put into a flame. If a scientist tests a material and sees that it glows a light purple, he or she may decide that it contains potassium.

A substance glows the same color whether it is heated in a firework, in a flame, or in a distant star. This fact is very useful for astronomers who want to know what makes up stars and other glowing objects in the universe. Although these objects are too far away to visit, the light they give off reaches Earth. Scientists use special telescopes to study this light. Then they compare what they find to substances that were tested in the lab. In this way, scientists have learned about substances that are found in the sun and in other stars across the Milky Way galaxy.

Scientists use flame tests to look for certain substances in minerals.

Astronomers study the colors of light from glowing objects in space. A substance glows the same color everywhere in the universe, so astronomers can identify substances that are far away.

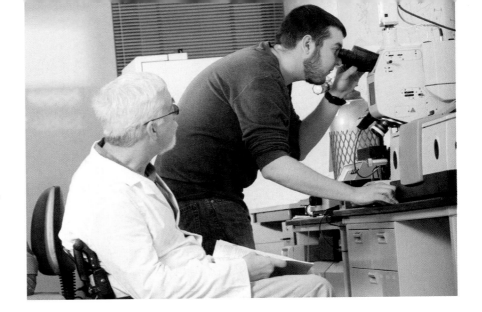

Scientists use tools in the lab to study substances that glow. The tools shine a light that is absorbed by the substance to show information that scientists cannot see with their unaided eyes.

Bright Ideas

Scientists are not the only people who look at the color a substance glows to identify a material. Have you ever seen a cashier shine a small flashlight on a 20 dollar bill before putting it in the cash register? The cashier is looking for substances in the money that glow. Business owners worry about people paying with fake bills. The government adds substances that can glow onto different bills. This way they can always be sure the money is not fake. These substances glow after they absorb energy carried by light.

Cashiers use a flashlight that shines a type of light called *black light*. The lit bulb looks dark purple, but most of the light it shines is invisible to people. Substances in the dollar bill absorb energy carried by this light and then glow as they lose this energy. Under a black light, a real 20 dollar bill has a glowing green strip.

Different substances are used in different bills to make the strips glow in a variety of colors. The strip in a ten dollar bill glows orange when a black light shines on it, while the strip in a 100 dollar bill glows pink. A cashier can identify which bill they have based on what substance is in the bill because it will glow a certain color!

The color a substance glows is a specific property of the substance. Scientists use this property to also to observe what substances are in different materials. Often they are not looking at dollar bills, but in different minerals they find in the world.

Glow On!

The substances in money stop glowing when the black light is turned off. However, some minerals glow even after the lights are turned off.

More than 400 years ago, an Italian shoemaker discovered stones that glowed at night. The stones became known as Bologna stones, after the city near where they were found. At the time, some people thought the stones were magical. Today, scientists know that a substance in the stones glows after being in sunlight. Because the substance slowly loses the energy it absorbs, it glows long after the sun sets.

You may not have seen a Bologna stone, but you have probably seen other things that glow in the dark. You can kick around a glow-in-the-dark ball or decorate your room with stars that glow after you turn off the lights. Glow-in-the-dark objects are not only for fun and games. There are also emergency exit signs that glow in the dark so that people can see them if the lights go out during an emergency. Many objects that glow in the dark contain a substance that can glow for hours. But these substances only glow after they absorb light. If you leave a glow-in-the-dark ball in dark closet all day, it will not glow at night.

Scientists spend a lot of time studying substances. Not only can they identify substances by their color, but also by what color they glow. Next time you see a material glow, you can use this property to try to identify the substances inside of it!

This soccer ball can glow for hours after it gets dark. Substances that glow for a long time are mixed into the ball.

How Do Scientists Know When Substances Change?

Science Vocabulary

reaction

state change

Substances' properties can change. Some of these changes can happen without the substance itself changing, like when solid ice melts into liquid water. Other changes form new substances, like mixing vinegar and baking soda. When you fry an egg, substances in the clear egg white change into new substances that are solid and white.

NGSS **5-PS1-3.** Make observations and measurements to identify materials based on their properties.
5-PS1-4. Conduct an investigation to determine whether the mixing of two or more substances results in new substances.

PS1.A. Measurements of a variety of properties can be used to identify materials.
PS1.B. When two or more different substances are mixed, a new substance with different properties may be formed.

Cause and Effect Cause and effect relationships are routinely identified, tested, and used to explain change.
Scale, Proportion, and Quantity Standard units are used to measure and describe physical quantities such as weight, time, temperature, and volume.

**Planning and Carrying Out Investigations**

1. Changes in Matter Can Be Seen

Take a moment to describe the glass in a window. You might say it looks smooth, shiny, and clear. You might even call it a solid. All the words you used to describe the glass are properties of the glass. Suppose you used a piece of sandpaper to scratch up the surface of the glass. What would you see? The glass may no longer be smooth and shiny, and if you scratched it enough, it may not even be clear. The properties of glass just changed!

Some changes in matter can be easily seen. Scratching glass to make it rough is an easy change to see. Other changes, like dissolving salt in water, can be more difficult to see.

Sometimes you can see the properties of matter change without the substance changing. Scratching and melting glass changes the properties of the glass, but does not change glass into a new substance. Just because you see a change in matter does not mean that the substance has changed.

Other times you can see a change in the properties of matter because a new substance forms. Every substance has different properties, so when a new substance forms it has different properties from the original substances. Some of these changes are easy to see. Iron is a gray solid and oxygen is an invisible gas. When they are mixed, they form rust, which is an orange solid.

Sometimes changes in matter can be hard to see. Baking soda is a white solid and vinegar is a clear or brownish liquid. When they are mixed, they form carbon dioxide, which is an invisible gas. When change is hard to see, scientists often will perform tests to see if a change has happened.

This substance may look like honey or syrup, but it is actually hot glass. When a substance like glass gets very hot, some of its properties may change, but it is still the same substance.

2. Substances Can Change State

You can watch some properties of matter change if you put a glass of ice cubes outside on a hot summer day. The ice in the glass will change from cube-shaped, solid pieces to a clear liquid. This is water changing from a solid state to liquid state.

A **state change** is a change of a substance from one state of matter to another. Some of the properties of a substance change during a state change, but the substance itself does not change. Four common state changes are melting, freezing, evaporation, and condensation.

Melting

Melting is the state change from solid to liquid. Ice is water in the solid state. When you watch ice cubes turn to water in a glass, you are watching the ice melting. As in all state changes, substances do not change but the arrangement of their particles do change.

The particles in a solid are close together and locked in position. During melting, the particles of a substance break away from each other. The particles stay close together, but they are no longer attached to each other. The particles slide past one another and form a liquid.

Freezing

Melting is a common state change. During a state change, the particles of a substance rearrange and start moving in different ways, but the substance stays the same.

Freezing is the state change from liquid to solid. If you put a container of liquid water into a freezer, the water will freeze and become solid ice. When a substance is in the liquid state, its particles are close together and move about. As the substance freezes, the particles slow down and begin to stick together. When the particles are stuck together and are locked in place, the substance is a solid.

Evaporation

Evaporation is the state change from liquid to gas. You can see evaporation if you heat a pot of water on a stove. When the water is hot enough, it will start to bubble. The bubbles form because liquid water is changing to water vapor, which is a gas. The bubbles are filled with this water vapor. This bubbling of a liquid as it changes to a gas is often called *boiling*. Evaporation happens when a liquid boils.

As you heat a liquid, the particles of the substance move faster and faster. The particles move farther apart and eventually break away from the particles that form the liquid. These particles that break away become the gas state of the substance. The particles in the gas state are far apart and move quickly in all directions.

When water boils, some of the water evaporates as a gas. If the gas starts to cool down, like when it touches the lid of a boiling pot, it condenses back into liquid water.

Condensation

Condensation is the state change from gas to liquid. If you cover a pot of boiling water with a glass lid, you will see drops of water forming on the lid. The drops form because of the condensation of water vapor to form liquid water. The water vapor cools down when it hits the lid. When the water vapor cools it turns from a gas to a liquid.

When a gas is cooled, the particles of the substance slow down. As they slow down, they also move closer together. When the particles are moving slow enough and are close enough together, they will start to stick together. When the particles are stuck together, but not locked in place, the substance becomes a liquid. The particles are close together and flow over each other.

3. New Substances Have New Properties

The properties of substances in egg white change when you cook it. Raw egg white is a slightly yellowish, clear liquid mixture. When an egg white is cooked, it turns into a white solid mixture. The properties of the egg white changed because the substances in the egg white changed into new substances.

When one or more substances are changed into new substances, a **reaction** is said to have happened. The new substances that form in a reaction have different properties than the original substances had. During a reaction, the particles of substances change, but you cannot see them changing unless you use very powerful tools. So, to tell if a reaction is happening, you have to look for certain signs. These signs include gas formation, solid formation, color changes, and energy changes.

Gas Formation

The formation of a gas is one sign of a reaction. When a gas forms in a liquid, you will see bubbles. These bubbles are full with the gas formed during the reaction. For example, you see bubbles when baking soda and vinegar are mixed together. These bubbles are filled with carbon dioxide gas that formed during a reaction between the baking soda and the vinegar.

When baking soda and vinegar are mixed together, carbon dioxide gas forms. The bubbles filled with gas are a sign that a new substance has formed and a reaction took place.

Solid Formation

The formation of a solid is another sign of a reaction. Burning is a kind of a reaction. If you burn a piece of paper, a crumbly, black material will be left behind. This black material is made of substances that were formed during burning. Solids can also form when liquids or gases are mixed together.

Burning is a reaction that can be seen by an energy change, formation of an ash solid, and formation of a gas. When something is burning, it gives off light and heat, and forms a solid and a gas.

Color Change

A color change is often a sign that a reaction happened. If you spill bleach on a colored shirt, the shirt will turn white. The shirt changed colors because of a reaction between the bleach and the dyes in the shirt that made a new substance.

Energy Change

Reactions often involve storing or releasing energy. Some reactions release energy. You can observe this when they give off light, heat, or sound. When something burns, you see a flame that gives off light and feel heat coming from the fire.

Other reactions store energy. An instant cold pack contains two substances—a solid and a smaller bag of liquid. When you squeeze the cold pack, the bag inside bursts, and the liquid mixes with the solid to start a reaction. The reaction takes in energy from its surroundings, which makes the cold pack feel cold.

Observing Signs Without a Reaction

Just because you see a sign of a reaction does not mean that a reaction has happened. Some of the signs happen even when no new substance is formed. For example, when you boil water, a gas forms and you see bubbles. Those bubbles are filled with water vapor, which is the gas state of water, not a new substance. When you freeze water, a solid forms. The solid ice is not a new substance either.

The signs of a reaction tell you that a reaction *may* have happened, but they do not tell you that a reaction has definitely happened.

Muffin batter is a mixture of different substances. While it bakes, different reactions occur to produce new substances that have different properties. Baked muffins have many different properties from muffin batter because of the reactions that created new substances.

4. Substance Changes in Your Kitchen

You may think that substance changes happen only in science labs. But changes happen all around you. In fact, many changes happen whenever food cooks or bakes.

Think about making muffins. You mix together different materials, including flour, butter, eggs, milk, salt, and baking powder. When the ingredients are all combined, you have a pale, liquid batter. You put the batter in the oven, and the batter puffs up, becomes a solid, and turns brown.

Muffin batter puffs up because of a reaction that occurs with the baking powder. During the reaction, substances in the batter form a gas that is trapped in bubbles in the batter. You can see these bubbles when you cut open a baked muffin. Muffin batter becomes a solid because different substances in the batter link together during a different reaction. A third reaction causes substances in the muffin to turn brown.

Reactions do not happen in all cooked food. If you make pasta, you first have to boil water. Boiling water is a state change, from liquid to gas, but it is not a reaction because no new substances have been formed.

Before you put pasta in water, it is a brittle solid mixture. After the pasta is cooked, the properties of the pasta change. The pasta is still a solid, but it can be bent. It seems like there was a reaction, but instead the pasta takes in water, which changes its properties. Cooked pasta is a mixture of the substances in dry pasta and water.

The next time you help someone cook or bake, study how the properties of the food change. Try to decide if new substances are being formed.

How Do Scientists Know When Substances Change?

1. Changes in Matter Can Be Seen   Sometimes, you can see the properties of matter change. These changes may happen without changing the substance. For example scratching glass will make it rough. The glass is no longer smooth and shiny, but it is still glass. However, some property changes happen because a new substance with new properties has formed. For example, iron, when mixed with oxygen, can change to rust, a new substance.

2. Substances Can Change State   A substance undergoes a state change when it changes from one state of matter into another. During a state change, the particles of a substance rearrange, but no new substance is formed. Melting, freezing, evaporation, and condensation are examples of state changes. For example, water as a solid, ice, will melt to become a liquid. During melting, the particles of water break away from each other to form a liquid.

3. New Substances Have New Properties   A reaction happens when one or more substances change into new substances. Each substance has different properties because the particles that make up a substance are unique. Some signs of a reaction are the formation of a gas, the formation of a solid, a change in color, or a change in energy. But sometimes a reaction is not actually happening, even if you see these signs.

4. Substance Changes in Your Kitchen   Substances change whenever food cooks or bakes. Some of these changes happen because new substances are being formed. Cooking muffin batter is an example of reactions forming a new substance. Other changes happen without new substances being formed. Cooking pasta is an example of creating a mixture, not a new substance.

Gold Quest

For centuries, alchemists have tried to make gold from other substances. You may have heard of their quest to find the philosopher's stone, which is supposed to be able to turn lead into gold. But what properties does gold have that make it so valuable?

Gold is a yellow, reflective metal. It has been used since ancient times for many purposes, including jewelry.

You may have seen gold before. Gold is a yellow metal that is very reflective. It is also easy to shape, because it is soft and not brittle. It is a solid at room temperature and changing its state into a liquid would require a large amount of heat. All of these properties make gold a valuable substance. Many people wear gold jewelry, such as necklaces or rings. Ancient kings and queens used to make their crowns out of gold. Some people even have gold teeth!

Gold has been valuable for thousands of years, so the alchemists that lived thousands of years ago wanted to find a way to make gold. You have learned that many substances can change into new substances during reactions. Alchemists mixed metals with different gases and liquids, hoping to make gold. This process could change the colors of metals. While alchemists were able to make new substances with different properties, they never succeeded in making gold.

Why did ancient alchemists try so hard to make gold? One reason is because gold was used for money. About 5,000 years ago, gold rings were used as money. Eventually, people began using gold coins as money. In fact, gold is called a *coinage* metal because it was used in money.

Gold Coins

These days, people use coins made of zinc, copper, or nickel. But many centuries ago, people used coins made of gold. You may have seen gold coins in a museum. Why did people choose to use gold instead of any other metal?

Gold is reflective and a solid at room temperature, but many other metals share that property. However, gold has a property that many other metals do not share. Gold does not react with other substances in the air. Have you seen silver before? If you have seen a piece of silver after it has been left outside for a few days, you may notice that the gray, shiny surface has turned black. The black substance is formed when silver is mixed with gases in the air. Iron will also react with gases in the air to form rust. In fact, many metals react with substances in the air to form new ones.

If you leave a gold coin out in the air, the coin will remain yellow and reflective. This property of gold, that it does not react with other substances easily, makes it more valuable. You can have a piece of gold for many years, and it will remain the same. People used gold for money because it is not reactive. If they had a gold coin, they could be sure that it would appear the same for their whole lifetime. Think about if you had to use iron coins. In a few years, the coin would rust and fall into pieces! It would be hard to save money if all of your coins were made of iron.

Many metals react with substances in the air to form new substances. Gold does not react with many substances in the air. Coins made of gold appear the same even after they have been used for many years.

Gold has a high electrical conductivity, so some manufacturers cover their plugs with a thin layer of gold. This USB cable has a thin coating of gold on its plug.

Coats of Gold

Gold has another property that makes it very popular. You have learned that gold is soft and not brittle, so it is easy to shape.

Ancient artists and jewelers discovered that they could pound gold into very thin, flat sheets. They could bend these thin sheets into shapes and press pictures into them. Because gold does not react with substances in the air, you can still see some of these decorations that were made by ancient artists today!

These days, people still use gold for jewelry and decorations, but they also use gold for another purpose. You have learned that metals have a high electrical conductivity. Gold is a metal that allows electricity to pass through it easily since it has a high electrical conductivity. Some very expensive machines have gold wires in them because the gold will conduct electricity, but will not react with substances in the air.

You may have never seen a gold wire before, but maybe you have seen a golden USB plug. These days, some manufacturers make plugs that are covered with a thin layer of gold. You might see these plugs with a television or a computer cable. The gold lets electricity pass through the cable to the computer. It also keeps the plug from reacting with substances in the air! That sure is a fancy computer plug!

Gold is easy to shape, so many people used it to made decorative objects, such as this gold mask.

Mining for Gold

People have been using gold for many different purposes for thousands of years, but where did this gold come from? Ancient Egyptians first found pieces of gold in the sands along rivers. They collected the gold pieces, but most of them were too small to make anything. Instead, they heated the tiny pieces over a very hot fire until the metal changed from a solid to a liquid. When they cooled the metal back down again, it turned back into a solid. They could gather gold in small pieces, and then use these state changes to form large pieces of gold.

These days, it is much harder to find gold. Instead, people dig deep into the ground in hope of finding gold. People often have to dig several kilometers underground in order to find gold. Often the gold that the miners find is still trapped in rocks as a solid mixture. To separate the gold, the rocks have to be smashed into a powder, and then mixed with a liquid substance called mercury. The gold dissolves in the mercury. Then the mercury is heated to make the mercury evaporate and leave pure gold behind.

But dissolving gold in mercury is not the only way to find gold. Scientists have also discovered bacteria that can take dissolved gold out of a solution to form solid gold pieces. In a way, the scientists are modern-day alchemists as they try to "make" gold. They have only gotten very small amounts of gold. Still, the ancient alchemists would be jealous—it is still more than they ever got!

Both ancient Egyptian miners and American miners searched rivers for small pieces of gold. They took the small pieces and melted them down to form larger pieces of gold.

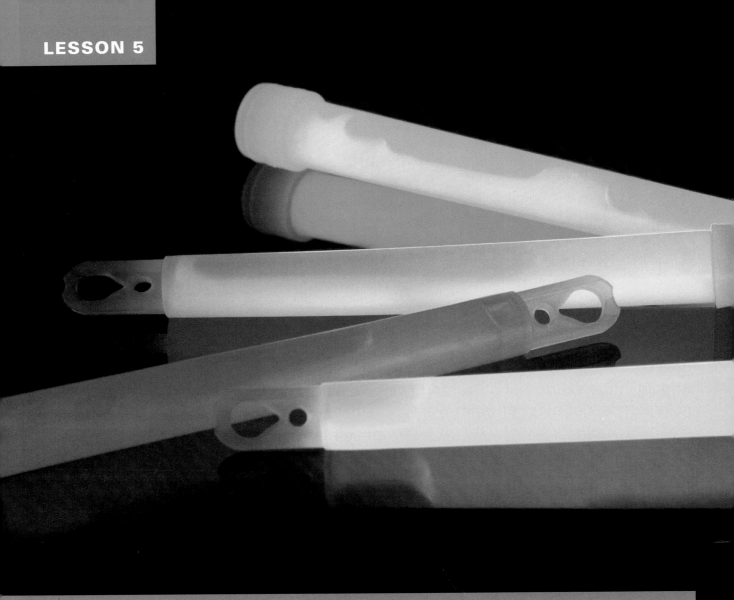

What Causes Substances to Change?

Science Vocabulary

contract

expand

Heating or cooling a substance can cause its properties to change. So can mixing many substances together. Glow sticks glow when substances mix and react to form new substances. In many cases, cooling matter can slow how quickly reactions occur. That is why putting glow sticks in the freezer makes them last longer!

NGSS   **5-PS1-3.** Make observations and measurements to identify materials based on their properties.
5-PS1-4. Conduct an investigation to determine whether the mixing of two or more substances results in new substances.

PS1.A. Measurements of a variety of properties can be used to identify materials.
PS1.B. When two or more different substances are mixed, a new substance with different properties may be formed.

Cause and Effect Cause and effect relationships are routinely identified, tested, and used to explain change.
Scale, Proportion, and Quantity Standard units are used to measure and describe physical quantities such as weight, time, temperature, and volume.

Planning and Carrying Out Investigations

1. Changes to Substances Have Consistent Causes

Will a pot of water on a stove boil if the stove is not on? Will a glass of water freeze if left on a table? Will baking soda and vinegar bubble and make carbon dioxide if kept in separate containers? The answers, of course, are no.

If you want the properties of matter to change, you have to do something to the matter. Only a few different things cause the properties of a substance to change: adding energy, removing energy, and mixing substances.

Adding energy to matter can cause the properties of matter to change. Heating matter is one way of adding energy. When you heat water, you can make it boil and evaporate. Heating substances also causes reactions. You heat food to cook or bake it and change the properties of the food.

Removing energy from matter can also cause changes. You can remove energy from matter by cooling it. Putting water in a freezer removes energy from the water, causing the water to become ice.

Mixing substances can also cause properties to change. Mixing substances can cause matter to dissolve and also allows reactions to happen. If you mix salt and water, no reaction happens, but the properties of the water have changed. If you mix vinegar and baking soda, a reaction happens to make a new substance with new properties.

However, heating, cooling, and mixing substances do not always lead to a reaction. Cooling plastic in a freezer will make the plastic colder, but will not cause a reaction. Mixing sand and salt together will not cause a reaction.

The properties of matter do not change on their own. Substances must be heated, cooled, or mixed to cause changes. Putting water in a freezer will change the properties of the water.

Heating things can make them expand. Many bridges are built with expansion joints like these that allow the bridge to expand in hot weather without breaking.

2. Heating and Cooling Cause Changes

If you went to a scientist's lab, you might see many tools to heat or cool substances. For example, Bunsen burners are used to heat up substances in experiments. You may also see tools to keep things cool, like refrigerators, freezers, or ice makers.

Heating Substances

Recall that the particles in a solid are close together, the particles in a liquid are a little farther apart, and the particles in a gas are very far apart. Heating a substance causes the particles in the substance to move faster. Heating a solid causes the particles to move fast enough to break away from each other to form liquid. Heating a liquid causes the particles to move fast enough to escape from the liquid to become a gas. Heating substances can cause changes in the properties of a substance without changing the identity of the substance.

Heating can change the size of a material. If you put a partly filled balloon in a hot car, the balloon will get bigger. The size of the balloon changed because the air inside it expanded. To **expand** means to get larger. Most things expand when heated. Bridges are often built with joints in them. The joints give the bridges room to expand. If the joints were not there, the bridge could break during hot weather.

Heating substances and materials can also change the properties of matter by causing a reaction to happen. You can start a fire by rubbing wood together to heat the wood and make it burn.

Cooling Substances

Cooling substances can also change the properties of matter. Some of these changes can happen without changing the substance into a new substance. For example, condensation and freezing are state changes that happen when substances are cooled. Cooling a substance causes the particles in the substance to slow down. As the particles in a gas slow down, they get closer to each other. They move close together and form a liquid. If the substance is cooled more, the particles slow down even more. Eventually, the particles lock together to form a solid.

Like heating, cooling a substance can change its size. When most substances are cooled they **contract**, or get smaller. If you put a balloon in a freezer, it will get smaller. The air inside the balloon contracts when it is cooled. The liquid inside a thermometer goes down in cold weather because the liquid contracts. However, water is different from most other substances. When it is cooled, water expands instead of contracts. That's why you should never put a completely full bottle of water in the freezer—the water will expand and the bottle could break!

Cooling certain substances can also cause reactions to happen. When you make gelatin, you pour a liquid mixture of water, sugar, gelatin, and other ingredients into a container. You put the container into a refrigerator to cool it. As it cools, the gelatin reacts and turns the mixture into a solid-like gel.

This scientist is pushing a balloon into a bucket of liquid nitrogen, which is −196° C (−321° F)! When he takes the balloon out, the air inside has contracted because it cooled.

When gold is heated to a very high temperature, it becomes a liquid. When it is a liquid, other metals can be dissolved into it, making a new metal with new properties. Mixing two substances can change their properties.

3. Mixing Substances Causes Changes

Some changes in the properties of matter will not happen unless substances are mixed together. Sugar will not dissolve unless it is mixed with water or another liquid. Baking soda will not react to form carbon dioxide unless it is mixed with vinegar or certain other substances.

Mixing Can Dissolve Substances

Mixing one substance into another to dissolve it changes the properties of both substances. When you think of dissolving something, you probably think about dissolving a solid into a liquid in which the particles of the solid break apart and mix with the particles of the liquid. The solid seems to disappear and the properties of the solid cannot be measured. It is not a solid anymore, but part of a liquid solution.

The properties of the liquid also change because it now has particles of the dissolved solid in it. The liquid is no longer a substance but a mixture with two substances. The liquid might change colors or taste different after a solid has dissolved in it.

Metals are also commonly dissolved in each other. You have learned that gold is a soft solid that is easy to scratch and bend. So jewelry made from pure gold is easily damaged. Other metals, such as copper and silver, are dissolved in gold to make a harder metal. Since gold is normally a solid, that means it must be heated up to a very high temperature so it melts. Then other metals like copper or silver can be dissolved in the liquid gold. This new metal is then used to make stronger jewelry. The new metal is much harder than pure gold. Other properties also change, like color and shininess.

Mixing Can Cause a Reaction

Many reactions happen when two or more substances are mixed. Recall that new substances are formed during a reaction. The new substances always have different properties than those of the original substances. So, when a reaction happens, new substances with different properties form.

You mix substances and cause a reaction whenever you activate a glow stick. A glow stick is a tube that contains a liquid. Inside the tube, there is a smaller glass tube that contains a different liquid. When you bend the glow stick, you break the smaller tube. When the smaller tube is broken, the liquid inside it mixes with the liquid inside the larger tube. A reaction between the two liquids happens, and the mixture glows. During this reaction, new substances with new properties are being formed, and light and energy are being released. The light stick eventually stops glowing once all of the substances have finished reacting with each other.

Rusting is also a reaction that happens when two substances are mixed. When you see an old car that is rusting slowly over time, you might wonder what substances are mixing to make the rust. One of the substances is iron in the car's body. The other substance is oxygen. The oxygen can come from the air that surrounds the car. It can also come from oxygen that is dissolved in rainwater. That is why many old iron tools that are left outside are rusty. Rusting is a slow reaction, but the rust that forms is a new substance with new properties. Rust has different properties from iron and from oxygen, the two substances that reacted to form it.

You activate a glow stick by breaking a tube inside the stick. The liquid in the tube mixes with liquid inside the stick, and a reaction happens. The reaction makes the mixed liquids glow.

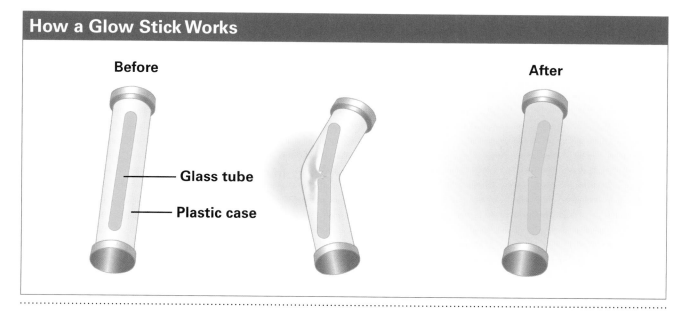

How a Glow Stick Works

Before

After

Glass tube

Plastic case

Food can be kept in the refrigerator to prevent it from spoiling quickly. Cooling down matter slows down its particles, so reactions happen less quickly.

4. Why You Use a Refrigerator

Imagine what life would be like without a refrigerator in your home. You could never pour yourself a glass of cold orange juice. You could not keep frozen fruit bars in the freezer to eat on hot summer days. But refrigerators have a more important job than keeping drinks cold and keeping fruit bars from melting. Refrigerators help keep food from spoiling quickly.

Food spoils partly because of reactions that happen in the food. When food spoils, its properties change. It may change colors and start to smell bad. Food that has spoiled is often not safe to eat. New substances are formed in the food by the reactions that caused the food to spoil. Some of those new substances can make you sick.

Keeping food in a refrigerator or a freezer can slow the reactions that make food go bad. Recall that particles in matter are always moving. Reactions between substances happen when particles of those different substances hit each other. When you cool matter, the particles in that matter slow down. When food is in a refrigerator or a freezer, the particles in the food slow down and do not hit particles of other substances as much. The reactions in the food that cause them to spoil do not happen as often, and the food does not spoil as quickly.

But keeping food cold does not completely stop it from spoiling. When you cool down matter, the particles slow down, but they do not stop completely. So, reactions still happen, they just happen more slowly. Food can still spoil in a refrigerator, but it spoils more slowly.

What Causes Substances to Change?

1. Changes to Substances Have Consistent Causes The properties of matter can change, but only a few different things can cause these changes. Adding energy and removing energy can cause changes. Heating and cooling matter are common ways to add and remove energy. Mixing substances can also cause changes in the properties of matter.

2. Heating and Cooling Cause Changes Heating and cooling a substance can change its properties. Heating and cooling cause substances to expand or contract and can even cause state changes. Heating and cooling can even cause reactions that create new substances. Rubbing wood together can cause it to heat up, burn, and form ash.

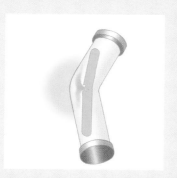

3. Mixing Substances Causes Changes Mixing substances to dissolve one substance into another causes changes in the properties of the substances. Mixing substances can also cause changes because of reactions that happen when certain substances are mixed. The reactions form new substances that have different properties.

4. Why You Use a Refrigerator Food can go bad partly because of reactions that happen in the food. These reactions cause new substances to form in the food that can make you sick. Cooling matter down slows down its particles. Reactions still happen, they just happen more slowly. That is why keeping food in a freezer or refrigerator makes the food spoil less quickly.

Science in the Kitchen

You do not have to be a scientist to work with substance changes. A chef makes a living changing the substances in food to make delicious meals. Chefs need to know the changes that happen when ingredients are mixed, heated, and cooled to be able to prepare the best dishes.

Chefs prepare meals at restaurants. Understanding the changes that happen to food as it cooks helps chefs make tasty meals.

Suppose you are sitting at a table and then smell the aroma of your favorite food. You take a bite, and the flavors explode in your mouth. Maybe your favorite food is crunchy, juicy, or gooey. It could be sweet or spicy. Whatever the reasons you love this dish, it must be prepared just right. If the wrong ingredients are used, your dinner could taste awful. If it is cooked too long, it could be dry or burnt. If it is not cooked long enough, it will not taste right either.

The substances in food ingredients change as they are cooked. In fact, you would not eat some foods unless they are cooked. Imagine biting into a raw potato. Yuck! The changes that happen to substances are the reason simple ingredients can be turned into a huge variety of foods, from tacos to pizza to a fancy dinner. Chefs need to understand what causes the changes in food when it cooks so they can make tasty dishes.

Chefs control ingredients and temperature to get the right substance changes for the meal they are preparing. Even a small change can make a big difference in a meal. For example, a dish may be too bland or too salty if the wrong amount of salt is added. Chefs also control changes so that the color and texture of the food come out the way they want. No one wants flavorless, mushy vegetables. Thankfully, chefs know how to cook vegetables so they are full of flavor and still a little crunchy.

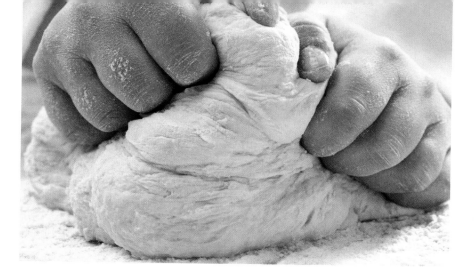

Bakers knead dough to cause changes that form gluten in the dough. Gluten is stretchy and strong. It helps trap gas bubbles in bread and gives it its chewy texture.

Bread and Water

People have eaten bread since ancient times. Bread can be made with a few simple ingredients: flour, water, yeast, sugar, and salt. But you would make a hard lump of bread if you simply stirred the ingredients together and baked them. Making a good loaf of bread takes some skill and knowledge. Bakers are chefs that make breads, cakes, and cookies, and they know the secrets of making good bread. Bakers can make all sorts of breads, from pita bread to naan to sandwich bread, by changing the ingredients and the way the bread is made.

Understanding the changes that happen to the ingredients helps bakers make good bread. First, yeast helps to produce a gas when it is mixed with sugar and water. Then, flour and salt are added to the yeast mixture to make bread dough. For the bread to rise, the gas bubbles need to be trapped inside the dough. Otherwise, the bread will be a flat lump. Bread needs gluten to trap the bubbles. Gluten is a substance in bread dough that makes the dough stretchy so that it can rise.

To form gluten, bakers knead bread dough. Flour contains substances that are shaped like loosely coiled strings. As dough is kneaded, these substances change. Short strings connect together to make longer strings. The longer strings stretch out and line up. They connect together to form gluten. Gluten is strong and stretchy. It allows bread dough to rise as yeast produces gas bubbles. When you slice into the baked bread, you see the holes where the gas bubbles were trapped.

Eggs do not have to be mixed with other ingredients for their substances to change. An egg is made of many different substances! When it is cooked, the substances inside an egg break apart into smaller pieces that then link together and form different substances.

Just Add Heat

Chefs do not always mix ingredients together before cooking them. Most ingredients are already made of several substances. So changes can happen when an ingredient is cooked by itself. Sometimes, cooking a single ingredient, such as eggs, causes the changes needed to make it more flavorful.

Eggs don't have to be mixed with other ingredients to be cooked. An egg can be divided into its yolk and its white. But did you know that each of those parts are mixtures containing many different substances? The substances in an egg yolk are different from the substances in an egg white. You can tell because the properties of egg yolk are different from egg white. When you see a sunny side up egg being cooked, you can see the substances in the egg white and egg yolk change as they react.

How do the substances in food change as they cook? When chefs cook food, they add heat to the ingredients. The heat makes the particles in the ingredients move around faster. Sometimes these particles hit each other and link together to form different, larger particles. Other times the particles shake so quickly that they end up breaking into a different substance with different properties! When a chef cooks an egg, the substances break apart into smaller substances. These smaller substances react to form new substances that give a cooked egg its appearance.

Chefs need to understand how substances change as the temperature changes. Heating ingredients can cause changes in the substances in ingredients— delicious changes!

Eat Your Vegetables

You may have eaten raw carrots, steamed carrots, and roasted carrots, but have you ever had juicy carrot beads? What about a light and airy foam made of peas or potatoes that are as creamy as pudding? Chefs are now using science to prepare food in surprising new ways. They are changing the way people eat their vegetables.

To make unexpected dishes, chefs are using new ingredients. Carrot beads are made by mixing carrot juice, which is not so unusual, and a substance that comes from seaweed. You won't find that ingredient in a lot of kitchens! The seaweed ingredient does not have a taste, but it undergoes an interesting change. To make juice-filled beads, the carrot juice mixture is dipped into water that contains a salt. The seaweed substance changes into a gel and forms a skin around the juice. The skin is similar to a thin layer of gelatin dessert. When you pop the beads in your mouth, the skin breaks to give you tiny bursts of carrot flavor.

Chefs are also using tools in new ways to make creative dishes. Whipped cream is a foam. You may have seen whipped cream come out of metal cans. Chefs are now using similar cans to make foams of other foods, such as peas and potatoes. To make a food foam, chefs put a liquid food mixture into the can. The can has a gas inside that does not react with food. When a button on the can is pressed, the gas comes rushing out. It mixes with the liquid, making an airy foam that seems to melt in your mouth. The foams are such fun to eat that they could become your new favorite food. Pass the pea foam, please!

Chefs are coming up with creative ways for you to eat your vegetables. These beads may look like orange gelatin, but they are actually carrot juice inside a thin skin made of a gel.

How Do Changes to Substances Affect Their Weights?

Science Vocabulary

conserve

Matter is always conserved, no matter what changes happen to it. When matter is heated, cooled, or mixed with other matter, changes can occur. However, the weight of matter always remains the same because matter is conserved. When ice is heated, it melts into water. But the weight of the ice is the same as the weight of the water it melts into.

NGSS

5-PS1-2. Measure and graph quantities to provide evidence that regardless of the type of change that occurs when heating, cooling, or mixing substances, the total weight of matter is conserved.
5-PS1-4. Conduct an investigation to determine whether the mixing of two or more substances results in new substances.

PS1.A. The amount (weight) of matter is conserved when it changes form, even in transitions in which it seems to vanish.
PS1.B. • When two or more different substances are mixed, a new substance with different properties may be formed.
• No matter what reaction or change in properties occurs, the total weight of the substances does not change.

Cause and Effect Cause and effect relationships are routinely identified, tested, and used to explain change.
Scale, Proportion, and Quantity Standard units are used to measure and describe physical quantities such as weight, time, temperature, and volume.

Planning and Carrying Out Investigations

Using Mathematics and Computational Thinking

1. Matter Is Conserved

You have learned that all matter is made of particles that are too small to be seen. You have also learned that matter can change. The properties of substances can change, and reactions between substances cause new substances to form. So what happens to the particles in matter during these changes? Are particles made? Are particles destroyed?

During any change, matter is *conserved*. To be **conserved** means to be kept at the same total amount. When you say that matter is conserved, you are saying that the total amount of matter stays the same. Thus, during any change of matter, the amount of matter always stays the same. Conservation laws like this one are powerful tools for making predictions in science. Another example of a conservation law is the conservation of energy, which you may have learned about previously.

You can check that matter is conserved by measuring the weight of the matter. The weight of a material is a measure of the amount of matter in the material. The tool used to measure weight is a scale. The scales you use at home usually measure weight in ounces (oz) and pounds (lb) or in grams (g) and kilograms (kg). If you find the weight of matter before and after a change, you will find that weight does not change.

Matter is conserved because matter is never made or destroyed. When matter changes, the particles that make up the matter may rearrange, join together, or break apart. But there is the same amount of matter that makes up those particles before and after the change.

The weight of an object is a measure of the amount of matter in the object. The amount of matter is conserved during any change of matter. So the weight of matter before and after a change will always be the same.

The total amount of matter of these frozen vegetables is conserved when they are thawed.

Matter is conserved during changes of state. So this glass of ice weighs the same now as it will when the ice melts into liquid water.

2. Weight and Changes in Temperature

Heating and cooling can cause different changes in matter. Matter can also change during reactions caused by heating and cooling. During all these changes, matter is conserved.

Weight Does Not Change When Heating Matter

Matter is conserved when matter is heated. Therefore, matter is not gained or lost during state changes. Suppose you weigh ice in a glass. If you let the ice melt and weigh the glass and the resulting water, you will find that they weigh the same as the glass and ice did. Matter is even conserved during boiling. However, it is hard to weigh water vapor after it is boiled off. The water vapor mixes with the air. But if you could collect all the water vapor, you would find that it weighs the same as the water that had evaporated.

The weight of matter also does not change when heating causes a substance to expand. When a substance expands, the particles of the substance spread out and take up more space. The number of particles does not change. So, the substance's weight remains the same.

Matter is also conserved during reactions that use heat. You can heat wood to cause it to burn. After wood burns, the resulting pile of ash is much smaller than the wood was. But burning did not destroy matter. Ash is only one thing that is formed when wood is burned. When wood burns, it uses oxygen gas from the air as part of the reaction. Other gases such as carbon dioxide and water vapor are also formed. If you captured all the gases formed by burning, you would find that the weight of the gases and the ash is the same as the original weight of the wood plus the oxygen from the air.

When substances in the wood react with oxygen while burning, they produce ash and various gases. Some of the gases are in the smoke that rises from a fire. If you could capture all of the substances made by burning wood, you would find that they weigh the same as the original wood and oxygen did.

Weight Does Not Change When Cooling Matter

Matter is conserved when it is cooled. Thus, no matter is gained or lost during freezing and condensation. When you cool water in a freezer to turn it into ice, the ice will weigh the same as the water did before it was frozen. Similarly, if you were able to weigh water vapor before it condensed, you would find that the resulting water weighs the same as the water vapor did. The weight of a substance stays the same during state changes because the number of particles does not change.

The number of particles also does not change when a substance contracts. So, matter is conserved when a substance contracts. The particles in the substance simply move closer together, and the substance takes up less space. No particles disappeared to make the substance smaller.

The amount of matter does not change when changes in the properties happen as the matter is cooled. To make gelatin snacks, you first make a mixture of hot water, sugar, gelatin, and other ingredients. As the mixture cools, particles of gelatin link together to form new, larger particles. The new particles mean that there are now new substances present in the gelatin. These larger particles trap other particles of water, sugar, and other ingredients. The whole mixture becomes a wiggly solid. The larger particles weigh the same as the smaller particles that were joined together. As a result, the wiggly solid weighs the same as the liquid mixture that you started with.

Gelatin is made of hot water, sugar, and gelatin. As the mixture cools, the gelatin and hot water forms a gel-like solid. If you measure the weight before and after the gelatin solidifies, you can see that the weight does not change.

Sugar and lemon juice are dissolved in water to make lemonade. The weight of the lemonade is equal to the sum of the weights of the sugar, lemon juice, and water.

3. Weight and Changes from Mixing

Like heating and cooling, mixing substances can cause the properties of matter to change. For example, mixing substances can cause one substance to dissolve in another. The properties of the mixture are different from the properties of the original substances. Mixing substances can also cause a reaction. During a reaction, one or more new substances are formed. These new substances have different properties than the original substances did. Whether substances dissolve or react when mixed, the matter involved is conserved.

Weight Does Not Change When Mixing Dissolves Substances

When a substance is dissolved into another substance, the amount of matter does not change. Recall that dissolving means that one substance is completely mixed with another substance. When a solid is dissolved in a liquid, the solid seems to disappear. But the solid is not destroyed. It is conserved. You can test this by weighing some salt before you dissolve it in water. Then, let the water evaporate off. The weight of the salt left behind will be the same as the weight before you dissolved it.

Matter is conserved when dissolving substances because the number and kinds of particles never change. Think about making lemonade. To make lemonade, you dissolve sugar and lemon juice in water. The sugar particles and the particles in the lemon juice separate. The particles spread out amongst the water particles. Although the sugar and lemon juice seem to disappear, all their particles are still there. No particles were destroyed. So, the weight of the lemonade that you made would be equal to the weights of the water, sugar, and lemon juice added together.

Weight Does Not Change When Mixing Causes a Reaction

One or more substances combine to form new substances when a reaction happens. Matter is conserved in any reaction that happens, even when substances are mixed. You can use a glow stick to easily prove that matter is conserved during a reaction. Start by finding the weight of the glow stick before you make it glow. Then, activate the stick by bending and shaking it to mix the contents. Once the stick is glowing, find the weight of it again. You will see that the weight of the glow stick does not change. If you weigh the glow stick again after it has stopped glowing, it will still have the same weight.

During any reaction, the particles of matter rearrange. Some particles break apart to make smaller particles. Other particles join together to make larger particles. But the parts that make up all these particles do not change. No matter is gained and no matter is lost. Thus, the total weight of the matter before and after a reaction is always the same.

Sometimes it is hard to see that matter is conserved in a reaction. When baking soda and vinegar are mixed together, one of the new substances made is a gas. This gas goes into the air. So it seems as though matter was lost during the reaction. But if you mix the baking soda and vinegar in a sealed bag, all the gas made by the reaction will be caught. You could then weigh the bag and see that it weighs the same before and after the reaction.

When baking soda and vinegar are mixed together, one of the new substances produced is a gas. If you trap the gas inside a balloon or a sealed bag and weigh it, you will find that the weight of the substances does not change.

Nature of Science

4. Science Assumes All Matter Is Conserved

How do scientists know that all matter is conserved? Do they check the weight of substances before and after every change of matter? That kind of testing is not possible. Some changes happen in nature. Some changes involve amounts of matter that are very difficult to weigh.

Scientists do assume that all matter is conserved without having to test it all the time. The French scientist Antoine Lavoisier is usually credited with coming up with the idea that all matter is conserved. To demonstrate the idea, he weighed a lot of substances before and after a reaction. He never found an exception to the rule.

Part of the study of science is to find patterns in nature. When a pattern is observed over and over again, and no exception to the pattern is found, scientists assume that the pattern is always true. Some of these patterns are called *laws*. One such pattern is the law of conservation of matter. This is the law that states that matter is never made nor destroyed.

Scientists do not spend time checking if the law of conservation of matter is always true. In fact, if scientists do an experiment that seems to go against the law, the scientists may conclude that there is a problem with the experiment. They do not conclude that the law is wrong.

However, if scientists do an experiment that goes against the law many times, in many places, they may check whether the law is wrong. If they all get results that go against the law, and none of them can find a problem with the experiment, then they may change or abandon the law.

Scientists assume that matter is always conserved, so they do not spend time testing the law of conservation of matter. Instead, scientists focus on testing substances to better understand the world around them.

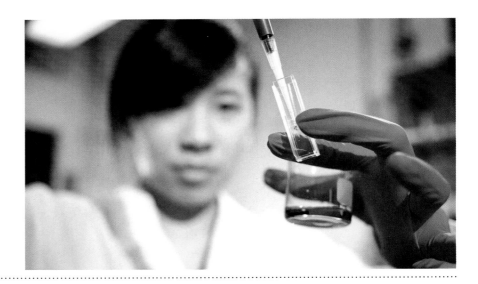

How Do Changes to Substances Affect Their Weights?

1. Matter Is Conserved During all changes of matter, matter is conserved. That means that matter is never made or destroyed. The particles that make up the matter may rearrange, join together, or break apart. But the amount of matter stays the same. Finding the weight of substances before and after a change will show that matter is conserved.

2. Weight and Changes in Temperature Heating and cooling matter can cause changes of state, can cause substances to expand or contract, and can cause reactions. During any of these changes, matter is conserved. No matter is gained and no matter is lost. The weight of the substances before and after always remains the same.

3. Weight and Changes from Mixing When you mix substances, it can cause one substance to dissolve or it can cause a reaction. Matter is always conserved during any of these changes. The particles of matter rearrange. But no matter is gained and no matter is lost. Checking the weight before and after a change shows that matter is conserved.

4. Science Assumes All Matter Is Conserved Scientists are not able to check that matter is conserved during all changes, but they assume it to be true. The fact that matter is conserved has been observed many times, and no exception to the rule has been found. When a pattern like this is observed again and again, scientists assume that the pattern is true and a law of science.

Star Stuff

You and everything around you, from your chair to the roof over your head, are made of matter. You know that the total weight of matter stays the same whenever matter changes. If matter is conserved, where did all the matter around you come from?

Everything around you, from the pencils and paper you use to the air you breathe, is made of matter.

Look around you. What matter can you see? Perhaps you see pencils and paper in a notebook. All of this is made of matter. The windows are made of glass, which are made of matter. The carpet is made of matter. Even you are made of matter. Everything you can touch is made of matter—tiny particles that make up substances that make up mixtures.

But what about matter that you cannot touch? The air around you is made of matter. You do not feel the weight of air pressing on you because you are used to feeling it every day. That does not mean that the air is not made of matter, or that it does not have weight. You can see the effect of the air particles on other objects around you. These tiny particles zip around and bounce off of objects.

Earth is full of matter, from the ground you stand on, the objects you use, and the air you breathe. You have learned that all of this matter is conserved, so the total weight of it stays the same. If you were to measure the weight of the Earth, it would be the same weight today as it was before you were born. But if all the matter on Earth is conserved, then where did it come from originally?

When a large star explodes, the explosion spreads out the matter made in the star. The matter drifts across space until it forms new stars and planets, such as Earth.

"Making" Matter

Most of the matter in the universe exists in the form of a substance called hydrogen, but that is not the case on Earth. In fact, Earth's most abundant substance is iron, and most of Earth's atmosphere is made of nitrogen. How did these substances form?

Stars are giant substance factories in space. Stars change hydrogen into the kinds of substances you see on Earth—the iron that makes up most of the planet, and the nitrogen and oxygen that you breathe.

But if all of this matter is inside of a star, then how did it reach Earth? For its entire life, a star turns hydrogen into these substances that you interact with on Earth. When you look into the sky at night, you may see hundreds of stars. These stars are light years away, and the matter inside of them is trapped inside for the star's entire life.

What happens when a star dies? Some stars simply fade quietly away, and other stars explode with a bang. When a star explodes, it is called a supernova. The star explodes in a burst of bright light that can outshine a whole galaxy, taking weeks or months to fade away. During a supernova, the exploding star spews out all of its matter across space, creating a shock wave across outer space.

The matter inside of a star drifts out in space until it comes together to form new stars and planets. All of the matter on Earth, that huge amount of matter, came from the insides of exploding stars.

The matter on Earth comes from many, many stars. These stars made particles that were sent into space by explosions billions of years ago.

Earth Matters

So which star formed the matter on Earth? Did the star fade quietly away or did it explode in a supernova? The truth is, Earth did not come from one star. It came from many different stars, and they did not all explode at the same time. When one star died, all of the matter inside of it spread out through space in a cloud. Gas and dust from other exploded stars mixed together with this cloud. For millions and billions of years, as more stars died, the matter inside the stars was pulled together by gravity. A huge spinning disk of dust and gas formed, and the matter in this disk clumped together to form new stars and planets.

But the matter in stars does not simply form the ground you are standing on, but also everything on the planet. All of the matter on Earth, including the ground, the table, even you and the air you breathe, are made from stars going supernova.

Take a look at your hands. Your right and left hands may look the same, but the matter that makes up your hands probably came from a different star. Each finger probably came from a different star. You are made from hundreds or thousands of different stars, exploding and sending matter to drift across the universe before it formed Earth.

Take a deep breath. The air you are breathing was made in different stars. The oxygen you breathe in one breath could have been formed in hundreds of different stars.

Earth did not come from just one star. It was formed by hundreds and thousands of stars exploding to form new stars that explode. It was formed by star stuff coming together, over billions of years, to form what you see now.

What's on Earth, Stays on Earth

Is the matter around you the same as it was hundreds of years ago? It took billions of years for Earth to form from the matter inside stars. But almost all the matter that came from the stars has been circulating around Earth for all of Earth's history.

When you take a deep breath, you breathe in hundreds of tiny particles, many that were formed in hundreds of different stars. But these particles have been around for all of Earth's history. The air you are breathing is the same air that the great scientists like Marie Curie, Sir Isaac Newton, and Aristotle breathed. When you take a deep breath, you are breathing the same air that the first humans breathed. You are also breathing the same air that the dinosaurs before them breathed.

But it is not just the matter in the air that has been around for billions of years. The pieces of matter that make your hands are made from different stars. Before they came together to form you, they made other people. Between the time when the matter was being formed in stars and reached you, the matter was part of Earth, and everything on it.

The matter on Earth is conserved, changing from one substance to another. For billions of years, the matter has remained on Earth, changing forms, but always being conserved. But before the matter formed Earth, it was in hundreds and thousands of stars many light years away. In the words of astronomer Carl Sagan, "The Earth and every living thing are made of star stuff!"

The matter on Earth has been here since Earth's early history. It may have changed into many different substances, but those changes did not change the amount of matter.

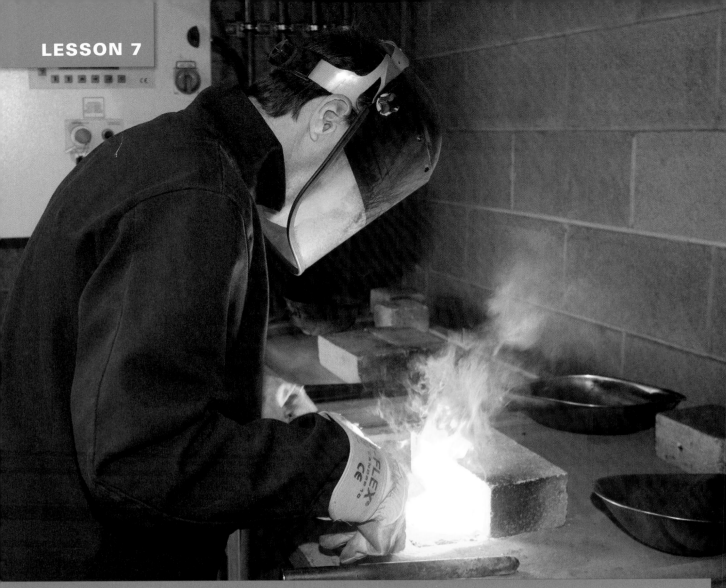

How Do Engineers Improve Materials?

Science Vocabulary

constraint

criteria

Engineers are able to make entirely new materials by mixing together old materials or even by rearranging the particles that make up matter. The new materials are tested to see how they function, and if they are successful, they are used to solve various problems.

NGSS

5-PS1-2. Measure and graph quantities to provide evidence that regardless of the type of change that occurs when heating, cooling, or mixing substances, the total weight of matter is conserved.
5-PS1-4. Conduct an investigation to determine whether the mixing of two or more substances results in new substances.

PS1.A. The amount (weight) of matter is conserved when it changes form, even in transitions in which it seems to vanish.
PS1.B. • When two or more different substances are mixed, a new substance with different properties may be formed.
• No matter what reaction or change in properties occurs, the total weight of the substances does not change.

Cause and Effect Cause and effect relationships are routinely identified, tested, and used to explain change.
Scale, Proportion, and Quantity Standard units are used to measure and describe physical quantities such as weight, time, temperature, and volume.

Planning and Carrying Out Investigations

Using Mathematics and Computational Thinking

1. Properties Have Different Uses

Suppose that you were camping and wanted to build a shelter in the woods that you could sleep in. What features would you want your shelter to have? What would you use to build your shelter?

Building a shelter for sleeping in the woods is an example of a problem that has different solutions. One solution would be to build a house and put a bed in it, but that solution may not be practical because of the constraints. A **constraint** is a limit that keeps you from doing certain things. Some constraints of building your shelter are that you cannot find tools or nails in the woods and building a house and a bed take a very long time. So, you can use only materials that you find in the woods, and you must build a shelter quickly.

When selecting materials to use for your shelter, you have to consider the properties of the materials. Some materials have better properties than other materials have. The properties that you want for a material or a solution are called **criteria**. For example, you want something strong to hold up the roof. A thick branch would work better than a thin one. You also want something soft for the floor. A pile of leaves would be more comfortable than just lying on the dirt ground. The strength of the branch and the softness of the leaves are your criteria for those materials.

Engineers approach problems similarly to how you approach the problem of building a shelter. They must work within the constraints of the problem and consider the criteria for their solutions.

When solving a problem, such as building a shelter in the woods, you have to work within certain constraints. You must also choose materials with properties that are suitable for their use.

When engineers solve a problem, they first understand it and identify constraints. If engineers had to design new eating tools, one constraint might be that the tools cannot be too expensive, so gold would not work.

Engineering Design

2. Engineers Choose the Best Material

Think about the utensils that you use to eat food. You probably use spoons, forks, and knives.

Suppose the world did not have utensils, and engineers were asked to design eating tools. The engineers would take certain steps in designing the tools. Engineers often use these steps to choose a material for a design.

Defining the Problem

The first step in choosing a material for a design is to define the problem that has to be solved. In the case of designing eating tools, engineers might start by saying that they need something that can move food from a plate to a mouth. They may then think about how people would use the tools. People would hold the tools in their hands. People would need something to cut food, spear food, and scoop up food. In other words, engineers start their process by making sure they completely understand the problem they are trying to solve.

Identifying Constraints

The next step in solving a problem is to identify the constraints to the problem. Often these constraints limit the kinds of materials that engineers can use. For example, a constraint in choosing the material for eating tools might be that the material must not be too expensive. That constraint would rule out using gold. Constraints may sometimes cause problems if they rule out too many choices. But the constraints are often useful for narrowing down choices.

Identifying Criteria

Next, engineers identify the criteria that they want a solution to fit. For example, engineers designing eating tools would want the tools to be easy to clean. After all, the tools will touch a lot of food and go inside people's mouths. Metals are easier to clean than wood. Wood is *porous*, which means that it has a lot of tiny holes in it. Bacteria and bits of food can get stuck inside wood utensils.

Engineers choosing a material have to consider many properties at once. Sometimes, the engineers identify constraints and criteria at the same time. Both constraints and criteria can help narrow down the choice of materials.

Wood is used for some kitchen tools, but it is not a good material for all of them. Engineers consider many different materials when solving a problem before choosing the one that best suits their needs.

Choosing the Best Material

Once engineers have identified the constraints and the criteria, they are often left with only a few materials to choose from. They then have to select the best materials from their choices. An engineer might consider using iron for utensils because it is not too expensive and is easy to clean. But iron rusts if it is exposed to oxygen. So the engineers might add a new criteria. The criteria would be that the material does not rust. Engineers might then consider a different material. Engineers will add additional criteria that they had not considered if they need to.

Often, engineers will improve old materials to fit criteria and constraints. Engineers improved iron by mixing it with different materials, such as carbon and chromium, to make stainless steel. Stainless steel is not expensive. It is also easy to clean and does not rust. By clearly defining a problem, they realized which materials would not work so they had to make new ones. Now many of our utensils are made with stainless steel.

3. Engineers Create New Materials

If you have ever watched a bicycle race on television, you know that the cyclists can go very fast. They can go so fast partly because their bikes are made of a special material called *carbon fiber*. Carbon fiber is very lightweight, which makes the bicycles easy to move. But carbon fiber is not a material that is found in nature. Instead, carbon fiber was designed by engineers to have specific properties.

Engineers sometimes design new materials to use to make objects. When engineers design a new material, they are often trying to make a material with specific properties. The new material usually has properties that work better than the properties of existing materials.

Engineers Study Existing Materials

Before engineers try to make a new material, they study materials that are already in use. They identify which properties of the materials are useful. They identify which properties cause problems. Suppose an engineer was trying to design a lightweight bicycle for racing. The engineer might study the metal aluminum. Aluminum is very lightweight, which is good. But aluminum is a soft metal. If a bicycle made out of aluminum crashed, it could be bent out of shape.

After studying known materials, engineers may make a list of all the properties they want in a material. They may want something as light as aluminum, as strong as steel, and as rustproof as gold.

The bicycles that racers ride are probably unlike your bicycle. Their bicycles are partly made from carbon fiber, which is a very strong and very lightweight material. Engineers chose carbon fiber because it has many of the properties a good racing bike needs.

Carbon fiber is made by rearranging carbon particles into long thin strands. Carbon fiber is thin and may not look very strong, but it is stronger and lighter than steel. Engineers make new materials by rearranging particles in old materials all the time.

Engineers Design New Materials

Once engineers know what properties they want in a material, they can go about trying to make a material that fits those properties. To do this, the engineers use what they know about matter. They think about how the particles of different materials are arranged. They think about how to rearrange those particles to improve a material's properties.

Engineers may try making a new material by mixing existing materials. For example, the aluminum foil that you use in your kitchen is not pure aluminum. Instead, it is a mixture of aluminum, iron, and silicon. This mixture is harder and stronger than pure aluminum but is almost as lightweight. In fact, this mixture of aluminum is strong enough to use as a bicycle frame.

But sometimes just mixing known materials is not enough. Sometimes engineers invent completely new materials. To do this, they take matter and rearrange the particles. Carbon fiber is made in this way. Carbon particles are taken from one material and rearranged. The rearranged particles form a material that is very lightweight and stronger than steel.

Engineers have to test different ways of making a new material. Sometimes a material is difficult to make. Sometimes a material is expensive to make. So, even after inventing a new material that has all the properties that they want, engineers sometimes have to continue working to find the best way to make their new material.

When engineering your own paint, you have to define your problem, identify constraints, and identify properties. Only then can you mix and test your paint.

 **Engineering Design**

4. Engineer Your Own Material

Can you follow the steps of the engineering process to design your own material? Suppose you want to engineer your own paint for painting a chair. How would you go about doing that?

When designing your own paint, you must first define the problem. Think about why you have to make your own paint. Why can you not use paint exactly as it comes from the store? Perhaps the store does not have the right color.

Next, identify the constraints and criteria for the paint. One constraint could be that you have to use ingredients that the store says are safe to combine. Some criteria might be that the paint should be quick drying, a certain shade of blue, and look old-fashioned.

Once you know your problem, constraints, and criteria, you can mix your own paint. You have to choose what materials you want to mix together to make your paint. You might need to add water. You need something that is the right shade of blue, and you need something to make the paint look old-fashioned. Now you have to test your paint to see if your problem is solved.

When testing your paint, you may find that it has unwanted properties that you had not thought of when you first designed the paint. Perhaps the paint you mixed is too thick and is difficult to spread evenly. If your paint does have problems, you will have to change your design. How can you make your paint better fit your criteria and constraints?

How Do Engineers Improve Materials?

1. Properties Have Different Uses   When developing a solution to a problem, engineers must work within certain constraints. The constraints are limits that keep them from doing certain things. They must also work to meet certain criteria. Engineers have to pick materials to use in their solutions that meet their criteria and work within the constraints.

2. Engineers Choose the Best Material   Engineers follow certain steps when choosing a material to use in a design. These steps include defining the problem, identifying constraints, identifying criteria, and then selecting the best material. Engineers consider many different materials during this process before choosing the one that best suits their needs.

3. Engineers Create New Materials   To design new materials, engineers start by studying existing materials. Then they use what they know about matter to make a new material that has the properties that they want. Even after inventing a new material, engineers sometimes have to continue working to find the best way to make the new material.

4. Engineer Your Own Material   You can follow the steps of the engineering process to design your own material. During this process, you define your problem and identify constraints and criteria. You then select or make your material. Finally, you test your material to see if your problem is solved. If not, then you go back to the beginning of the design process.

Plenty of Polymers

Look around your classroom. You might see plastic chairs and tables. The materials that make up these chairs and tables were designed by engineers. Many materials that make up the things you use every day are made of materials that were designed by engineers.

Many things that you use every day are made of polymers. These sports uniforms, the soccer ball, and eyeglass frames are all made of polymers.

A ball bounces up and down on the playground. You jump as high as you can to catch it. Good thing you are wearing your sneakers to cushion your landing! It's a hot, summer day, so you are wearing a shirt that helps keep you cool and dry. But if it were a cool, fall day, you might wear a cozy jacket. What do the ball, your sneakers, your shirt, and your jacket have in common?

All of those objects can be made of polymers. A *polymer* is compound that is made of many particles of smaller pieces that are linked together. Many kinds of polymers exist, and they are found almost everywhere. Some polymers are natural substances, including rubber that comes from trees. But most polymers around you are made by engineers. Engineers can design polymers to have many different properties.

Some polymers are bouncy, like the rubber used to make balls and the soles of sneakers. Others can be spun into thread that is used to make fabric, such as the shiny fabric of sports uniforms or the soft polar fleece of a jacket. Engineers can form polymers into almost any shape. Anything made of plastic is made of a polymer, from toys to plastic bags and from water bottles to the plastic parts of a pen. Engineers can add different colors to polymers. They can also make clear polymers, such as those used to make eyeglass lenses.

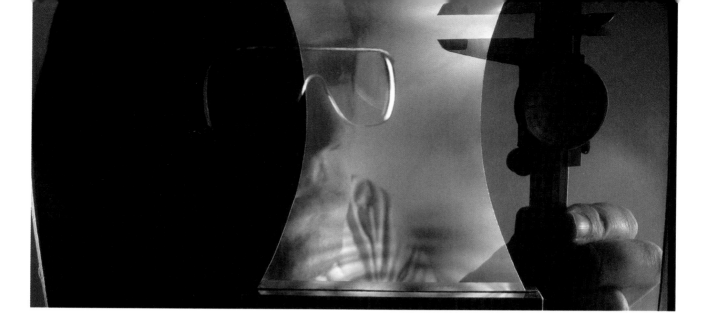

Manufacturing Polymers

How can polymers have such different properties and be used to make so many different products? Scientists and engineers study different substances and mix them with each other to see the new substances that form from the reaction. They also modify existing polymers to change their properties.

Nylon is a polymer that you may have heard of. Many clothes are made of this silky material. Many umbrellas are also made of nylon. Engineers manufacture nylon by pouring two different substances together. These two substances are clear, colorless liquids that do not mix, just like how oil and water do not mix. However, a thin film forms where they meet. That thin film is nylon!

How does that thin film turn into thread that can be woven into a cloth? Machines carefully pull the thin film out of the mixture. As it pulls the film out, the film stretches and appears threadlike. The film moves away from where the two liquid substances met each other, and the substances continue to mix and form more nylon.

Engineers try to design new polymers to improve materials. They might try mixing the substances at a different temperature and seeing what polymer forms. They might try mixing different substances. After they form a polymer, they run tests on it to see if it has the properties they want.

A scientist tests a polymer he made. He is seeing what properties that polymer has to see if it can be used in certain materials.

Polymers have a wide range of properties. The polymers used in the clothes worn by firemen help prevent the clothes from tearing and burning.

Perfecting Polymers

Engineers have been trying to control the properties of polymers for over 50 years. At first, they tried to make polymers similar to the ones found in nature, such as rubber. One of the first engineers who tried to make synthetic rubber made a polymer that was more interesting. It was bouncier than rubber and very stretchy. But, the polymer could not be used to make car tires. So it did not seem very useful. Then, someone realized that the polymer would make a fun, silly toy. You can still find this bouncy, stretchy putty in toy stores.

Engineers have become very good at making new polymers. They know how to make polymers that can be shaped into thin threads to make warm jackets or light sports jerseys. They can also make plastics that can be melted and poured into a mold to make car parts or toys. They can even make polymers that absorb 300 times their weight in water, which is very useful in a baby diaper.

Some polymers have amazing and useful properties. One polymer is stronger than steel and can stop bullets. Because the polymer is also lighter than steel, it is used in bulletproof vests and in clothes that protect firefighters. Firefighters' gear also includes a polymer that protects them from the heat of the fire. These polymers are extremely light, but they are so strong that they do not get squashed when put under a car. The things that polymers can do seem limitless!

Problems with Polymers

Polymers are very useful and usually inexpensive, but they also create a big problem: trash. Many of the polymers you use every day do not easily break down into new substances. This property makes them useful for products that need to last a long time. It also means that a plastic bottle or bag that you use only once will be around for a very long time after you throw it away.

Plastic trash seems to turn up everywhere. You have probably seen plastic bags and bottles on the side of the road. Many plastics float and can travel long distances across the ocean. Plastic trash has even been found on the ocean floor and on remote islands where no people live!

Scientists and engineers are working on the polymer trash problem by finding ways to recycle plastics. Plastics can be recycled into a variety of products, from carpets to flower pots. Even clothes can be made from recycled plastic!

Recycling plastic is a good way of keeping plastic trash out of the environment. But the process of changing old plastic into new materials takes a lot of energy resources. So reusing plastic objects is often better than immediately recycling them after you are done with them. Another way that you can help with the plastic problem is to give away old toys and clothes that are still in good shape. Who knows? The bouncy ball that you chased on the playground could keep bouncing along for years to come!

Plastic can be recycled. These beads are made of recycled plastic. They can be used to make new products.

Earth, the Moon, and the Stars

It is a clear summer night. You gaze at the shining stars. You see the Big Dipper and even Orion's belt. You wonder, what are the other star patterns in the night sky? Later, you go back outside to show your parents the Big Dipper. But it has moved! If you watched the stars throughout the night, they and the moon would all appear to move. In this unit, you will discover how the moon and stars change and move in patterns. These patterns can be explained. And you will read about the tools scientists use to discover these objects.

Unit Contents

Unit 4 Overview

Graphic Organizer: This unit is structured to first provide an overarching **understanding of gravity**, which is supported by **five patterns caused by gravity**, and then end with an **engineering connection**.

1. What Does Gravity Do?

2. Why is the Sun Brighter Than Other Stars?

3. Why is There Day and Night?

4. How Do Shadows Change During the Day and Year?

5. How Do Stars Seem to Move During the Night and Year?

6. How Does the Moon Seem to Move and Change Shape?

7. What Tools Do Scientists Use to Observe Space?

NGSS Next Generation Science Standards

Performance Expectations

5-PS2-1. Support an argument that the gravitational force exerted by Earth on objects is directed down.

5-ESS1-1. Support an argument that differences in the apparent brightness of the sun compared to other stars is due to their relative distances from Earth.

5-ESS1-2. Represent data in graphical displays to reveal patterns of daily changes in length and direction of shadows, day and night, and the seasonal appearance of some stars in the night sky.

Disciplinary Core Ideas

PS2.B: Types of Interactions

• The gravitational force of Earth acting on an object near Earth's surface pulls that object toward the planet's center.

ESS1.A: The Universe and Its Stars

• The sun is a star that appears larger and brighter than other stars because it is closer. Stars range greatly in their distance from Earth.

ESS1.B: Earth and the Solar System

• The orbits of Earth around the sun and of the moon around Earth, together with the rotation of Earth about an axis between its North and South poles, cause observable patterns. These include day and night; daily changes in the length and direction of shadows; and different positions of the sun, moon, and stars at different times of the day, month, and year.

Crosscutting Concepts

Patterns

• Similarities and differences in patterns can be used to sort, classify, communicate, and analyze simple rates of change for natural phenomena.

Cause and Effect

• Cause and effect relationships are routinely identified and used to explain change.

Scale, Proportion, and Quantity

• Natural objects exist from the very small to the immensely large.

 **Analyzing and Interpreting Data**

 **Engaging in Argument from Evidence**

Have you ever wondered...

From your place on Earth, you can observe the patterns of the moon, see movement of the stars, and wonder about your place in the universe. This unit will help you answer these questions and many others you may ask.

What causes the length of shadows to change during the day?

Why can I sometimes see the moon during the day?

Why is it daylight in some parts of the world when it's nighttime for me?

What Does Gravity Do?

Science Vocabulary

gravity

meteor

orbit

What is causing this skydiver to fall downward? You will learn about a force called gravity. Gravity pulls you and all objects near Earth's surface toward Earth's center, but it is stronger and weaker at different places. Earth's gravity can also pull objects in space, such as meteoroids, down to Earth. Objects in space, like the sun and moon, have gravity, too.

NGSS

5-PS2-1. Support an argument that the gravitational force exerted by Earth on objects is directed down.

PS2.B. The gravitational force of Earth acting on an object near Earth's surface pulls that object toward the planet's center.

Cause and Effect Cause and effect relationships are routinely identified and used to explain change.

Engaging in Argument from Evidence

1. Gravity Pulls You Toward Earth's Center

When you jump into the air, you fall back to the ground. When you drop an egg, it falls to the floor. When skydivers jump from planes, they fall to Earth. You, the egg, and the skydivers all fall because you are all pulled downward by the force called gravity.

Gravity is a force of attraction. This means that gravity is a force that pulls on objects but does not push on them. All objects on or near Earth's surface are pulled down by Earth's gravity toward Earth's center. If you throw a ball up in the air, you know that the ball will fall. Objects fall because gravity pulls them toward Earth's center. Gravity keeps objects on Earth's surface from floating away into space.

Like magnetic force, gravity works without objects having to touch. Recall that a magnet has a magnetic field around it. Similarly, Earth has a gravitational field around it. This is why objects not touching Earth's surface are still pulled toward the center of the planet.

How you sense "up" and "down" is related to the pull of gravity. Suppose Earth was made of glass, and you could see all the way through it. People standing on the other side of Earth would appear to be upside down to you, and you would look upside down to them! Yet people on Earth, no matter where they stand, feel like they are standing right side up.

Wherever you stand on Earth, gravity is pulling you straight down toward its center. So, "down" is always in the direction gravity pulls. "Up" is always the direction opposite to the pull of gravity.

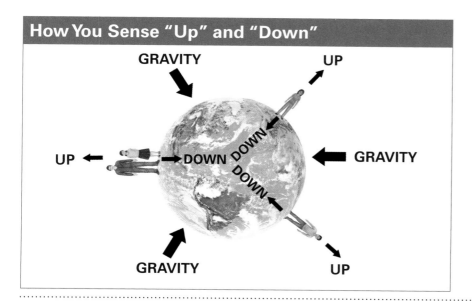

How You Sense "Up" and "Down"

GRAVITY — UP — UP — DOWN — DOWN — DOWN — GRAVITY — GRAVITY — UP

Gravity is a force that pulls objects on or near Earth's surface toward Earth's center. Wherever you are on the planet, Earth's gravity pulls you toward its center. So, "down" is always toward the center of Earth, and "up" is always away from the center of Earth.

2. Gravity Causes Meteors

When space objects come near Earth, they are pulled toward the center of Earth because of gravity. Meteors, such as the one in this image, are streaks of light that occur when chunks of rock fall through the atmosphere.

On a clear night, you might look up at the sky to observe the moon and stars. If you are patient, you may see a streak of light in the sky. What is the source of the light?

This streak of light begins as a chunk of rock, or *meteoroid*, floating in space. There are lots of these objects in space. When one comes close enough to Earth, gravity pulls it through the atmosphere toward Earth's center. As the objects get closer to Earth's surface, Earth's pull gets stronger, and they fall faster and faster. As they fall through the atmosphere, they squeeze the air in front of them together. The object gets very hot as it falls through the air. This air then also gets very hot and begins to glow. So, as these meteoroids speed through the sky, they look like bright streaks of light. The streak of light that a falling meteoroid produces is called a **meteor**. From Earth, a meteor can look like a star shooting across the sky. That is why you might hear people use the term *shooting star* to describe them.

The leftover chunks of meteoroids that cool after they hit Earth form meteorites.

Most meteoroids burn up in Earth's atmosphere and never reach the ground. But sometimes really large meteoroids do not burn up all the way. They hit the ground at very high speeds, and the leftover chunk of material cools and forms a rock called a *meteorite*. Meteorites are usually as small as grains of sand. But sometimes meteorites are much larger. The largest one ever found was discovered in Africa and weighs more than 54,000 kg (about 119,000 lbs).

3. Gravity Is Strongest at Earth's Surface

You know that Earth has a gravitational force that reaches from its center to beyond Earth's surface. How far does it reach? And how strong is it when it is far away from Earth?

Earth's gravity acts like magnetic and electric forces. Recall that these forces between objects get stronger when the objects are closer to each other. Similarly, the strength of the force of gravity changes when objects move closer together or farther apart. Earth's gravity pulls strongest on objects resting near sea level. This is because these objects are closest to Earth's surface. If you climb to the top of a mountain, Earth's gravity pulls on you a little bit less. But you must go very high before you will be able to notice gravity's pull weakening. Even in an airplane or on top of Mount Everest, the difference in the force of gravity will be hardly noticeable.

Think about throwing a ball up in the sky really hard. You throw it so hard that it flies up higher than airplanes fly and goes into outer space. As the ball flies higher and higher, Earth's gravity pulls on it less and less. If you threw the ball hard enough, eventually Earth's gravity would not be pulling on it enough for it to fall back to Earth's surface. It would float off into space. But no one is strong enough to throw a ball that high.

Scientists and engineers send vehicles to explore outer space. They design rockets with powerful engines. The engines push the rocket up with much more force than a person can throw a ball. The force is greater than Earth's gravity pulling back to Earth. As a space vehicle moves farther and farther away from Earth, Earth's gravity becomes weaker and weaker.

The pull of Earth's gravity is strongest on objects at sea level. As a space vehicle moves away from Earth's surface into outer space, the force of Earth's gravity becomes weaker and weaker.

4. All Objects Have Gravity

You have learned about how Earth's gravity pulls objects down toward its center. What other objects do you think have gravity?

All objects have gravity that pulls other objects toward their center. But the strength of an object's gravity depends on the object's size. Larger objects have stronger gravity and smaller objects have weaker gravity. The force of gravity of most objects around you is very weak. It is so weak that you do not notice it. The force of gravity from very large objects, on the other hand, is strong enough to cause effects that you can notice. You might think that a truck or a house is very large. But they are not big enough for you to feel their gravity. Even mountains are too small for you to feel their gravity. Other than Earth itself, there are no objects on Earth big enough for you to feel the force of their gravity. But there are objects you are familiar with whose gravity pulls noticeably on other objects. Can you guess what they are?

From Earth, the sun looks small, but it is actually over one million times larger than Earth. Like all other objects, the sun has gravity that pulls other objects toward it.

The Sun's Gravity

When you see the sun in the sky, it does not look very large. But the sun is actually much larger than Earth. The sun is so big that over one million Earths could fit inside of it. This means that if the sun were the size of a basketball, Earth would be smaller than a sesame seed.

Earth   150,000,000 km   Sun

Since the sun is so large, its gravity is very strong. The sun's gravity is much stronger than Earth's gravity. So, why are we pulled toward Earth's center instead of the sun's? The reason is the same as the reason that the sun appears so small in the sky. It is that the sun is very far away from Earth. If you had a piece of string long enough to stretch from Earth to the sun, it would be long enough to wrap around Earth nearly 3,733 times! Since the sun is so far from Earth, its gravity pulls on objects on Earth less than Earth's gravity does.

The sun's gravity has another very important effect on Earth. The sun's gravity makes Earth follow an *orbit* around the sun. An **orbit** is a curved path that an object makes around another object. If the sun's gravity were not as strong as it is, Earth would not follow an orbit around the sun. Instead, it would drift off into space, far away from the sun.

Astronauts are able to walk on the moon because the moon's gravity pulls them towards the moon's center.

The Moon's Gravity

The moon is another familiar object whose gravity is noticeable. You do not feel the moon's gravity when you are on Earth, but if you stood on the moon you would feel it. So, the force of the moon's gravity is not as strong as the force of Earth's gravity. If you were standing on the moon, you could jump much higher than when you jump on Earth. But you would still fall back down to the surface because the moon's gravity would pull you toward the moon's center.

The sun's gravity is strong because the sun is very large. Without the sun's gravity holding it in its orbit, Earth would drift away into space.

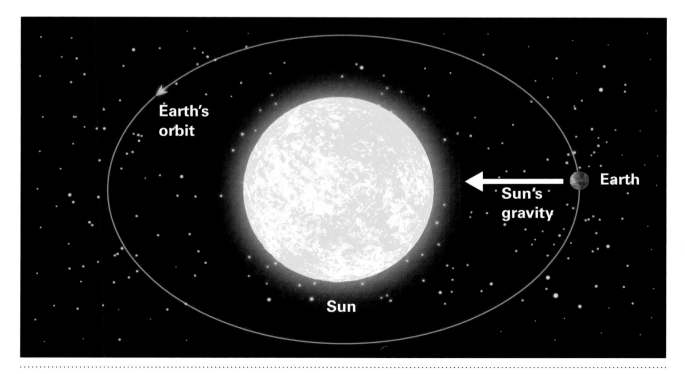

Earth's orbit

Sun's gravity

Earth

Sun

The weight of an object describes how much gravity is pulling on it. A person's weight changes depending on where he or she is weighed. In this photo, an astronaut, his spacesuit, and seat are weighed together.

5. Weight Is the Force of Gravity

Your weight can go up and down depending on the foods you eat and the activities that you participate in. Did you know that your weight also changes depending on where you are?

When you step onto a scale, the weight it shows is how much the force of gravity is pulling on you. So, if you stepped on a scale at sea level and then stepped on the same scale at the top of a ladder high above the Earth, there would be a small difference in your weight. You would weigh slightly less on top of the ladder than at sea level. This is because Earth's gravity is strongest at the surface of the Earth. It gets weaker as you move away from the surface of the Earth.

Suppose you are an astronaut going on a trip to the moon. What will happen to your weight during the trip? First, you would weigh yourself on Earth's surface. If you watched the scale as the rocket carried you up and out of Earth's atmosphere, you would see your weight slowly drop. It would drop more and more as you got farther from Earth. If you were far enough from Earth, it would drop all the way to zero, and you would be weightless. But as you approach the moon, your weight would start to increase. It increases because of the moon's gravity. When you landed on the surface of the moon, you would not weigh the same amount as you do on Earth. You would weigh about one-sixth as much as you do on Earth. This is because the moon's gravity is not as strong as Earth's gravity.

What Does Gravity Do?

1. Gravity Pulls You Toward Earth's Center   Gravity is a force that pulls objects on or near Earth's surface toward Earth's center. Objects fall to the ground because of gravity's force. Gravity also keeps objects on Earth's surface from floating away into space. What many people think of as "down" is actually the direction that gravity is pulling.

2. Gravity Causes Meteors   When a meteoroid in space comes close enough to Earth, gravity pulls it toward Earth. As they fall through the atmosphere, meteoroids heat up and give off light. The streaks of light are meteors. Those that do not burn up sometimes land on Earth's surface and are called meteorites.

3. Gravity Is Strongest at Earth's Surface   The force of gravity is strongest between objects when they are closest together. Earth's gravity is strongest at Earth's surface. So, it pulls the most on objects at sea level. It pulls less on objects that are further from Earth's surface, such as objects in outer space.

4. All Objects Have Gravity   All objects have gravity that pulls other objects toward their center. For objects on Earth, only Earth's gravity is strong enough to have a noticeable effect. But the sun's gravity is strong enough to make Earth follow an orbit around the sun. The moon's gravity is also noticeable on objects that are close to it.

5. Weight Is the Force of Gravity   A scale is used to measure weight. Weight describes how much the force of gravity is pulling you down. Astronauts that go to the moon experience weight changes as they travel. Their weight goes down to zero once they get very far from Earth. But their weight goes back up as they get to the moon because it has gravity.

Your Mission— Explore Other Planets

You may not think about characteristics of Earth very much, such as its gravity, length of its days, and temperature and weather. But these characteristicss affect you all the time. You know what it feels like to live on Earth. But what would it be like to stay on other planets?

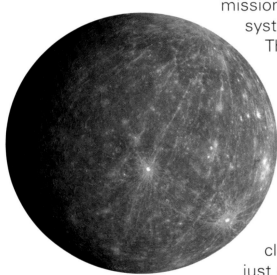

Mercury has a lot of craters on its surface. In this way, Mercury looks a lot like the moon.

Suppose that you are chosen to be a part of a mission to travel to the other planets in the solar system. Including Earth, there are eight planets. The spacecraft that you will ride in is very fast so you will be able to zip from one planet to another in no time.

Before you go on your mission, you must train. Each planet has a different force of gravity. Each planet's gravity will affect your weight and the way you move there. You may not be able to get around the same way that you do on Earth.

Your mission starts with a visit to the planet closest to the sun: Mercury. Mercury's gravity is just over one-third of Earth's gravity. So, you weigh a little more than one-third as much as you do on Earth. As you walk around on Mercury, you spring up with each step. Your leg muscles are used to moving the weight of your body on Earth. So on Mercury, the muscles push too hard, which causes you to bounce up.

As you have fun bouncing around, you notice that you are getting very hot. Mercury has long days. A day on Mercury is 176 Earth days long! So the temperature during the day can climb to 430 °C (806 °F). But the nights are also long. At night the temperatures drop to −180 °C (−292 °F). People would not be able to live on Mercury. It is both too hot and too cold!

Visiting Venus and Mars

The next stop on your mission is Venus. Once you land, you cannot leave the spacecraft. The air pressure on Venus is so dense that it would crush you. The air also contains a dangerous acid that could eat through your spacesuit and then your skin. It is not a place for a relaxing outdoor stroll! But as you walk around inside the spacecraft, you notice that Venus's gravity is about the same as Earth's. You weigh just a little less than you do on Earth. If not for the harmful air, people could easily move around on Venus.

A day on Venus is 116 Earth days long. If you stayed on Venus for one of its days, you would see something strange. The sun would rise in the west and set in the east, which is opposite from what happens on Earth. This backward motion happens because Venus spins in the opposite direction from Earth.

After a short stop on Earth, the next planet you visit is Mars. Like on Mercury, the gravity on Mars is a little more than one-third of Earth's gravity. So, you bounce around on Mars, too. Unlike Mercury, Mars is much more people-friendly. It is very, very cold at about –63 °C (–81 °F). The air is thin and does not contain oxygen to breathe, but it will not crush you.

Mars is like Earth in many ways. A day on Mars is just a little longer than a day on Earth. Mars has mountains and volcanoes and looks like a rocky desert on Earth. Mars also has clouds, wind, and seasons. Mars does not have oceans, lakes, or other bodies of water, but it does have polar ice caps.

Venus is covered in thick clouds. But these clouds are not made of water like the clouds on Earth. Venus's clouds are made of acid!

Jumping to Jupiter and Saturn

Next, you head to the gas giants. These planets are made up mostly of gases. They do not have hard surfaces. A spacecraft couldn't really land on a gas giant, so your spacecraft might just hover near the surface of each one.

You arrive at Jupiter, a gigantic planet. Jupiter is so large that more than 1,300 Earths could fit inside it. Its gravity is more than twice as strong as Earth's. So, in your spacecraft at Jupiter's surface, you weigh more than twice what you weigh on Earth!

You head over to look at Jupiter's Great Red Spot. The Great Red Spot is a huge storm that has been swirling on Jupiter for more than 300 years. The spot is large enough to cover Earth and Mars at the same time.

You then go to Saturn, taking time to look at the planet's rings. All of the gas giants have rings, but Saturn's rings are impressive. The rings are made of dust, rocks, and ice. Saturn's rings are wide. If you put the rings next to Earth, they would almost reach the moon. But the rings are also very thin. Some are only about 10 m (almost 33 ft) from top to bottom.

As your spacecraft hovers on Saturn's surface, you notice that you weigh only a little more than you do on Earth. How can such a big planet have about the same gravity as Earth? Remember: The strength of an object's gravity depends on the object's size. And size equals how much matter the object has. Although Saturn takes up a lot of space, it does not contain much matter. The matter inside it is very spread out. The matter is so spread out, if you put Saturn in a big bathtub of water, the planet would float!

This computer drawing of Jupiter shows the Great Red Spot. This is a huge storm swirling on Jupiter that is bigger than both Earth and Mars together.

Underway to Uranus and Neptune

The seventh stop on your tour of the planets is Uranus. Uranus is an odd planet. Although Uranus is not the farthest planet from the sun, it is as cold as Neptune. The inside of the other gas giants are very hot. But for some reason the inside of Uranus is cold in comparison, which makes the whole planet cold. But the oddest thing about Uranus is that it is turned on its side. Instead of spinning horizontally like a top, Uranus spins vertically, like a wheel.

Similarly to Saturn, the matter that makes up Uranus is very spread out. As a result, Uranus's gravity is a little less than Earth's gravity. Your weight on Uranus is about nine-tenths of your weight on Earth. In your hovering spacecraft, you find that heavy things are a little easier to lift.

The final stop of your mission is Neptune. When your spacecraft gets close to Neptune, you find that you cannot keep the craft steady because the winds are too strong. They blow nine times faster than the strongest winds on Earth.

Although Neptune is about the same size as Uranus, it contains more matter. So, Neptune's gravity is stronger than both Uranus's and Earth's. You weigh more than you do on Earth, but not by much.

On your way back to Earth, you think about what you have seen. Although the gravity of some planets is similar to Earth's, people could not live on the planets. Some are too hot, others are too cold, and some have no place for you to stand. They are not places for extraterrestrial vacations!

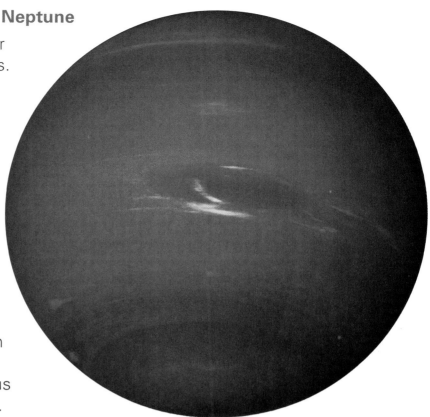

Neptune has dark spots similar to Jupiter's Great Red Spot. But the spots on Neptune last only a few years.

Why Is the Sun Brighter Than Other Stars?

Science Vocabulary

apparent brightness

light-year

On a clear night, you might look up at the sky and see thousands of glimmering stars. You will discover how stars give off light and that several factors affect how bright they look. The distance between most stars and Earth is so great, scientists measure it in a different way than they measure things on Earth.

NGSS

5-ESS1-1. Support an argument that differences in the apparent brightness of the sun compared to other stars is due to their relative distances from Earth.

ESS1.A. The sun is a star that appears larger and brighter than other stars because it is closer. Stars range greatly in their distance from Earth.

Scale, Proportion, and Quantity Natural objects exist from the very small to the immensely large.

Engaging in Argument from Evidence

1. Light from Stars Travels to Earth

When you look up at the night sky, you probably see glimmering stars. They look like tiny points of light. What makes stars look like tiny points of light?

Because stars are so hot, their energy produces bright light. This energy comes from the center, or *core*, of the star. Slowly, the light travels from the star's core to its surface. From the surface, light travels outside of the star into space, where there is little matter. The light travels in straight lines, or *rays*, in all directions away from the star until it hits some form of matter. As light rays move away from a star, the rays spread out over more and more space. So, when a star is very far away, only a small portion of its light reaches Earth. The rest of its light spreads out in different directions.

The sun looks so big compared to other stars because it is the closest star to Earth. This means light rays from the sun do not spread as far as rays from other stars before they reach Earth. This is why the sun appears brighter than other stars.

At night, when the sun is not visible, you can look up at the night sky and see hundreds or even thousands of stars —too many to count! Each star looks like a tiny point of light. But, as you have learned, stars only look small and dim because they are so far away. So, only a very small portion of their light reaches Earth.

The farther that light from a star travels, the more the light rays spread out. So, star A would look brighter from Earth than stars B and C. This is because star A is the closest of the three to Earth.

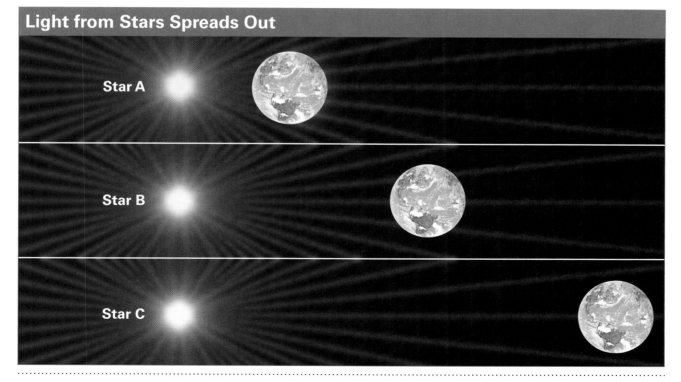

Light from Stars Spreads Out

Star A

Star B

Star C

2. Measuring Distances in Space

You use different units to measure different distances. You may live only steps away from your neighbor. That distance might be measured in meters. But you might use kilometers to explain how far away the next town is. What unit do scientists use to measure the distance between stars?

Distances between stars are much larger than a few meters or kilometers. In fact, the distances are so large that everyday units are too small to describe them easily. Instead, scientists use a unit called a *light-year*. A **light-year** is the distance that light travels in one year.

The word *light-year* sounds like a unit of time. But it is actually a unit of distance. It is similar to saying that your school is a ten-minute walk from home. You know how far you can walk in ten minutes. That distance is a ten-minute walk. In the same way, light needs a whole year to travel about 9.5 trillion kilometers, which is one light-year. Sirius is 8.6 light years away, so it takes light 8.6 years to reach Earth from Sirius.

Light travels faster than anything else. It moves so fast, you cannot even see that it is moving. The light from a lamp seems to reach you instantly when you turn the switch. But light takes longer to travel greater distances. Light from the sun travels for more than 8 minutes before it reaches Earth. So, if another space object near the sun blocks the sun's light, it would take more than 8 minutes for people on Earth to know!

Because distances in space are so great, scientists use a special unit called a light-year. Light-years are used to measure distances between stars or the distance between Earth and a star, such as Sirius.

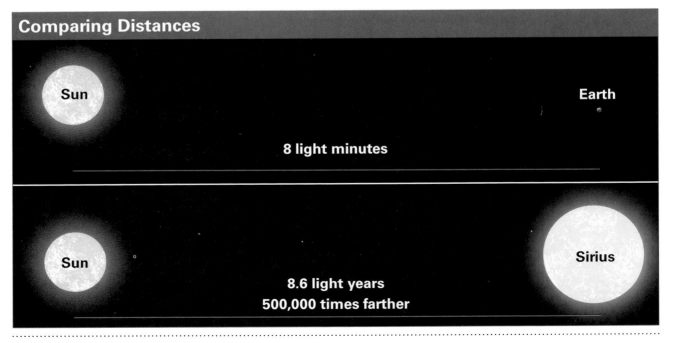

Comparing Distances

Sun

Earth

8 light minutes

Sun

Sirius

8.6 light years
500,000 times farther

3. Distance Affects a Star's Apparent Brightness

There are billions upon billions of stars in space. On a clear night, you can easily spot some stars in the sky. They are bright against the dark night sky. But most stars are harder to see. These stars are much dimmer.

The **apparent brightness** of a star is a measure of how bright it looks from Earth. One factor that affects a star's brightness is how far away it is from Earth. This is why the sun is so much brighter than other stars. Compared to other stars, it is very close to Earth.

Although all other stars are very far away from the sun, some stars are closer than others. One of the closest stars is called Alpha Centauri A. It is about 4.3 light-years away from both Earth and the sun. This means the light you see left the star 4.3 years ago! So, Alpha Centauri A is much farther from Earth than the sun. Most stars are much farther away than Alpha Centauri. They are up to tens of thousands of light-years away, or even farther.

Stars that are a great distance from Earth look dimmer than stars that are closer. This is because the farther light travels, the more it spreads out. Less of their light reaches Earth, so their apparent brightness is lower. The sun is so close that its apparent brightness is enough to light up the sky. More of its light falls on Earth than does the light of other stars. Alpha Centauri A gives off about as much light as the sun. But, at 4.3 light-years away, it only looks like a tiny bright dot in the night sky. Most stars are so far away that by the time their light reaches Earth, it is so spread out, they cannot be seen without a telescope.

Star	Distance from Earth (in light-years)
Proxima Centauri	4.2 ly
Alpha Centauri A	4.3 ly
Sirius	8.6 ly
Betelgeuse	643 ly
Rigel	773 ly

As this chart shows, stars are different distances away from Earth.

The sun and Alpha Centauri are stars that give off about the same amount of light. But the sun appears brighter than Alpha Centauri because it is closer to Earth. This is because distance is a factor that affects a star's apparent brightness.

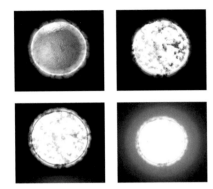

Temperature affects a star's apparent brightness. Blue stars are the hottest, and red stars are the coolest.

Each star is pictured as if it were the same distance from Earth. The size of a star affects its apparent brightness. The sun is bigger than Proxima Centauri, so it looks brighter from Earth. But it is smaller than Betelgeuse, so it looks dimmer.

4. Other Factors Affect a Star's Apparent Brightness

Distance is not the only factor that affects a star's apparent brightness. There are two other factors.

A second factor that affects a star's apparent brightness is size. Large stars are brighter than small stars. A star's size is described by its *radius*. The radius of a ball-shaped object, such as a star, is the distance from its center to its outside. The star Proxima Centauri is small. Its radius is about 100,000 km (62,100 mi). Betelgeuse is one of the largest stars known. Its radius is at least 90 million km (56 million mi). The sun is bigger than Proxima Centauri, but smaller than Betelgeuse. The sun's radius is about 700,000 km (435,000 mi). As a result, the sun is brighter than Proxima Centauri, and Betelgeuse is brighter than the sun.

A star's temperature also affects its apparent brightness. Hotter stars are brighter than cooler stars. Scientists use a star's color to measure its temperature. Blue stars are the hottest. White stars are also very hot. Sometimes stars are considered more than one color. The star Rigel is a blue-white star. Rigel's temperature is almost 11,000 °C (about 20,000 °F). Red stars are cooler. A red star can have a temperature of about 2,500 °C (4,500 °F). Yellow and orange stars have medium temperatures. The sun is a yellow star and is about 5,500 °C (10,000 °F). So, blue-white Rigel is brighter than the sun, and the sun is brighter than a red star.

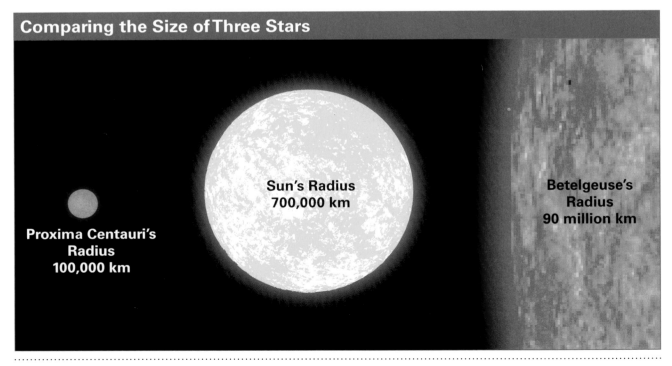

Comparing the Size of Three Stars

Proxima Centauri's Radius 100,000 km

Sun's Radius 700,000 km

Betelgeuse's Radius 90 million km

Why Is the Sun Brighter Than Other Stars?

1. Light from Stars Travels to Earth   Stars give off energy in the form of light. This light spreads out in all directions. As the light moves away from a star, it spreads out over more and more space. So, when a star is very far away, only a tiny amount of its light reaches Earth. The sun looks bigger and brighter than other stars because it is closer to Earth.

2. Measuring Distances in Space   Distances between the sun and other stars are measured in units called light-years. One light-year is the distance light can travel in one year. The sun is much less than one light-year way from Earth. It is about 8 light minutes away from Earth. This means it takes about 8 minutes for light from the sun to travel to Earth. Despite sounding like a measurement of time, a light-year is a measurement of distance.

3. Distance Affects a Star's Apparent Brightness   The apparent brightness of a star is a measure of how bright it looks from Earth. One factor that affects a star's apparent brightness is its distance from Earth. The sun is close to Earth, so it has a greater apparent brightness than other stars. Stars that are farther have a lower apparent brightness and look dimmer. This is because light spreads out more the farther it travels.

4. Other Factors Affects a Star's Apparent Brightness   Two other factors that affect a star's apparent brightness are its size and its temperature. A star's size is described as its radius, or its distance from its center to its outside. From Earth, larger stars appear brighter than smaller stars. Hotter stars also appear brighter than cooler stars. Scientists use a star's color to measure its temperature. Blue stars are the hottest, and red stars are the coolest. So, blue stars are hotter than red stars.

The Life and Death of a Star

When you look in the night sky, you see stars. They vary in their brightness, color, and size. Each star has a life of drama. There is an explosive birth, colorful periods of change, and a spectacular death. What exactly is this life of a star?

Picture yourself as a young adult. Now picture yourself as a senior citizen. You might have imagined yourself taller as a young adult and with white hair as a senior citizen. What caused you to predict those changes in your body? You probably based your predictions on observations of how young adults and senior citizens look. You can look at people of different ages and predict how you will grow and change over your lifetime. Scientists who study stars use a similar method to predict how stars will change over their lifetimes.

Stars may live for millions or billions of years. Because they live for so long, scientists cannot watch a single star to see how it is born, how it changes, and how it dies. So, scientists study many stars at once. The stars in the universe are at various stages in their lives. A star's life cycle depends on how much matter is in it. Scientists find stars of different ages that are made of the same amount of matter and put together a timeline of what happens.

A star is born in a huge cloud of gas and dust called a nebula. The particles of gas and dust float in space until a force pushes the particles together. As the particles move closer together, the gravity between them pulls them even closer together. More and more particles come together, and they form a big spinning disk. As the disk continues to spin and grow, it gets hotter and hotter. This heat helps start the birth of the star.

The gas and dust in nebulas will eventually become stars.

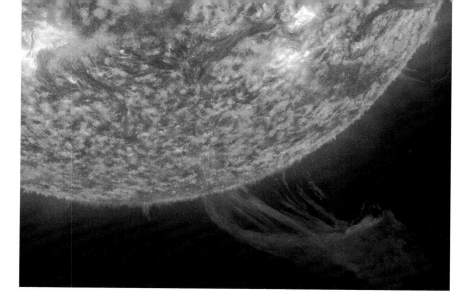

The sun is in the main sequence. All the energy that it sends out comes from the fusion of hydrogen particles.

Birth and Life

Eventually, the temperature of the disk becomes high enough for a process called *fusion* to start. During fusion, particles of matter come together and release a lot of energy. A star is born when hydrogen particles come together. Fusion is the process that produces all the light and heat energy given off by stars, including our sun.

The next step in a star's life is the main-sequence stage. If you think of a nebula as a star's infancy, and the disk as its childhood, the main-sequence stage can be thought of as its adulthood. The main sequence is the longest part of a star's life cycle. A star stays in the main sequence as long as it has particles of hydrogen that can undergo fusion.

How long a star stays in the main sequence depends on how much matter it contains. The more matter a star has, the shorter the amount of time it spends in the main sequence. Bigger stars have more gravity and hotter temperatures than smaller stars. So, a bigger star burns through its matter faster. For example, the sun and other stars that contain the same amount of matter will spend about 10 billion years in the main sequence. But a star that has ten times more matter than the sun may stay in the main sequence for only 20 million years.

A star leaves the main sequence when all of the hydrogen inside its center is used up. Once a star leaves the main sequence, it enters old age and begins to die. Scientists estimate that the sun will be in the main sequence for another 6.5 billion years. So, don't worry. The sun will eventually die, but not in your lifetime!

Fade Away

When a star leaves the main sequence it starts to cool down. As stars cool down, they change from blue or white, to a reddish color. The stars also grow bigger—a lot bigger. Stars that have entered this part of their life cycle are called *red giants*. Red giants are 100 to 1,000 times bigger than the sun. In fact, scientists estimate that when the sun is a red giant, its outer edge will reach beyond Earth's current orbit. You certainly do not want to be on Earth when that happens!

The red giant stage is not quite the end of the road for a star. What happens next depends on the amount of matter in the star. A star like the sun will eventually stop producing energy through fusion. The gases that make up the outer layers of the stars will drift away and form a nebula. Remember, a nebula is a huge cloud of gas and dust. The gases continue to drift outward, and the nebula grows bigger over time.

The matter from the center of the star will pack tightly together to form a small, hot ball called a *white dwarf*. Because a white dwarf is very hot, it still gives off some light. If you have a good telescope, you might be able to see a white dwarf glowing inside of a nebula.

But no fusion happens in a white dwarf. So the dwarf slowly cools down. Eventually, the dwarf will cool down so much that it stops giving off light. When that happens, the former star is called a *black dwarf*.

The red, white, and blue clouds in this photo make up a nebula formed after a red giant died. The tiny blue dot in the center of the nebula is the white dwarf that remains from the star.

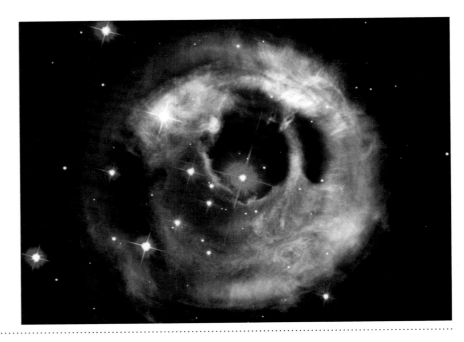

Going out with a Bang

Our sun, and the stars like it, will die quietly. But stars that contain much more mass will have more spectacular deaths. After these huge stars go through the red giant stage, their matter will pack together tightly and become very hot. Eventually, the star will explode and form a *supernova*, a star that suddenly increases in brightness. In the year 1054, people saw one that was so bright that it could be seen even during the day. During a supernova, a lot of matter from the star spews outward to form a nebula.

The amount of matter left behind by a supernova determines what happens next. If a small amount is left behind, the leftover matter forms a *neutron star*. The matter in a neutron star is packed together very tightly. In fact, if you had a piece of neutron star the size of a raindrop, it would contain as much matter as all the people on Earth squished together!

If a larger amount of matter is left behind, the leftover matter forms a *black hole*. A black hole is not actually a hole. It is an object that has such strong gravity that anything that comes near it is pulled in and can never escape. A black hole is called "black" because its gravity is so strong that even light cannot escape.

Black dwarves, neutron stars, and black holes are the corpses of stars. But before these stars died, they did something to ensure that a new generation of stars could be born. As the stars were dying, they sent out matter in nebulas. These nebulas could become the birthplace for new stars, making the life cycle of a star truly a cycle!

As the stars die, they send out matter in nebulas. These nebulas could become the birthplace for new stars.

Why Is There Day and Night?

Science Vocabulary

axis

rotate

rotation

time zone

From space, Earth looks like a blue marble. Why is part of the marble always in a shadow? You will learn about Earth's rotation, and how it causes the patterns of night and day and sunrise and sunset. These daily patterns also change over the course of a year, so sometimes it is daytime for longer than on other days.

NGSS

5-ESS1-2. Represent data in graphical displays to reveal patterns of daily changes in length and direction of shadows, day and night, and the seasonal appearance of some stars in the night sky.

ESS1.B. The orbits of Earth around the sun and of the moon around Earth, together with the rotation of Earth about an axis between its North and South poles, cause observable patterns. These include day and night; daily changes in the length and direction of shadows; and different positions of the sun, moon, and stars at different times of the day, month, and year.

Patterns Similarities and differences in patterns can be used to sort, classify, communicate, and analyze simple rates of change for natural phenomena.

 **Analyzing and Interpreting Data**

1. Earth Spins on Its Axis

If you watch the sky during the day, you will see the sun rise in the east. It seems to move slowly across the sky all day, and in the evening, it will set in the west. This pattern happens every day.

To people standing on Earth, it seems that the planet is still and that everything around it in space—including the sun—is moving. But the sun only looks like it is moving across the sky. In fact, the sun stays in one place in the center of the solar system, and it is Earth that moves.

To understand why the sun appears to move, think about riding on a carousel. As you watch the people standing around the spinning carousel, they appear to move. But they are not moving. You are moving. In a similar way, the sun appears to move in the sky because Earth is moving.

Because you are moving in a circle on the carousel, you see the same people over and over again. Similarly, the sun seems to rise and set in the same pattern every day because you move in a circle when you are on Earth.

You move in a circle because Earth *rotates* around an *axis*. To **rotate** means to spin. Earth's **axis** is an imaginary line going through the middle of the planet from its North Pole to its South Pole. Earth makes one complete spin, or **rotation**, about its axis every 24 hours. So, each rotation is one day on Earth.

The sun appears to move in the sky because, like a carousel, Earth is rotating.

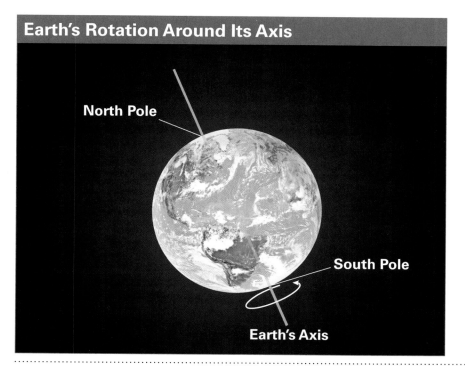

Earth's Rotation Around Its Axis

North Pole

South Pole

Earth's Axis

The sun appears to move because Earth rotates around an axis. Earth makes one rotation about its axis every 24 hours, which means that day on Earth is one complete rotation.

The horizon is the line that appears to separate Earth and the sky.

Earth's rotation causes day and night. In this diagram, the part of Earth that is facing the sun is experiencing daytime. The part that is not facing the sun is experiencing nighttime.

2. Earth's Rotation Causes Day and Night

What is the difference between day and night? To answer this question, you might look at the sky. *Day* is any time that the sun is in the sky, and *night* is any time that the sun is not in the sky.

Day and night are caused by Earth's rotation. Because Earth rotates, the sun seems to change its position in the sky throughout the day. In the middle of the day, the sun is at its highest point and the part of Earth you are standing on is facing directly toward the sun. As the day continues, Earth continues to rotate, and the part of Earth you are on is no longer facing the sun. As a result, the sun seems to be lower in the sky. Eventually, Earth rotates so much that the part you are standing on is facing away from the sun. This causes the sun to drop below the horizon, and a sunset occurs.

After sunset, Earth continues to rotate. Just after sunset, there is usually a little light in the sky because the part of Earth you are on is still almost facing toward the sun. As it gets later into the night, Earth rotates more. In the middle of the night, the part of Earth you are on is facing directly away from the sun. During this time, the sky is usually very dark. Then Earth rotates more, and the sky starts to get lighter. Eventually, it rotates enough so that the sun rises up over the horizon again. But the sun is still low in the sky. Earth continues to rotate, and by the middle of the day, it is directly overhead, just like the day before. Because Earth rotates once every 24 hours, you see this pattern of the sun's movement once every 24 hours.

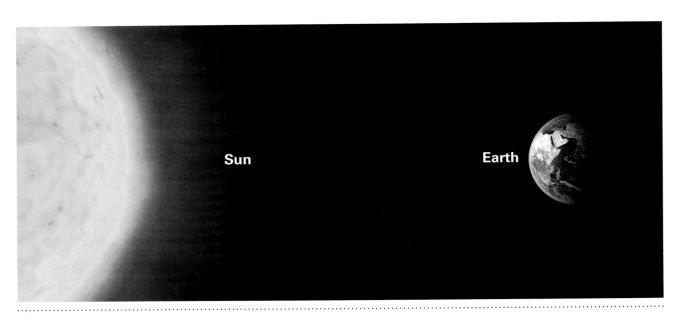

Sun

Earth

3. It Is a Different Time of Day in Different Places

Suppose that you live in Hawaii. You text a photo of the sunset to your cousin in New York. Your cousin replies, "Why are you texting me after midnight?" How can it be after midnight in New York when it is not even 7:30 P.M. in Hawaii? New York and Hawaii are in different time zones, so it is never the same time in both places.

A **time zone** is a part of the world where the same standard time is used. For example, Iowa and Arkansas are in the Central time zone. So, when it is 5:00 P.M. in Iowa, it is also 5:00 P.M. in Arkansas.

The time in each time zone is based on the pattern of the sun's position in the sky. The moment when the sun is at its peak, or highest point in the sky, is called *noon*. But the time that the sun is at its peak differs from place to place. The sun's position in the sky changes because Earth rotates. For a given spot on Earth, the sun is at its peak when that spot is pointed directly at the sun. So, it will always be noon in New York before it is noon in Hawaii. Time zones are set up such that the sun is at or near its highest point at 12:00 P.M.

The world is divided up into 24 time zones. The times in these time zones are one hour apart. The United States spans six time zones. New York is in the Eastern time zone. Hawaii is in the Hawaii-Aleutian time zone, which is five hours behind the Eastern time zone. So, when it is midnight in New York, it is 7:00 P.M. in Hawaii.

The time in each time zone is based on the pattern of the sun's movement. The United States is divided into six different time zones, as shown on this map. Which time zone are you in?

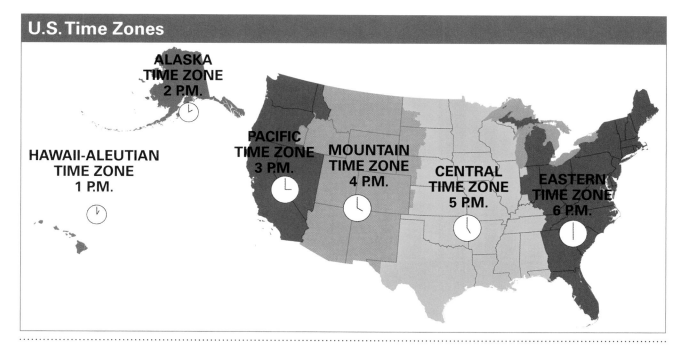

U.S. Time Zones

ALASKA TIME ZONE 2 P.M.

HAWAII-ALEUTIAN TIME ZONE 1 P.M.

PACIFIC TIME ZONE 3 P.M.

MOUNTAIN TIME ZONE 4 P.M.

CENTRAL TIME ZONE 5 P.M.

EASTERN TIME ZONE 6 P.M.

4. The Amount of Daylight Changes During the Year

Every day, the sun rises and sets in a predictable pattern. But the sun does not rise at the same time each day, and it does not set at the same time each day. So, there is another pattern about sunrise and sunset that you can observe—a pattern of changes through the year.

You can observe the time that the sun rises and sets and see how it changes. During summer, you might notice that the days seem very long. This is because the sun rises early in the morning and sets late in the evening. The sun might rise at 6:00 A.M. and set at 8:00 P.M. The sun would be in the sky for 14 hours. There are more hours of daylight than hours of night in the summer.

During fall, there are fewer daylight hours than during summer. There are about the same number of hours of daylight as hours of night. The sun might rise at 7:00 A.M. and set at 7:00 P.M., so would be in the sky for 12 hours.

There are the fewest hours of daylight during winter. There are fewer hours where the sun is in the sky than hours of night. The sun might rise at 7:30 A.M. and set at 5:00 P.M. There would be only nine and a half hours of daylight.

During spring, the sun is in the sky for a longer period of time than during winter. There are about the same number of daylight hours in spring as in fall. There are more daylight hours in spring and fall than in winter, and fewer hours than in summer.

The sun does not rise and set at the same time every day. It rises and sets in a pattern of changes that is different for each season. In which season does the sun rise the earliest? Which is the latest?

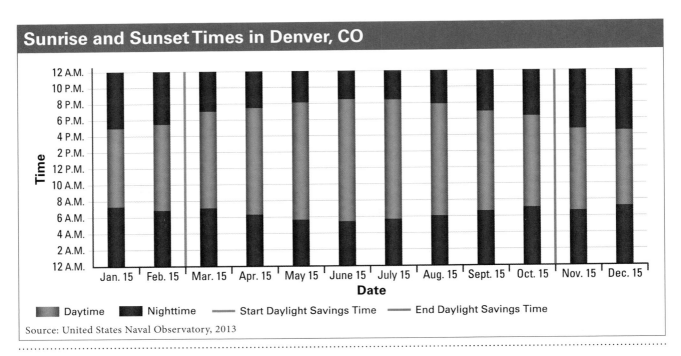

Sunrise and Sunset Times in Denver, CO

Legend: ■ Daytime ■ Nighttime — Start Daylight Savings Time — End Daylight Savings Time

Source: United States Naval Observatory, 2013

Why Is There Day and Night?

1. Earth Spins on Its Axis   The sun appears to move in the sky, but it is not actually moving. Rather, it is Earth that is moving. Earth rotates around an axis. Earth's axis is an imaginary line running through its North and South pole. Earth takes 24 hours to rotate around this axis. Each rotation is 24 hours, or one day on Earth.

2. Earth's Rotation Causes Day and Night   Day and night are caused by Earth's rotation. When it is day, the part of Earth you are on faces the sun, and when it is night, the part of Earth you are on faces away from the sun. Because Earth rotates around its axis every 24 hours, you see this pattern of day and night every 24 hours.

3. It Is a Different Time of Day in Different Places   People in a time zone use the same standard time. There are 24 time zones in the world, six of which are in the United States. The time in each time zone is based on the pattern of the sun's position in the sky. In each time zone, the sun is at or near its highest point at 12:00 P.M.

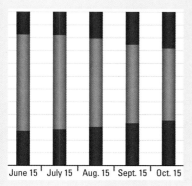

June 15   July 15   Aug. 15   Sept. 15   Oct. 15

4. The Amount of Daylight Changes During the Year   The time that the sun rises and sets changes in a pattern. If you observed the time that the sun rises and sets, you would see this pattern. Spring and fall have about the same number of daylight hours. It is daytime for the longest during the summer, and it is daytime for the shortest during winter.

Hang onto Your Hat

People once thought that Earth did not move. The sun, moon, and stars seemed to move in the sky, and no one felt Earth moving. Now, we know that Earth turns once a day and goes around the sun once a year. So, how fast does Earth move?

Try to answer this brainteaser: Which is moving faster—a tree in Alaska or a tree in Hawaii? It seems like a trick question because trees do not seem to move at all. They just stand planted in one place. But trees are on Earth, and Earth is moving. So, trees move along with Earth as it moves. To figure out which of the two trees is moving faster, you have to think about Earth's rotation and shape.

Earth spins, or rotates, once every day. Every point on Earth's surface moves with Earth as it rotates. And each point on Earth's surface moves at a different speed.

The speed of an object describes how fast the object moves. To find the speed of any object, you divide the distance the object travels by the time needed to travel that distance. So, to find Earth's speed of rotation, you have to find how far a point on Earth's surface moves in one day and divide that distance by 24 hours, the length of one day. Earth's circumference is the distance around the equator. The equator is the imaginary line that marks the widest part of Earth. It is equal to a little more than 40,000 kilometers (25,000 miles). A point at the equator travels a distance equal to Earth's circumference once every 24 hours. So, the speed of a point on the equator is about 1,670 kilometers per hour (1035 miles per hour)! That's much faster than a jet plane. But that speed is just the speed at the equator. The speed at other points on Earth is not quite as fast.

The equator is the imaginary line that marks the widest part of Earth. You can see the equator on this globe. Every point on Earth's surface moves with Earth as it rotates.

The Need for Speed

To understand why different points on Earth travel at different speeds, think about a playground merry-go-round. A merry-go-round is a disk that spins. Suppose that you sit at the edge of the merry-go-round and your friend sits near the center. Then, imagine that the merry-go-round spins once every 5 seconds. During the 5 seconds, you move in a complete circle. Your friend also moves in a complete circle in the same amount of time. But the circle you follow is bigger than the circle that your friend follows. So, you move farther in 5 seconds than your friend moves in the same amount of time. That means that you are moving at a faster speed than your friend because you are sitting further from the axis.

The same thing happens when Earth rotates. During every 24 hours, a point at the equator travels in a circle. A point near the North Pole also travels in a circle. But the point at the equator traces a bigger circle than the point near the North Pole. So, the point on the equator travels at a higher speed than the point near the North Pole.

Can you figure out the answer to the brainteaser now? Hawaii is close to the equator, and Alaska is close to the North Pole. So, Hawaii traces out a bigger circle in one day than Alaska does. That means that Hawaii and its tree move faster than Alaska and its tree. But neither the tree in Hawaii nor the tree in Alaska moves as fast as a tree planted right on the equator.

Objects travel in a circle during a merry-go-round's, or Earth's, rotation. However, an object at the edge travels farther in the same amount of time than an object in the center. This means it moves faster!

People on this spin ride are moving fast due to the ride's rotation. The Earth's rotation gives rockets an extra boost of speed when they take off in the direction that Earth spins.

Spin Out

You probably do not live on the equator, so you do not move 1,670 kilometers per hour (1035 miles per hour) when standing still. But you are still moving fast. Why don't you feel that you are moving so quickly? The answer has to do with the fact that everything around you, including the air, is moving at the same speed that you are moving. Suppose you are on a bus. You and your friends are moving at the same speed as the bus. You do not feel wind on your face. Unless you looked outside, you might feel as if you are not moving at all. The Earth is like your bus, and all that is on Earth are its passengers.

Because you cannot feel Earth move, the fact that the Earth rotates so quickly is not very important to you. But Earth's speed does matter to rocket engineers. For a rocket to get into space, it has to be traveling very fast. Engineers make a rocket travel quickly by using a lot of fuel to send it up. However, engineers realized that they could use Earth's rotation to give a rocket even more speed.

Think about throwing a ball as hard as you can. You can give the ball a certain speed if you throw it while standing still. But, if you throw the ball out the window of a moving train, the ball will move faster because it was already moving at a fast speed before you threw it.

In a similar way, engineers learned that if they launch a rocket from a place on Earth that was already moving fast, they could make the rocket move faster. That is why rockets in the United States take off from Florida. Florida is closer to the equator than most of the rest of the United States.

Slow Down

To launch a rocket properly, engineers have to know exactly how fast Earth is rotating. But the speed that Earth rotates is always changing. Typically, Earth is slowing down, but it sometimes speeds up. Earth's rotation changes because of the gravity between Earth and the moon. This gravity pulls on Earth and slows it down. Weather and earthquakes can also change Earth's speed. These factors cause the speed of Earth's rotation to shorten by 1.8 millionths of a second each day! But don't adjust your clocks. That time change is much too tiny for you to notice.

Tiny amounts of time eventually do add up. Because Earth's rotation is mostly slowing down, every few years, scientists add a leap second to the length of a year. A leap second is an extra second that adjusts the world's clocks to account for the change in Earth's rotation speed. People do not usually add the second to their clocks at home, but clocks on computers, cell phones, and other devices add the second automatically. Adding those seconds is important for devices that communicate with each other. Problems may happen if the devices are not telling the exact same time. For example, if the time on a GPS device is not exact, it will no longer tell you your correct location on Earth.

Because so many people depend on electronic devices, how fast Earth rotates is very important. Luckily, you do not have to keep track of the speed. Also, since you do not feel how fast Earth turns, you do not actually have to hang onto your hat.

If your GPS device did not add a leap second when it was supposed to, you could not use it to find your way on a hike. It would not know where you are.

How Do Shadows Change During the Day and Year?

Science Vocabulary

shadow

sundial

If you observe shadows outdoors throughout the day, you will notice that they change in two different ways. You would discover that the length of the shadows changes and that the direction the shadows point also changes on a daily basis. Cultures throughout history have used these patterns in different ways.

NGSS

5-ESS1-2. Represent data in graphical displays to reveal patterns of daily changes in length and direction of shadows, day and night, and the seasonal appearance of some stars in the night sky.

ESS1.B. The orbits of Earth around the sun and of the moon around Earth, together with the rotation of Earth about an axis between its North and South poles, cause observable patterns. These include day and night; daily changes in the length and direction of shadows; and different positions of the sun, moon, and stars at different times of the day, month, and year.

Patterns Similarities and differences in patterns can be used to sort, classify, communicate, and analyze simple rates of change for natural phenomena.

Analyzing and Interpreting Data

1. Shadows Follow a Daily Pattern

When you're outside, you might notice that your shadow changes. It might be short or tall. It might in front of you or behind you. Why does your shadow change?

A **shadow** is an area of darkness created when an object blocks light. Shadows can form where any light source is blocked. Shadows formed by the sun change in patterns.

If you watch the shadow of a tree during the day, you will see that it changes length and direction. When the sun rises, the shadow is long and points mostly toward the west. As the sun rises higher, the shadow gets shorter. At around noon, it is very short and at the base of the tree, and in the afternoon, the shadow gets long again. But this time it points mostly toward the east. Just before sunset, the shadow is about as long as it was at sunrise.

The length of shadows follows this pattern of changes each day. Recall that even though the sun seems to change positions, it is not actually moving. The pattern of changes of a shadow is caused by the sun's *apparent* position. Shadows are long when the sun is low in the sky. As Earth rotates, the sun moves higher in the sky, and shadows continue to get shorter until the sun is at its highest point in the sky. At this time, shadows are shortest because the sun shines straight down or almost straight down on objects. In the afternoon, the sun moves lower in the sky, and shadows get longer.

The direction that a shadow points also depends on the sun's apparent position in the sky. Shadows always point away from the sun because the object causing the shadow is always between the shadow and the sun.

A Shadow's Pattern of Changes

8 A.M. — Sun

12 P.M. — Sun

4 P.M. — Sun

Any object's shadow that is caused by the sun follows a daily pattern of changes. The shadow is longer if the sun is low in the sky and shorter if it is high in the sky. Shadows also change direction in a pattern since they always point away from the sun.

2. Shadows Follow A Yearly Pattern

You can easily see the daily patterns of shadows by looking outside several times during the day. But seeing yearly patterns is not as easy. You have to make observations for a whole year before you see the pattern repeat. To see this pattern, you must observe the shadow of a stationary object at the same time of day for a year.

If you watched a shadow caused by the sun for a year, you would see two changes. One change is that the length of the shadow changes with the seasons. The other is that the direction that the shadow points changes. During the summer, a shadow is shorter than it is in other seasons. If you observe a morning shadow, you will see that it points mostly to the west. If you observe an afternoon shadow, you will see that it point mostly to the east. During the winter, a shadow looks different. It is longer than it is during other seasons. It also points in a different direction. At all times of the day, it points slightly more to the north than it does during the summer.

Some ancient cultures used the yearly pattern of shadows to track the seasons. For example, historians believe that the Maya used this pattern in El Castillo, a pyramid built for the god Kukulkán. At certain times during the spring and fall, the sun hits the steps, creating a shadow on the pyramid. Many historians believe that the shadow was used to mark important times during the spring and fall. The Pueblo also built monuments that used sunlight and shadow to help track the seasons.

A shadow cast by an object in sunlight follows a yearly pattern. During summer, a shadow is shortest and points to the east and west. During winter, a shadow is tallest and points slightly north at all times of the day.

The Yearly Pattern of Shadows

10:00 A.M. | Summer | N W E S

10:00 A.M. | Winter | N W E S

Shadow

Shadow

Engineering Design

3. Using Shadows to Measure Time

If someone asks you for the time, you would probably look at a clock or a watch to find out. But telling time was not as easy before clocks were invented. So, how did ancient cultures keep track of time?

Many ancient cultures used a *sundial* to track time. A **sundial** is a tool that uses the shadow cast by an object in sunlight to keep track of time during the day. The oldest known sundial was found in Ukraine and was made in the 13th century B.C.E.

Sundials come in different shapes and sizes, but all have two parts. One part is a thin stick or wedge that casts a shadow. The other part is a base with marks on it. The marks show time intervals. The marks are spaced so that the time needed for the shadow of the stick to move from one mark to another is equal between all marks.

Many modern and ancient sundials have 12 marks that divide daytime into 12 pieces. But recall that the length of daytime changes with the seasons. So, the hour marks on sundials are not the same length throughout the year. For example, during summer, it might be daytime for 12 hours. So, each mark on the sundial would represent one hour. But during winter, each mark might only represent 45 minutes.

Not all sundials have 12 marks. For example, the Pilgrims used a sundial with only one mark, the noon mark. The sundial was hung above a door or window. When its shadow reached this mark, the Pilgrims knew that it was noon, or about the middle of the day.

Many ancient cultures used a sundial, a tool that uses a shadow and sundial to track time during the day. All sundials, like this one pictured, include a long stick that casts a shadow on a base with markings on it. Notice that the markings are equal distance apart.

Sundials come in many different forms. This bowl-shaped sundial is from Seoul, South Korea and uses both horizontal and vertical lines to indicate the time of year and the time of day.

4. Shadows Point in Different Directions in Different Places

You have learned that as the sun seems to move across the sky, the direction that your shadow points changes. But there is another factor that affects which direction it points—location.

You learned that at noon, your shadow is very short. It is short because the sun is nearly straight overhead, and so you cast a shadow almost straight down. But it is not quite straight down. Your shadow points a little bit in one direction. Does it always point in the same direction?

The direction that your shadow points changes in a pattern based on where you are on Earth. It is easiest to see which direction it points at noon. How north or south you are on Earth determines your shadow's direction. If you are on the Northern Hemisphere, the sun will seem to be slightly to the south. Since shadows always point away from the sun, your shadow will point north. If you are on the Southern Hemisphere, the sun will seem to be slightly to the north, so your shadow will point south.

Near the equator, the sun is very close to straight overhead in the middle of the day. If you are on this part of Earth, your shadow will not point noticeably north or south. It would stay mostly in a circle around your feet. So, the farther you are from the equator, the more north or south your shadow points.

The direction that your shadow points at noon depends on where you are on Earth. In the Northern Hemisphere, a shadow caused by the sun points more to the north, but in the Southern Hemisphere, a shadow points more to the south.

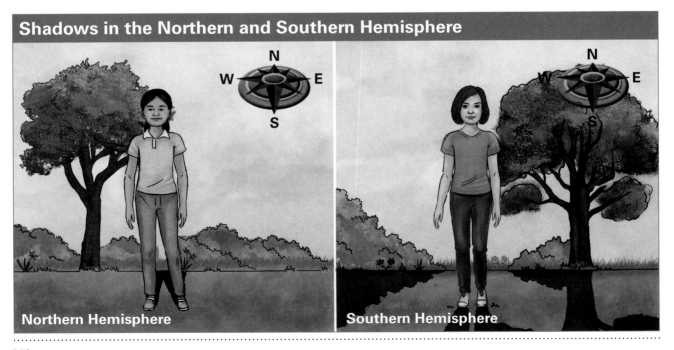

Shadows in the Northern and Southern Hemisphere

Northern Hemisphere

Southern Hemisphere

How Do Shadows Change During the Day and Year?

1. Shadows Follow a Daily Pattern   When a shadow is caused by the sun, it follows a daily pattern of changes. The length and the direction that the shadow points change. These changes are caused by the apparent position of the sun. An object's shadow is shortest at noon, when the sun is directly above. As the sun moves in the afternoon, the shadows get longer.

2. Shadows Follow a Yearly Pattern   Shadows caused by the sun follow a yearly pattern of changes. Throughout the year, their length and the direction they point change. In summer, shadows are shorter than shadows in winter. In the summer, shadows point to the east and west. In the winter, shadows point more north than in other seasons.

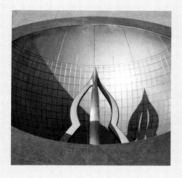

3. Using Shadows to Measure Time   A sundial is a tool that uses a shadow's pattern of changes to keep track of time during the day. All sundials have two parts. One part is a thin stick or wedge that casts a shadow. The other is a base with marks on it that represent time intervals. Because the amount of daylight changes with the seasons, the intervals that the marks represent also change.

4. Shadows Point in Different Directions in Different Places   The direction that your shadow points at noon depends on where you are. In the Northern Hemisphere, your shadow would point more north. In the Southern Hemisphere, your shadow would point more south. Near the equator, your shadow would not point very north or south.

Ancient Skywatchers

During a year, the seasons change on Earth. Keeping track of seasonal changes was important for ancient people. How did they know what time of year it was without calendars?

The sun sets between two stones of Stonehenge on the first day of summer. Scientists think people may have used this event to keep track of the time of the year.

If someone asked you when your birthday was, you would be able to say the exact day and month that you were born. You could probably even tell the person how long it is until your birthday. You can give all this information because you know how to use a calendar.

Calendars are tools for marking the passage of time. A calendar can tell you when your doctor's appointment is, when the last day of school is, or when the first day of spring is. Ancient people may not have had to worry about these things, but they did have to pay attention to the seasons. Weather changes with the seasons, and the lives of ancient people depended on the weather. They needed to know when to plant crops or when to prepare for winter. But those people did not have paper calendars. Instead, they used the changes in the sun's motion to keep track of the passage of time throughout a year.

Throughout history, different cultures built structures that may have been used to track the sun. One such structure is Stonehenge in England. The huge stones that still stand at the site were placed around 2500 BCE. Scientists are unsure what the exact purpose of Stonehenge was. However, the stones are positioned such that the sun rises between two stones on the first day of summer and sets between two different stones on the first day of winter. It is hard to believe that is just a coincidence.

The large steps on the side of El Castillo cast a snake-like shadow on the sides of the staircases, but only at certain times of the year.

The Castle with the Snakes

Another structure that tracks the sun can be found in Mexico. The structure is called El Castillo, which is Spanish for "the castle." The Maya who lived in the area built El Castillo in the ancient city of Chichén Itzá around 1000 CE.

El Castillo is a pyramid that has steep sides and a flat top. The sides are built like large stair steps, but they also have stairways that people can climb. On certain days, the large steps and the stairways combine to show something interesting. At sunset on the first day of spring and on the first day of fall, the large steps cast a snake-like shadow on the stairways. At the bottom of the stairways, carved snakeheads connect with the wavy snake shadow. If the Maya did this on purpose, they had to have known how the position of the sunset changed throughout the year.

Scientists think that the Maya could have used the changing shadows on El Castillo to track the seasons. That means that the huge pyramid may have been a calendar for the Maya who lived in Chichen Itza.

Another building in Chichén Itzá gives evidence that the Maya watched the skies. The building is round and has small windows. At first, the windows seem to be randomly placed. But scientists realized that the windows can be used to track the motion of Venus. The Maya thought that Venus was a war god, and may have used the position of the planet to plan battles.

The spiky circle near the bottom of this rock is thought to be a carving of a supernova.

Canyon Carvings

The ruins of an ancient Native American community in what is now New Mexico also contain evidence that the people who lived there watched the skies. The ruins are located in a place called Chaco Canyon. Instead of using buildings and shadows to mark the seasons, the people of Chaco Canyon used carvings and sunlight.

Sometime between 850 and 1250 CE, the people living in Chaco Canyon built what is now known as the Sun Dagger. The Sun Dagger has two parts. The first part is a pair of spirals carved into a rock. One spiral is large and the other is small. The second part of the Sun Dagger is three slabs of stone arranged in front of the carvings. Sunlight shining through the slabs forms thin strips of light that look like daggers. The daggers shine on the rock that has the spiral carvings.

On the first day of summer, a dagger goes through the center of the large spiral. On the first day of winter, a dagger shines on each side of the large spiral. And, on the first day of spring and the first day of fall, a dagger goes through the center of the small spiral. At the same time, a second dagger hits halfway between the center and the edge of the large spiral. Scientists think that the Sun Dagger was used to keep track of the seasons.

Other carvings in Chaco Canyon show that the people living there paid attention to changes in the sky. One carving is thought to show the sun during a solar eclipse. Another carving is thought to be of a supernova that was so bright people could see it during the day.

A Well-Built Temple

Scientists who study ancient cultures will never know why the people of those cultures did certain things. Scientists think the carvings in Chaco Canyon show an eclipse and a supernova. But they will never know for certain if that is the case. All scientists can do is study what was left by the cultures and look for patterns that might explain what the ancient people thought.

Scientists who studied a temple in Cambodia found a lot of patterns in its design that seem to match patterns in the sky. The temple is called Angkor Wat. It was built between 1113 and 1150 CE. Angkor Wat has many towers, hallways, and rooms. It is decorated with large carvings and is surrounded by a moat. Scientists measured many parts of the temple and found that the lengths used match numbers found in astronomy. For example, some measurements are equal to the number of days in the year. Others are equal to the number of days the moon needs to complete its phase cycle. Scientists also think that one of the carvings is a calendar that ties in with the seasons.

The people who built Angkor Wat and people from other ancient cultures seemed to understand that time passed in cycles. They also understood that they could keep track of the cycles by watching the sun and other objects in the sky. Today, you use calendars to keep track of time. These calendars may seem more accurate than those of ancient people. But remember, the calendars you use are based on the same changes in the sun's position that ancient people watched.

The people who built Angkor Wat seem to have had knowledge of the changes that the sun and the moon go through over time.

How Do Stars Seem to Move During the Night and Year?

Science Vocabulary

astronomer

constellation

On a clear night, you can look up at the sky and see thousands of stars. You might even see star patterns, or constellations, that form shapes and pictures. Many cultures have stories to explain constellations. You will learn about constellations, and how they seem to move during the night and year. Scientists use constellations to help map the sky and communicate their observations.

NGSS

5-ESS1-2. Represent data in graphical displays to reveal patterns of daily changes in length and direction of shadows, day and night, and the seasonal appearance of some stars in the night sky.

ESS1.B. The orbits of Earth around the sun and of the moon around Earth, together with the rotation of Earth about an axis between its North and South poles, cause observable patterns. These include day and night; daily changes in the length and direction of shadows; and different positions of the sun, moon, and stars at different times of the day, month, and year.

Patterns Similarities and differences in patterns can be used to sort, classify, communicate, and analyze simple rates of change for natural phenomena.

Analyzing and Interpreting Data

1. Star Patterns Form Pictures in the Sky

When you look at the night sky, you can probably see some familiar star patterns. Perhaps you see the Big Dipper or the Little Dipper. If you connect the star patterns, you might see pictures of familiar objects.

These patterns mark the *constellations* in the night sky. A **constellation** is a section of the sky that has a recognizable star pattern. People have been seeing pictures in the stars for thousands of years. For example, one constellation is called Orion, named after a hunter from ancient Greek mythology. Some people see a person hunting with a bow or holding a shield when they look at this constellation. Another constellation called Scorpius has a star pattern that looks like a scorpion. Scorpius is also from ancient Greek mythology.

The brightest stars in the sky are usually part of the most recognizable star patterns. The star Betelgeuse and other bright stars form Orion. Some star patterns with bright stars make up only part of a larger picture. For example, one of the most well-known constellations is the Big Dipper, which is also part of the larger constellation Ursa Major, or the Big Bear. The stars of the Big Dipper are seven of the brightest stars in Ursa Major. The stars of Ursa Major form a picture of a bear. The handle of the Big Dipper is the bear's tail, and the bowl is part of its body. Other stars in Ursa Major form the rest of the bear's body, legs, and head. But many people cannot see the rest of Ursa Major because those stars are not as bright. So, their pattern is not as noticeable.

A constellation is a section of the sky that has a recognizable star pattern. The constellation Orion is made up of very bright stars, which makes it one of the most easily seen constellations.

Some star patterns are part of larger constellations. This picture shows the Big Dipper, which is part of a larger constellation called Ursa Major.

2. Stars Seem to Move During the Night

Suppose you are outside one evening and find Orion shining just above a tree near your home. A few hours later, you go outside again and look for Orion in the same spot, but it is not there! You search the sky again and finally find it lower in the sky. What happened? Why did Orion move?

If you observe the stars several times during a night, they will seem to move in an arc, or semicircle. If you could see the stars for an entire day, they would appear to move in a full circle. If you face north, the stars move in a counter-clockwise direction, and if you face south, the stars move in a clockwise direction. But they are not actually moving. Rather, the stars only look like they are moving because Earth is rotating.

Think about riding a moving bus. If you look at the seats on the bus, they do not seem to be moving, and you do not seem to be moving either. Everything on the bus seems still because these things are moving with you. Similarly, if you look around you while standing on Earth, everything on Earth, including you, seems to stay still.

If you look out the window of a moving bus, buildings and trees appear to move past it. But you know that the buildings and trees are not moving. They only seem to move because you are moving in relation to everything outside of the bus. Like on the bus, if you look "outside" of Earth at the sky, you see that stars and other objects in space seem to be moving. But stars do not move in relation to Earth. Rather, you are moving in a circle as Earth rotates which makes objects that are not on Earth appear to move.

If you observed the stars throughout the night, they would appear to move. Each star trail in this picture shows the path of a star. But they only look like they are moving because Earth rotates.

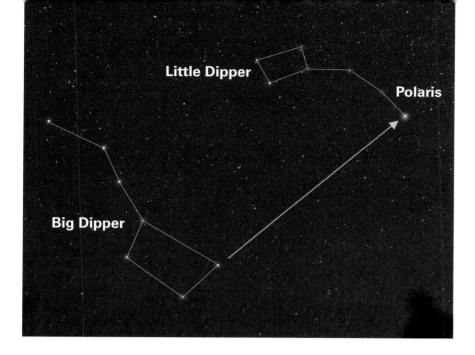

Polaris, the last star in the handle of the Little Dipper, is one star that does not seem to move in the sky. Since it does not move, you can use Polaris to help you navigate.

3. Using Stars and Star Patterns to Navigate

Oh, no—you are lost! What are you going to do? The first thing you should do is find out which direction is which. In the morning and evening, you can use the sun to determine the directions since it rises in the east and sets in the west. But what can you do when you are lost at night? Like people have been doing for thousands of years, you can use the stars to find your way around.

You just learned that the stars seem to move in the sky. So, how can you use them to find direction? Not all stars appear to move, so you can use these stars to help you determine which direction is which. One star is easy to see and always seems to stay in the same place. That star is Polaris, or the North Star, and can be seen from the Northern Hemisphere. There is another star that does not move in the sky, but it is much more difficult to see. That star is Polaris Australis, which can be seen from the Southern Hemisphere. Since it is not a very bright star, using it to navigate is not as easy as using Polaris.

Finding Polaris is easy if you are in the Northern Hemisphere. First, look at the night sky and find the Big Dipper, and then locate the last two stars that form the bowl of the Big Dipper. In your mind, draw a line connecting those two stars. Continue your imaginary line away from the bowl, going up from the top of the bowl. The first bright star that your line meets is Polaris. When you find Polaris, you will know which direction is north.

This picture shows the movement of stars over time with Polaris, or the North Star, in the center. Notice that Polaris does not appear to move, unlike the other stars around it.

4. Constellations Seem to Change With the Seasons

Orion is large and made of some of the brightest stars in the sky. So, it is one of the easiest star patterns to find. On a winter night in the Northern Hemisphere, you can probably see its brightly glowing stars. But if you look for Orion in the summer, you will not be able to find it at all. In fact, many stars that you can see in the winter are not visible in the summer, and many stars that you can see in the summer are not visible in the winter.

As you have learned, stars appear to move because Earth rotates. But another reason why they appear to move is because of Earth's orbit around the sun. If you observe a star pattern, such as Orion, at the same time of night for several weeks, you will see that its position in the sky changes. It may move higher or lower in the sky. Some stars, such as the stars around Polaris, never disappear from the sky. But other stars, such as those that form Orion, will rise and set as the seasons change.

The stars you see at night depend on which direction the part of Earth you are on is facing. As Earth moves around the sun in its orbit, the night side of Earth looks out into a different part of space. The night side of Earth is the part of Earth that faces away from the sun. During the winter, the night side of Earth faces the part of space that contains Orion. In the summer, the day side of Earth faces Orion. So, Orion is in the sky during winter nights and summer days. But you cannot see Orion when it is in the day sky because the sun is so bright that other stars are not visible.

Constellations seem to change positions in the sky with the seasons. This happens because of Earth's orbit around the sun. This illustration shows how Betelgeuse, the brightest star in Orion, cannot be seen in the summer.

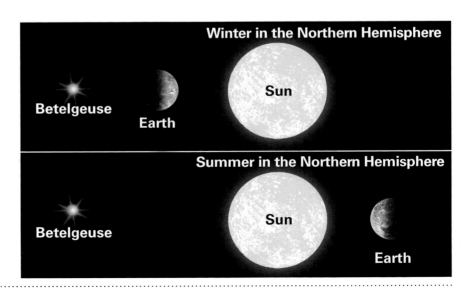

Winter in the Northern Hemisphere

Betelgeuse

Earth

Sun

Summer in the Northern Hemisphere

Betelgeuse

Sun

Earth

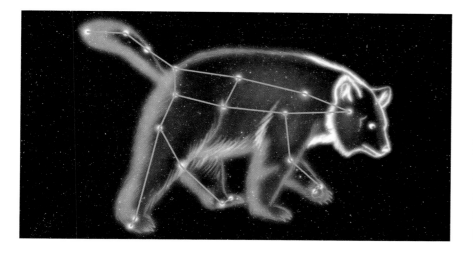

Stars do not actually form pictures in the sky. People just see pictures in the stars, which is why different people see different pictures. Many cultures have myths that go with constellations, such as Ursa Major.

5. People Use Constellations to Tell Stories

Have you ever looked at clouds and seen shapes of objects? Perhaps you saw a cloud that looked like a cat. Maybe your friend looked at the same cloud and saw a duck. People like to find familiar objects in things that do not have regular shapes. So, it is not surprising that people all over the world find pictures in the star patterns. But just as you and your friend saw different shapes in a cloud, different people see different pictures in the same patterns of stars.

You and your classmates probably call the seven bright stars in Ursa Major the Big Dipper. But people in England call it the Plough (spelled "Plow" in the United States). A plough is a tool used in farming. Slaves from the American South called the same pattern of stars the Drinking Gourd. Some cultures see a wagon or a coffin. So, the stars in a constellation do not actually form a picture in the sky. People just see pictures in the stars.

The Greek Myth of Ursa Major

Many cultures have myths about the pictures that they see in the sky. Many myths revolve around Ursa Major.

One Greek myth explains how Ursa Major formed. The myth says that Zeus, the king of the gods, fell in love with a woman named Callisto. Zeus's wife became jealous and turned Callisto into a bear. Callisto's son, who was a hunter, saw Callisto in bear form and tried to kill her. To stop the killing, Zeus turned her son into a bear and put both the mother and the son in the sky. They became Ursa Major and Ursa Minor—the Big Bear and the Little Bear.

Different groups of people see different pictures in the same constellation. Many groups, such as the Blackfoot Nation, see pictures based on myths in their culture.

The Blackfoot Myth of Ursa Major

The Blackfoot Nation is a group of American Indian tribes that originally lived in parts of what is now the United States and Canada. Like the Greek myth of Ursa Major, the Blackfoot myth involves people becoming stars.

According to the myth, a young woman fell in love with a bear. When her father learned of this, he became angry and told his sons to kill the bear. When the bear died, the woman was turned into a bear by magic. As a bear, the woman became angry and chased after her little sister and seven brothers. When she chased them, her youngest brother shot an arrow into the sky so that he and his siblings could escape. The brothers and sister followed the arrow and became the stars of the Big Dipper.

Other American Indian myths about Ursa Major are also about bears. But what happens in each story is different. In some stories, the stars in the handle of the Big Dipper are hunters chasing a bear.

The Arab Myth of Ursa Major

Ursa Major does not represent a bear in Arab culture. Instead, the bowl of the Big Dipper is a coffin. The stars in the handle are grieving people following the coffin. According to the Arab myth, the person in the coffin is a man named al-Naash. Two of the stars in the handle represent his son and daughter. Al-Naash was killed by a person named al-Jadi, who is represented in the sky by the North Star.

6. Scientists Use Star Charts to Map the Sky

Most people use the word *constellation* to describe parts of the sky with recognizable star patterns. But to the ancient Greeks, constellations were more than just pictures formed by star patterns. They were also areas in the sky around these star patterns. Today, **astronomers**, or scientists who study objects and energy in space, still think of constellations as areas in the sky.

When you look at a map of the United States, you see that the land is divided up in to different states. The map shows where borders are between states. These borders can help you describe places in the United States. For example, suppose you wanted to explain where the Great Salt Lake is. You would find it on the map and say that it is in Utah. Astronomers use constellation borders in a similar way that we use the state borders on a map.

Like the ancient Greeks, astronomers today divide the sky into areas called constellations. The constellations have borders. The entire sky is divided into constellations, just like how all of the United States is divided into states.

When astronomers describe where stars or other objects in space are, they use star charts. For example, M81 is a group of stars that is visible from Earth. M81 is not part of the star pattern Ursa Major. But astronomers describe it as being in the constellation Ursa Major because it is located in that part of the sky. Astronomers describe it as in this place because they divide the sky into constellations. So, a constellation and the sky around it are grouped together.

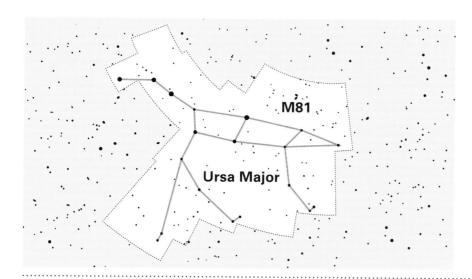

The constellation Ursa Major is an area in the sky surrounding the star pattern also known as Ursa Major. Although the group of stars M81 is not part of the star pattern Ursa Major, astronomers describe it as located in the constellation Ursa Major.

Astronomers worldwide have agreed on the names of the constellations. This makes communicating information to each other easier.

Different cultures see different star patterns. They have also come up with different systems for mapping star patterns. But astronomers around the world have agreed on the borders and names of the constellations.

This agreement helps astronomers communicate information. An astronomer can name an area in the sky, and others will understand what he or she is talking about. In casual conversations, astronomers have different names for constellations. Astronomers in the United States talk about the Big Dipper. Astronomers in England talk about the Plough. But astronomers from both countries use the same name when describing something they are studying in the night sky. They all use the name Ursa Major. This common name lets astronomers easily understand each other. It lets them know that they are talking about an area in the sky, not about a star pattern.

Star patterns still help astronomers find the various constellations. Think about a map of the United States that does not show the state's borders. It is not easy to find where the states are on this map. But you can use landforms and bodies of water to locate states. For example, the eastern border of Iowa has a "nose," or a place where the land sticks out and looks like a nose. This nose is formed by a bend in the Mississippi river. If you find this bend on a map of the United States, you can find the eastern border of Iowa. Astronomers can use star patterns in the same way. They can find Ursa Major by finding the Big Dipper or other stars in the constellation.

How Do Stars Appear to Move During the Night and Year?

1. Star Patterns Form Pictures in the Sky   Sections of the sky have star patterns that create recognizable pictures. These sections of the sky are called constellations. People have been seeing these patterns in the sky for thousands of years.

2. Stars Seem to Move During the Night   When you look at the stars from Earth, they appear to be moving in an arc. If you could see the stars for an entire day, they would appear to move in a full circle. But the stars are not actually moving. They only appear to be moving because Earth rotates.

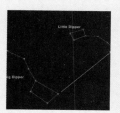

3. Using Stars and Star Patterns to Navigate   Not all stars appear to move in the sky. Polaris, or the North Star, can be seen from the Northern Hemisphere, and does not appear to move in the sky. So, you can use the North Star to determine which direction is north.

4. Constellations Seem to Change With the Seasons   Star patterns change positions in the sky over time. So, many constellations can only be seen during certain seasons. They appear to move because of Earth's orbit around the sun over the course of a year.

5. People Use Constellations to Tell Stories   Many people see pictures in star patterns because people like to see familiar objects in things that do not have a regular shape. Different people and cultures see different objects in the same constellation.

6. Scientists Use Star Charts to Map the Sky   Astronomers use maps that divide the sky into areas called constellations. They use constellations to describe where objects are in the sky. Astronomers around the world have agreed on the names of these constellations so that they can communicate their findings.

Animal Navigators

When you travel to some place new, you might use a map or a GPS device to get where you are going. Many animals travel to different places without the help of a map or GPS. How do these animals know where to go?

Suppose you have a friend who lives on the block next to yours. You could get to your friend's home easily without a map. But what if your friend lived farther away? Would you be able to go across town without a map? What if you had to go to another city? Traveling long distances without a map and without getting lost is not very easy. But many animals do it all the time.

Some animals migrate. To migrate means to move from one area to another at different times of the year. Animals of all kinds migrate. Some animals walk, some fly, and others swim. Animals often migrate hundreds or thousands of kilometers at one time. And, they can do it without getting lost. Scientists who study migrating animals think that the animals use clues in nature to help them get from one place to another. For example, some animals might use familiar landmarks to figure out where they are. Other animals may use Earth's magnetic field to navigate.

However, scientists have learned that some animals navigate in the same way that people do: by using the stars. The stars in the night sky form predictable patterns. Like people, some animals can recognize these patterns and use them to find their way around.

Wildebeest are animals that live in Africa. They migrate thousands of kilometers each year without getting lost.

Dung beetles roll balls of animal droppings until they find a safe place to eat. At night, the beetles use the Milky Way to keep them moving in a straight line.

Bug Eyes

One animal that navigates by starlight is the dung beetle. Dung beetles are African insects that eat—you guessed it—dung! Dung is the droppings from animals. When a beetle finds a dung pile, it rolls the dung into a ball. It then quickly rolls the ball away to keep it from other dung beetles. The beetle runs in a straight line to get as far away as possible in the shortest amount of time. Scientists observing dung beetles wondered how the beetles manage to keep running in a straight line despite obstacles.

A group of scientists ran several tests to see how the beetles navigated. The scientists thought that the beetles used objects in the night sky to guide them. So they tried different ways of blocking the beetles' view of the moon and stars. They even put little hats on the beetles that kept them from seeing any sky! With the beetles' views blocked, the scientists put the beetles in the middle of an enclosed area. Then they timed how long the beetles took to get to the edge of the area.

Eventually, the scientists determined that the dung beetles were using the Milky Way as a guide. The Milky Way is the glowing band of stars that you can see in the night sky. As long as the beetles could see the Milky Way, they ran quickly to the edge of the area.

Bird Brained

Although dung beetles use the stars to navigate, they do not depend on the stars to guide them for very long distances. Other animals, however, do use the stars to travel far. Birds are known to migrate thousand of kilometers from season to season. Scientists have several ideas on how birds navigate, some of which they have tested. Scientists have found that different kinds of birds navigate in various ways. For example, a scientist showed that indigo buntings, a kind of bird, use the stars to find their way.

To determine whether indigo buntings used the stars, the scientist studying them had to control the stars. But of course, he could not control the real stars. So, he used a planetarium. A *planetarium* is building that has a dome-shaped ceiling. A machine in the middle of the building projects points of light onto the ceiling. The points of light look like the stars in the sky.

The scientist put groups of indigo buntings into the same planetarium, but showed the groups different things. One group saw a normal night sky. The stars rotated around the North Star. Another group saw the stars rotating around a star called Betelgeuse. When it was time for the birds to migrate to the south, the scientist put the birds in special cages inside the planetarium and observed which way the birds wanted to fly. The birds in the first group turned away from the North Star to fly south. The birds in the second group turned away from Betelgeuse thinking that it was the North Star. The experiment showed that indigo buntings recognized north by the motion of the stars.

A scientist studies whether indigo buntings migrate using the stars. The five circular containers are special birdcages. The machine on the right projects the stars onto the ceiling of the planetarium.

A Whale of a Time

Another animal that may use the stars to navigate is the humpback whale. It is hard to believe because whales spend so much time underwater. But scientists who study humpback-whale migration think that the whales use several methods of navigation, including using objects in the night sky. Whales do have to come to the surface of the water to breathe. Perhaps they take a peek at the sky when they do.

To study whale migration, scientists put electronic tags on several humpback whales. The tags sent out radio signals that were tracked using satellites. The scientists found that the whales traveled in very straight lines for thousands of kilometers. The scientists think that the whales could not keep such straight lines by relying on only one method of navigation. They think the whales use a combination of the sun, the moon, the stars, and Earth's magnetic field to navigate. However, the scientists will have a hard time testing whether whales navigate by starlight. They cannot put the whales in a planetarium!

Migration and navigation are two curious animal behaviors. Scientists use different methods to learn how animals travel around with out getting lost. They know that some animals navigate in the same ways that people can. But with all of today's detailed maps and GPS devices, most people no longer use the stars to navigate. So, maybe dung beetles and indigo buntings have a skill that you do not have!

A scientist uses a long pole to attach a tag to the back of a humpback whale. The tag sends out a radio signal that the scientists can track using satellites.

How Does the Moon Seem to Move and Change Shape?

Science Vocabulary

full moon

moon phases

new moon

waning

waxing

If you observe the moon for several days, you would see that it appears to change in two different ways. You will discover that these changes happen in a pattern. The first is that the moon rises and sets in a regular pattern, just like the sun. The second is that the moon appears to change shape over a month. These two patterns of the moon are related to each other.

 **NGSS** **5-ESS1-2.** Represent data in graphical displays to reveal patterns of daily changes in length and direction of shadows, day and night, and the seasonal appearance of some stars in the night sky.

ESS1.B. The orbits of Earth around the sun and of the moon around Earth, together with the rotation of Earth about an axis between its North and South poles, cause observable patterns. These include day and night; daily changes in the length and direction of shadows; and different positions of the sun, moon, and stars at different times of the day, month, and year.

Patterns Similarities and differences in patterns can be used to sort, classify, communicate, and analyze simple rates of change for natural phenomena.

Analyzing and Interpreting Data

1. The Sun Lights Up the Moon

When you look at the moon, what do you see? Some nights, you might look up and see a full circle or an oval lighting up the night sky. Other nights, you might see only a sliver of the moon glowing amongst the stars. Why does the moon appear to glow?

The moon does not give off any of its own light. Instead, the moon appears to glow because it reflects the sun's light that shines on it. The sun casts its light on the surface of the moon, lighting up an area of it. The moon then reflects the sun's light. Some of the light goes toward Earth, so from Earth, the moon appears to give off light. But if you were to observe the moon in space, it would appear to glow, too.

Just like Earth, the moon is shaped like a ball, so only part of the moon can be lit up by the sun at once. Recall that the sun shines its light on Earth, causing day and night. Also, remember that the sun only casts its light on the part of Earth that is facing it. Similarly, the sun cannot cast its light on the entire surface of the moon at once. The sun can only cast its light on the part of the moon that is facing it, which is similar to how the sun causes day on Earth. The part of the moon that is facing away from the sun is not lit up and is completely dark, which is similar to night on Earth. So, just like Earth, the moon always has one side that is lit up by the sun and one side that is dark.

Even though the moon appears to glow from Earth, it does not give off its own light. Instead, the sun casts its own light on the moon. Like Earth, only part of the moon can be lit up by the sun at once.

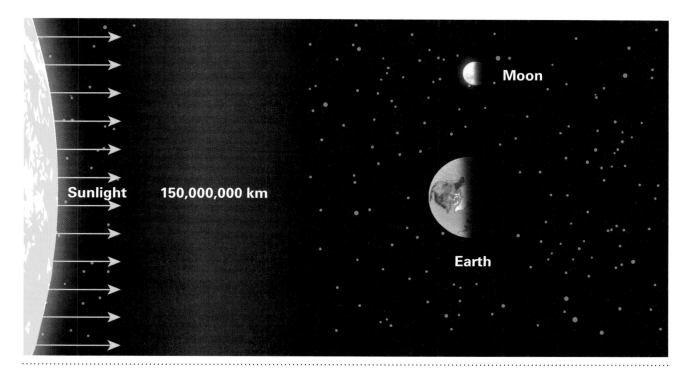

Sunlight   150,000,000 km   Moon

Earth

2. The Moon Rises and Sets in a Pattern

When you think about the moon, you probably picture it glowing in the night sky. But if you were to observe the moon, you would see that it is only visible at certain times because it rises and sets. Why does the moon rise and set?

Earth's Rotation and the Moon

Like the sun, the moon rises and sets in a pattern. It rises in the east and sets in the west. Also like the sun, the moon rises and sets because Earth rotates about its own axis. This causes a different part of Earth to always be facing the moon. When you are on the part of Earth that faces the moon, the moon is in the sky. When the part of Earth you are on faces away from the moon, the moon has already set.

The Moon's Orbit

The moon does not rise and set at the same time as the sun. It also does not rise and set at the same time every day. Some days, the moon rises when the sun rises, and other days, it rises when the sun sets. The moon can also rise at midnight or in middle of the afternoon. Why does the moon rise and set at a different time each day?

The moon rises and sets in a pattern, but it does not rise and set at the same time every day. Some nights it might rise in the afternoon, and other nights it might rise at night. It rises and sets at different times each day because the moon orbits Earth.

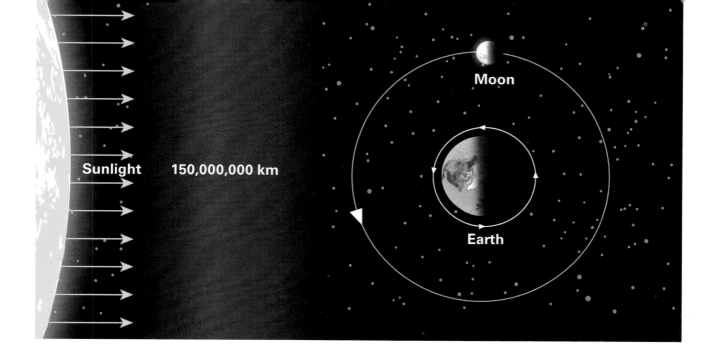

Two factors affect the way that the moon appears to move. The first is Earth's rotation. Since it takes Earth 24 hours to complete its rotation, it takes the moon about 24 hours to rise, set, and rise again, just like the sun. But this pattern of the moon rising and setting takes slightly more than 24 hours. This is because the moon's orbit around Earth is the second factor that affects the way the moon appears to move. So when Earth completes one full rotation, the moon appears to have moved from its initial position. It appears in a slightly different part of the sky. For example, if the moon rose at 10:00 P.M. one day, the next day it would rise at about 11:00 P.M.

Each day the moon rises a little bit later. After about a month, these time changes eventually add up so that the moon rises at about the same time as it did a month before. This causes the moon cycle to repeat. For example, if the moon rose at 10:00 P.M., a month later it would rise at about 10:00 P.M. again.

The moon appears to take longer to rise and set than the sun. Think about riding in a car. If you look out the window at a still object, like a street sign, you pass it quickly. But if you look at a car going in the same direction as you, but moving slower, it takes longer for your car to pass the other one. Like the street sign, the sun is moving slowly relative to Earth. But the moon is like the other car. It is moving faster than the sun relative to Earth. So, the moon seems to take a longer time to rise, move across the sky, and set than the sun.

Every day, the moon appears to rise and set. This happens because the moon orbits Earth, and Earth rotates. Because a full rotation takes Earth 24 hours, it takes slightly more than 24 hours for the moon to rise, set, and rise again.

3. Moon Phases Follow a Pattern

When you look up at the night sky, the moon might look like a round disc. At other times, the moon might look like a half circle or a thin C shape. On some nights, you might not be able to see the moon at all!

If you keep track of the shape of the moon each night, you will notice that its shape changes in a pattern. The moon's shape seems to get thinner and less round over time and eventually disappears for a night. When it reappears the next night, it seems to get thicker and rounder until it looks completely round again. This pattern repeats about every month.

The actual shape of the moon does not change, but the lit part of the moon that you can see from Earth does change shape. These different shapes of the lit part of the moon are called **moon phases**. The moon phases change in a monthly pattern because the moon moves around Earth about once each month.

The pattern of moon phases begins when the moon appears completely dark, and you cannot see the moon at all. In this phase, the moon is a **new moon**. Over the next few days, you can see a sliver of the lit part of the moon, which appears in the shape of a backward-C. Whenever the moon appears to be in a backward-C shape or a C shape, it is a *crescent moon*. For about two weeks after the new moon, the moon appears to get bigger. During this time, people say that it is **waxing**, or growing slowly. The backward-C-shaped moon is therefore a *waxing crescent moon*.

The first of the moon phases is the new moon, which is when the moon cannot be seen. For about two weeks after the new moon, the moon appears to be waxing.

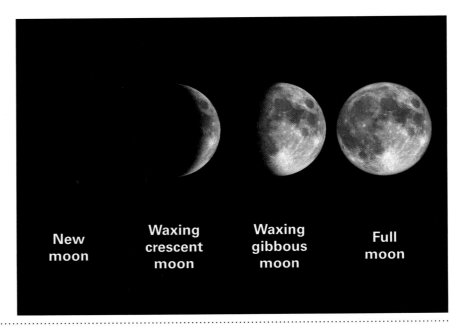

| New moon | Waxing crescent moon | Waxing gibbous moon | Full moon |

About a week after the new moon, the moon looks like a half circle. At this point, the moon is one quarter of the way through the cycle of moon phases, so this phase is called the *first quarter*. Over the next week, the lit part of the moon appears to grow and more of the moon can be seen from Earth. During this time, the moon looks like an oval. An oval-shaped moon is a *gibbous moon*. The gibbous moon that appears after the first quarter is a *waxing gibbous moon* because it still appears to be getting bigger.

About two weeks after the new moon, the side of the moon facing Earth is completely lit, and the moon looks like a perfect circle. This moon phase is the **full moon**. During a full moon, the moon is halfway through its cycle of phases. For about two weeks after the full moon, the moon appears to shrink. During this time, people say that it is **waning**, or getting smaller.

After the full moon, the moon is a gibbous moon again. This time, it is a *waning gibbous moon*. Then, about a week after the full moon, the moon looks like a half circle again. This moon phase is the *last quarter* because the moon is three quarters done with its cycle.

Over the last week of the cycle, the shape of the moon narrows and appears to be a thin C shape. This C-shaped moon is called a *waning crescent moon*. The waning crescent moon slowly grows smaller as time passes. Finally, the moon seems to disappear because it is a new moon again, and the pattern of moon phases starts over and repeats.

Waning gibbous moon　　**Waning crescent moon**　　**New moon**

Halfway through its cycle of phases, the moon looks like a perfect circle and is called a full moon. Then, the moon appears to be waning. In the last quarter, the moon is called a waning crescent moon.

4. The Moon's Patterns Are Related

You have learned about two of the moon's patterns. The first pattern is that the moon rises and sets at different times, just like the sun. The second pattern is that the part of the moon lit up by the sun changes, so the moon seems to change shape in a pattern. Both of these patterns take about a month to complete a full cycle.

These two patterns are very closely related to each other. If you know when the moon will rise on a certain day, you can predict what phase it will be on that day. Similarly, if you know what the moon's phase will be, you can predict when it will rise.

Here's how the two patterns work together. When the moon is in the new moon phase, it rises at about the same time as the sun. The moon is in the sky through the daylight hours and sets at around the same time as the sun. As the moon rises later in the day, it grows into a crescent. When the moon rises at about noon, it is at first quarter moon. During this phase, it sets at around midnight. A waxing gibbous moon rises in the afternoon and sets after midnight. When the moon is full, it rises at around the same time that the sun sets, and it sets at around the same time that the sun rises. A full moon is in the sky all night, but it is not during the day.

This pattern continues for all of the waning moon phases. Waning gibbous, last quarter, and waning crescent moons all rise during different parts of the night, and set during different parts of the day.

The two patterns of the moon are related to each other. So, during each phase, the moon rises at the same time. For example, a waxing crescent moon rises at about the same time as the sun rises. But a full moon rises when the sun sets.

Waxing Crescent Moon

Full Moon

How Does the Moon Seem to Move and Change Shape?

1. The Sun Lights Up the Moon   The moon does not give off its own light. Instead, it appears to glow because the sun casts its light on the moon. The sun can only cast its light on one part of the moon at once. This is similar to how the sun shines its light on Earth, causing day and night. So, like Earth, the moon always has one side that is lit up and one side that is dark.

2. The Moon Rises and Sets in a Pattern   The moon rises in the east and sets in the west, just like the sun. It rises and sets because Earth rotates. It takes about 24 hours for the moon to rise, set, and rise again. The moon rises and sets a little bit later each day until the moon is rising and setting at the same time as before. This pattern takes about one month to repeat.

3. Moon Phases Follow a Pattern   The moon's shape changes over the course of about a month. The phases are new moon, waxing crescent moon, first quarter, waxing gibbous moon, full moon, waning gibbous moon, last quarter, and waning crescent moon. As the moon passes through these phases, it seems to get more round until it is completely round. Then it seems to get less round until it is no longer visible.

4. The Moon's Patterns Are Related   The two patterns of the moon are closely related to each other. So, if you know what time the moon will rise on a certain day, you can also predict which phase it will be in. Likewise, if you know which phase the moon will be in, you can predict when it will rise. Different phases of the moon rise during different parts of the day or night and set during different parts of the day or night.

Apollo 8's Journey to the Far Side

The full moon always looks the same because one side of the moon always faces Earth. The other side of the moon is often called the far side of the moon. Who were the first to see the far side, and how did they get there?

One side of the moon always faces Earth. The other side is called the far side of the moon. In 1962 President John F. Kennedy set a challenge to go to the moon before the end of the 1960s.

"We choose to go to the moon. We choose to go to the moon in this decade." Those words were spoken by President John F. Kennedy on September 12, 1962. With the words he set a challenge and a deadline. He wanted an astronaut from the United States to set foot on the moon before the end of the 1960s. The challenge was huge. At the time of the speech, the longest that an American astronaut had spent in space was just under five hours. Traveling all the way to the moon seemed impossible.

Nevertheless, the engineers at NASA embraced the challenge. They began the Apollo space program. Not quite seven years later, in July of 1969, as part of the Apollo 11 mission, Neil Armstrong became the first person to stand on the moon. But many things had to happen before Apollo 11 met Kennedy's challenge. The early years and missions of the Apollo program were all about testing the equipment and procedures that would be used to get a man on the moon.

For years, NASA engineers designed, built, and tested various parts of the moon program. They tested the rocket, the spacecraft, and the lander that would take the astronauts to the surface of the moon. Finally, in December 1968, NASA was ready to send people to the moon.

William Anders, James Lovell, and Frank Borman made up the crew of Apollo 8.

Where No One Has Gone Before

Contrary to what you might think, Apollo 11 was not the first crewed mission to the moon. Apollo 8 was. People do not remember the Apollo 8 mission the same way that they remember Apollo 11 because the astronauts on the mission did not step on the moon. However, the mission was still very important and had its own share of "firsts."

Apollo 8 lifted off from Cape Kennedy in Florida (now the Kennedy Space Center) on December 21, 1968. The astronauts on board were Frank Borman, William Anders, and James Lovell. Borman and Lovell had been in space before, but this mission was Anders's first trip. However, all three had been training for years for this moment. The astronauts orbited Earth twice and then set off for the moon. They were the first people to leave Earth's orbit. They were traveling farther than any human had ever traveled. On the way to the moon, they were the first people to see the Earth as a globe. The three astronauts were really going where no one had gone before!

The main goal of the Apollo 8 mission was to test that the spacecraft—and the people inside—could travel to the moon and come back again safely. The mission achieved that goal and many others. The astronauts showed that they could correctly adjust the direction of the spacecraft, that they could put the spacecraft in orbit around the moon, and that they could send radio and television signals from the moon back to Earth. They also took photos of the moon's surface to find good landing sites for future missions.

Blackout!

Apollo 8's trip to the moon lasted seven days, and the spacecraft worked perfectly. All the astronauts had to do was wait and take photos. But, as they got close to the moon, they prepared for one of the most frightening parts of the mission. They were going to the far side of the moon. The far side of the moon was a mystery. A Soviet space probe had taken blurry photos of the far side in 1959, but no person had ever looked directly at it. That was about to change.

Of course, for the Apollo 8 astronauts, looking at the far side was not as important as the other things they had to do. When the spacecraft was behind the moon, they had to fire the engines just enough to put the craft into orbit around the moon. If the engine burn did not go correctly, they might crash into the moon. What made the engine burn even more nerve-wracking was that the astronauts could not talk to engineers on Earth as they did it. Radio signals that the astronauts and engineers used to talk to each other could not go through the moon. So, the entire time that Apollo 8 was behind the moon, they were in radio blackout.

On board Apollo 8, the astronauts worked quickly, making calculations and doing the procedures that they had practiced in training. On Earth, NASA's engineers could only wait. They knew how long Apollo 8 was supposed to be behind the moon. If Apollo 8 appeared too early, they would know that the astronauts could not put the spacecraft into orbit and that the mission was aborted. If Apollo 8 did not appear on time, it meant that the astronauts were not coming home.

The most famous photo from Apollo 8 is the Earthrise photo. William Anders took the photo during one of the times that the spacecraft came around from the far side of the moon.

On the Flip Side

The engineers on Earth cheered. Apollo 8 had indeed appeared from the far side of the moon right on schedule. The engine burn had gone as planned, and the spacecraft was orbiting the moon. The astronauts orbited the moon 10 times during the next 20 hours. During this time, they took a lot of photos and video of the moon's surface. As the first people to actually go to the far, or dark, side of the moon, they took the first clear photos of that hidden side.

The common term *dark side* of the moon is misleading. Some might think that *dark* means "no light." In reality, both the near and far sides receive almost equal amounts of light from the sun. Only during a full moon (as you see it from Earth) is the far side of the moon physically dark.

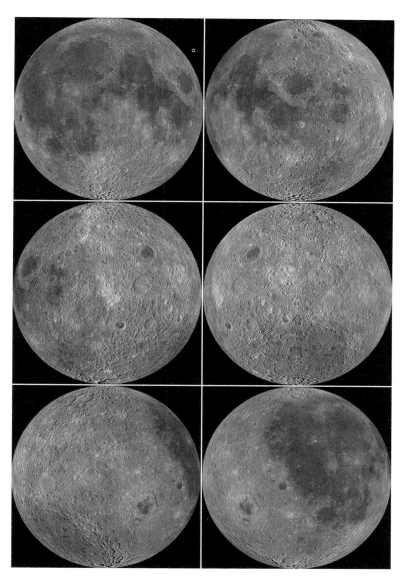

The dark splotches that you see on the face of a full moon are called seas. The far side of the moon does not have very many seas.

Apollo 8's photos and those taken by later Apollo astronauts show that the moon's far side looks very different from its near side. Both sides are covered with craters where the moon had been hit by asteroids and meteorites. But, the moon's near side also has many large, dark, flat areas. The moon's far side has only a few of these flat areas, and they are much smaller.

The Apollo 8 crew returned to Earth on December 27, 1968. The mission was a huge success. The moon landings of later Apollo missions would not have been possible without the work of those on Apollo 8. Because of Anders, Lovell, and Borman, President Kennedy's goal and dream were fulfilled. And, they finally got to see a world that no one had ever set eyes on before.

What Tools Do Scientists Use to Observe Space?

Science Vocabulary

lens

radio telescope

reflecting telescope

refracting telescope

space telescope

telescope

Have you ever looked up into the sky and wondered what is in space? You can probably see the stars and moon in the night sky, but these objects look very small. You will learn about telescopes, tools that make detailed images of objects in space so that scientists can study them. Scientists have designed different types of telescopes to observe different objects in space.

 NGSS

5-ESS1-1. Support an argument that differences in the apparent brightness of the sun compared to other stars is due to their relative distances from Earth.

ESS1.A. The sun is a star that appears larger and brighter than other stars because it is closer. Stars range greatly in their distance from Earth.

Scale, Proportion, and Quantity Natural objects exist from the very small to the immensely large.

 Engaging in Argument from Evidence

1. Tools Help Scientists See Light from Stars

Suppose that you are outside on a summer day and that the sun is shining so brightly, you have to wear sunglasses. What makes the sun shine?

Deep inside of all stars, including the sun, a reaction happens that releases a lot of energy, which causes stars to shine. Some of this energy is carried away from the star by light. Much of the light travels away from the stars to Earth, where it can be seen. But because the stars are so far away from Earth, they only look like tiny points of light.

Stars give off different types of light. You cannot see some of these types, even if they travel to Earth. This is because some types of light are not visible to humans. Infrared light is one example of a type of light that you cannot see. However, scientists have developed tools that can detect infrared. These tools let scientists study stars and other objects in space that they could otherwise not see.

Every star's light travels away from the star in all directions. Although stars produce a lot of light, most of it is not headed toward Earth. So, only a small amount of a star's light reaches Earth. Since so little light from stars reaches Earth, scientists build tools that bend and gather as much light as possible to observe them. A tool that bends light is called a *lens*.

Light carries energy away from a star. It travels in all directions. So, some of this light reaches Earth, but most of it does not. So, scientists need tools to see the light more clearly.

Stars give off different types of light. Some of the light from stars reaches Earth, but most of it does not.

2. Lenses Refract Light

Suppose you and your family are camping. When it gets dark, you use a flashlight. The beam of light shines straight in the direction that the flashlight is pointing.

The beam from a flashlight makes a straight line because light travels in a straight line. Since light travels in straight lines, scientists often use arrows, called rays, to model light.

Light can travel through different materials. It can even cross from one material into another. For example, the light from a flashlight first passes through the air that surrounds the light bulb and then passes through the glass on the front of the flashlight. Finally, it passes through the air around the flashlight. When light moves from one material to another, it can change directions, or bend. The bending of light as it passes from one material to another is called *refraction*.

Refracting light can make images easier to see. A **lens** is a clear object that refracts light. Some lenses refract light so that light rays come together, or focus. Other lenses refract light so that light rays spread apart. All lenses form images. For example, when you watch a movie, you see images on a screen. Those images form when light from the projector passes through a lens and travels to the screen. The lens focuses the light on the screen, and you can see an image.

Everything you see can be seen because lenses focus light. Each of your eyes has a lens that focuses light on the back of your eye. Nerves detect this light, and your brain interprets it as images.

A lens is a tool that refracts, or bends, light. Here, a lens bends three beams of light so that the light rays come together. Other lenses refract light so that the light rays spread apart.

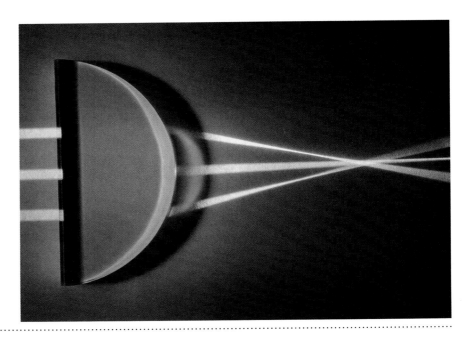

Refracting telescopes, like this one, use a lens to collect and focus light. They are useful for studying objects that are bright and not very far away.

Nature of Science

3. Refracting Telescopes

If you search the Web, you can find many detailed images of stars and other objects in space. But if you look up in the sky, you will not see these details. You will not even see most of these objects! This is because many of these images were taken with telescopes.

A **telescope** is a tool that collects light and focuses it to make an image. Telescopes make objects that are far away look larger. A telescope allows people to observe objects that they cannot see with just their eyes.

One type of telescope is called a refracting telescope. It was the first type of telescope ever invented. A **refracting telescope** is a telescope that uses lenses to collect and focus light. A simple refracting telescope has a large lens at the front of the telescope. This lens gathers light from distant objects and focuses it inside the telescope tube. You can look through the telescope's eyepiece to see the image inside the telescope tube.

Refracting telescopes are useful for studying objects in space that are bright and not very far away. For example, you can look at the moon with a refracting telescope. But refracting telescopes are not good for looking at dim objects or objects that are very far away. To collect light from these objects, a refracting telescope needs a very big lens. Big lenses are heavy and hard to make. Heavy lenses do not hold their shape, so they cannot focus light properly.

A telescope collects and concentrates light to make large images of distant objects. These large images allow people to see more details than they can with just their eyes.

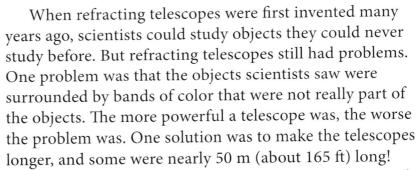

Engineering Design

4. Isaac Newton and Reflecting Telescopes

Sir Isaac Newton solved the problems of the refracting telescope by designing the reflecting telescope.

When refracting telescopes were first invented many years ago, scientists could study objects they could never study before. But refracting telescopes still had problems. One problem was that the objects scientists saw were surrounded by bands of color that were not really part of the objects. The more powerful a telescope was, the worse the problem was. One solution was to make the telescopes longer, and some were nearly 50 m (about 165 ft) long!

Sir Isaac Newton was an English scientist who wanted another solution to this problem. So, he decided to design one. His first step was to clearly define the problem. Then he had to think about the solution. His *criteria*, or requirements, for a successful solution were that the telescope needed to be small but still make objects look larger. His *constraint*, or restriction, was that he could only use a certain type of mirror.

In 1672, Newton published his idea about why refracting telescopes had problems with color. He correctly thought that lenses bend different colored light differently. So, his solution had to include a material other than a lens. Newton used a mirror instead. He made a curved mirror, which bends colors of light in the same way. The result was the first reflecting telescope! A **reflecting telescope** is a telescope that uses a mirror rather than a lens to gather and focus light.

Reflecting telescopes have other advantages. Large mirrors do not have the same problems with color as large lenses. This is why most large modern telescopes are reflecting telescopes, not refracting telescopes.

Reflecting telescopes use curved mirrors instead of lenses to gather and focus light. They have many advantages and can be much larger than refracting telescopes.

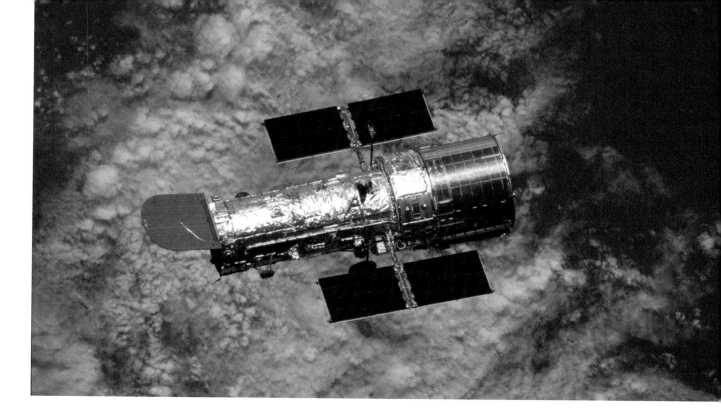

5. Space Telescopes

One reason astronomers use telescopes in space is because a layer of gases surrounds Earth. This layer is called the atmosphere. Although the atmosphere is good for supporting life, it is not good for studying space because it blocks a lot of the light that travels from the stars to Earth. The atmosphere also causes images gathered by telescopes to be blurry. To avoid these problems, scientists and engineers have put some telescopes into space.

A **space telescope** is a telescope that works in space, beyond Earth's atmosphere. The most famous space telescope is the Hubble Space Telescope. Hubble was sent into space in 1990. It is a reflecting telescope that orbits Earth. Hubble lets scientists see farther into space than any telescope on Earth's surface.

By using data from Hubble, scientists have learned a lot about space. Hubble has photographed galaxies that had never been seen before. A galaxy is a large group of stars. Data gathered by Hubble has even shown that galaxies can collide and join together.

Hubble has also taken a lot of images of nebulas, which are clouds of gas and dust in space. Some nebulas form when a star explodes. From Hubble's photos, scientists have learned that stars die.

The Hubble Space Telescope is a telescope that orbits Earth, beyond Earth's atmosphere.

Only space telescopes can gather light from nebulas and other distant objects in space. This image of a nebula was captured by the Hubble Space Telescope.

Radio telescopes gather radio waves, or light that we cannot see. The Very Large Array is a group of antennas in Socorro, New Mexico. It is the largest radio telescope in the world.

6. Radio Telescopes

So far, you have learned about telescopes that gather visible light, which is light that you can see. These telescopes are used to see stars in space. But some telescopes gather light that you cannot see.

Stars give off many kinds of light, but not all of the light is visible light. For example, infrared light and radio waves are types of light that your eyes cannot see, even with lenses. So that scientists can further study stars, some telescopes are built to gather these other types of light.

A **radio telescope** is a telescope that can gather radio waves. Radio waves are a kind of light you cannot see with your eyes. These telescopes do not look like those that collect visible light. They also do not use lenses or mirrors. Instead, radio telescopes are large antennas. The Very Large Array in New Mexico is a group of 27 antennas. It is one of the most powerful radio telescope in the world.

When scientists use radio telescopes, they cannot look into eyepieces and see images. This is because radio waves are invisible. Instead, scientists use computers to create images. Computers receive radio waves as data, which are analyzed. The computers are then used to make pictures. With images, scientists are able to observe stars and other objects in space that give off radio waves.

What Tools Do Scientists Use to Observe Space?

1. Tools Help Scientists See Light from Stars All stars shine because they give off light. Some of this light travels to Earth, but most of it does not. In order to see this light, scientists use a lens, or a tool that gathers and bends light.

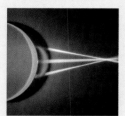

2. Lenses Refract Light Light travels in a straight line. It can pass through many materials and can cross from one material to another. When light crosses materials, it can bend, or refract. A lens bends light and focuses it or spreads it apart to form an image.

3. Refracting Telescopes A telescope is a tool that collects and focuses light. A refracting telescope uses a lens to collect and focus light. Scientists use refracting telescopes to observe objects in space that are bright or not very far away.

4. Isaac Newton and Reflecting Telescopes Large telescopes use curved mirrors instead of lenses to collect and focus light. Telescopes that use mirrors are called reflecting telescopes. Scientists use reflecting telescopes to observe objects in space that are dim or very far away.

5. Space Telescopes Earth's atmosphere makes it difficult to see some objects in space. So, scientists place some telescopes in space beyond Earth's atmosphere. These telescopes are called space telescopes. The most famous one is the Hubble Space Telescope.

6. Radio Telescopes Stars give off many types of light. We can only see visible light. Radio telescopes gather radio waves, a type of light we cannot see. Radio telescopes use antennas that send data to a computer. The computers then make images.

The Best Place for a Telescope

Scientists use telescopes to study distant stars. But scientists cannot simply place telescopes wherever they want. Different factors affect how well a telescope can gather light. Where is the best place on Earth for a telescope?

Using a telescope just outside of a city is better than using it inside the city. But moving it far away from the city would be even better.

Suppose that you get a telescope for your birthday. Where would you set it up to get a good view of the stars? Just outside your home would be convenient and easy to get to. A nearby park might work if it did not have too many trees. But, if you live in a city, you might find that you cannot see very many more stars using your telescope than you can see without it. Instead, you could pack up your telescope and head out to the country, where you can get a better view.

You can easily carry a small telescope around until you find a good place to stargaze. But the telescopes that scientists use to do research are much too big to move. Once they are built, they have to stay where they are. So, scientists have to carefully pick where they put their telescopes. Space is an excellent place for a telescope, but putting telescopes in space is difficult and expensive. As a result, many telescopes are built on Earth.

Most telescopes that scientists use for research are built in remote locations. That means the telescopes are placed far away from any large cities. Several factors determine why these locations are good for telescopes.

Less Light

The biggest reason why telescopes are placed in remote locations is to keep them away from light pollution. Light pollution is any unwanted light. The light pollution that bothers people studying the stars is light that shines up into the sky. Light from cities causes the air and sky above the city to glow. This glow is light pollution. It reduces the visibility of stars and other objects in space. The more people that live in an area, the more light pollution that area has. This is because more people means more buildings, more cars, and more streetlights. So, putting telescopes far away from where people live means that the telescope is also far away from sources of light pollution.

The Mauna Kea Observatories, which has thirteen telescopes, is an example of an observatory placed far away from light pollution. Mauna Kea is located on the Big Island of Hawaii. The number of people living in Hawaii is not very high, which helps reduce light pollution. Hawaii is a group of islands far away from any other land. So, light pollution from beyond the state is not a problem. Finally, the Mauna Kea Observatory is located in the middle of the island. That means it is away from the cities and the places where most people live. As a result, the sky above Mauna Kea is very dark. Because the sky is so dark, many faint stars can be seen clearly. Even without a telescope you would see many more stars from Mauna Kea than you could from outside your own home.

The round buildings on the top of this mountain contain some of the Mauna Kea telescopes.

The Atacama Observatory is located on a desert mountain in Chile. It is also far away from sources of light pollution.

High and Dry

Another factor that affects how well a telescope works is the air. The air around Earth, while good for people who want to breathe, is not helpful for people who want to look through telescopes. Looking through air can distort what you see.

For example, if you look down a long, straight road on a hot day, you might see a shimmering that looks like water. What you are seeing is a mirage. Mirages are caused when the temperature of the air you are looking through is uneven. The hot road heats the air above it, but not the cool air higher up. A similar thing happens when scientists look at stars through a telescope on Earth. The air temperature between the telescope and the star is uneven and they cannot see the star clearly. The air around Earth also contains a lot of water vapor. This water vapor can make the changes worse.

Scientists must find places where the problems caused by air and water vapor are as small as possible. To reduce the problems caused by looking through air, scientists put telescopes on tall mountains. The higher the mountain is, the less air the scientists have to look through. Then, to reduce the problems caused by water vapor, scientists place telescopes in areas that are very dry. Telescopes are put in deserts and places that do not get much rain. The drier the area is, the less water vapor the air has.

The Atacama Observatory in Chile is located in just such an area. The observatory is at the top of a tall mountain that just happens to be in a desert. The air is thin and dry around the observatory, making the site perfect for a telescope.

It Is Cold Out There!

For years, scientists have used observatories like Mauna Kea and Atacama because those places were some of the best places on Earth for telescopes. But in 2009, scientists used information from satellites to find the absolute best place on Earth for a telescope. Unfortunately, no one had ever been there, and getting there would be hard. The place is called Ridge A. It is located in Antarctica, not far from the South Pole.

What makes Ridge A so wonderful? For one thing, it is very cold and very dry. You might think that Antarctica is wet because it has so much snow. But Antarctica is a desert—a very cold desert. The air in Antarctica contains very little water vapor. Ridge A is also a good location because it is a very tall mountain. Furthermore, the weather at Ridge A is perfect for stargazing. There are hardly any clouds to block your view. And, of course, Ridge A is far, far away from people. That means it is far away from light pollution. What is more, the sun does not even rise for six months in the year, so the sky is dark and stays dark all day long.

Scientists have set up the first observatory on Ridge A. It does not have big telescopes like those found at Mauna Kea or Atacama, but they are already collecting new information about space. But it is cold! Even if it *is* the best place for a telescope, it might not be the most comfortable place for stargazing.

These three observatories are found in remote parts of the world. Where is the best place for a telescope on Earth?

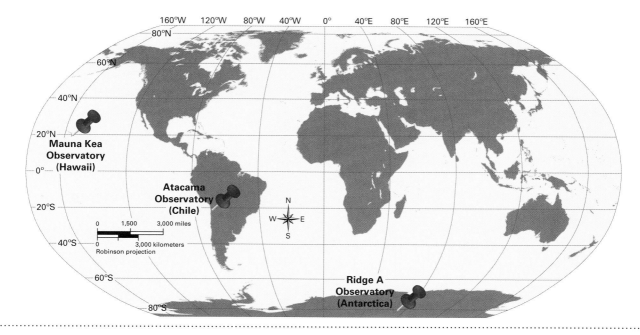

Science and Engineering Resources

In Science and Engineering Resources, you will learn how to conduct safe investigations using the skills scientists and engineers use, called "practices." You will also learn how to use metric units and measurement tools.

So, what are science and engineering? *Science* is a way of understanding the natural world. Science involves asking questions and gathering evidence. It also involves constructing models and explanations. Science explanations depend on evidence. This evidence must be able to be observed or measured. But as scientists make new discoveries, scientific understandings can change.

Engineering is a way to solve real-world problems. Engineers use their understanding of science to do this. Engineering solutions include a new way of doing something, a new machine, or new structures. Engineering solutions are always changing as engineers test and improve their designs and apply new scientific ideas.

Science Safety

Science investigations are fun. Use these rules to keep yourself and your classmates safe before, during, and after an investigation.

Classroom Science Safety

✓ Wear safety goggles when needed to protect your eyes.

✓ Wear safety gloves when needed to protect your skin.

✓ Wear protective aprons when needed.

✓ Tie back long hair and loose clothing so that they do not touch investigation materials.

✓ Keep tables and desks cleared except for investigation materials.

✓ Carry and handle equipment safely to avoid accidents.

✓ Handle living things with care and respect to protect them and yourself.

✓ Do not eat, drink, or place anything in your mouth during science investigations.

✓ When you work in a team, make sure all members of the team follow safety rules.

✓ Tell your teacher right away if materials spill or break.

✓ Tell your teacher right away if someone gets injured.

✓ Place leftover materials and waste where your teacher tells you to.

✓ Clean up your work area when finished.

✓ Wash your hands with soap and water after cleaning up.

✓ Know your school's safety rules for classroom behavior and follow them.

Outdoor Science Safety

✓ Wear clothing that is good for walking on wet, rocky, or rough ground.

✓ Wear clothes and a hat to protect you from ticks, insects, sun, wind, and rain. It is best to wear shoes that cover the whole foot, have low-heels, and have non-skid soles.

✓ Wear sunscreen if your class plans to be outdoors for more than a few minutes.

✓ Check the weather and sky. Go indoors if lightning may be nearby.

✓ Do not touch plants or animals, alive or dead, without your teacher's permission. Know what plants and animals to be careful of in your area.

✓ Some things are poisonous when eaten. Never taste or eat anything you find outdoors without permission.

✓ Wash your hands with soap and water after any outdoor science activity.

✓ Make sure an adult brings along a first-aid kit.

Planning Investigations

✓ Choose materials that are safe to use.

✓ Plan how you will handle the materials safely.

✓ Include safety steps when writing your procedure.

✓ Always get your teacher's permission before carrying out your investigation plan.

Science and Engineering Practices in Action

Asking Questions and Defining Problems

Questions about the world drive science. A science investigation tries to answer a question. So, a scientist must be able to ask good questions. Questions can be based on observations. For example, "Why do some of my plants grow taller than others?" They can also be based on models, such as the question "Why do most habitats have more living things that make their own food than living things that eat food?" Scientists also ask really big questions like "What happened at the beginning of the universe?"

Asking Scientific Questions

There are many different kinds of questions. One kind is a scientific question. This is question with a definite answer that can be learned through investigation. A question like "Which color is the prettiest?" is not a scientific question. Each person can have their own opinion. So, all answers are correct. But "Which of these two glue recipes makes the strongest glue?" is a scientific question. This is because it has a definite answer.

These students are working to answer a scientific question. They want to know which glue recipe makes the strongest glue. So, they glued a plastic bag to a craft stick. Now they are adding washers to the bag to see how many it can hold.

Questions are also important to engineers. An engineer might ask, "Why did that bridge collapse in the earthquake?" or "Which material is best for a raincoat?"

The goal of engineering is to solve problems to make life better for people. They solve problems by building things or finding new ways to use things. But first they must define the problem they are trying to solve. Asking questions is important for defining problems. Then they can determine how good their solutions are.

Engineers might ask why a bridge collapsed during an earthquake.

Defining a Problem

Defining a problem has two parts. The first is defining the criteria for a successful solution. The *criteria* are the things the solution needs to do. Suppose you are designing a magnetic latch for a box. One of the criteria would be that the latch does not open unless you pull on it. Engineers might explain how much force you need to pull on it with.

The second part is defining the constraints. *Constraints* are the limits on the design. Constraints include limits on time, materials, or costs. A NASA engineer might design a shuttle to carry astronauts. But the shuttle needs to take less than one year to build. So, the time it takes to build is one constraint.

These students are observing that their box comes open when they shake it. So, they are defining a problem. Then they will design a solution using their knowledge of magnets.

Developing and Using Models

Models in science represent ideas in the real world. Diagrams and mathematical representations are examples of models. So are physical copies and computer simulations. Models are not perfect copies of the ideas they represent. They make some parts of the concept clearer. But they make some parts less clear.

A Spring Toy Model

One example of a model is a spring toy being pushed back and forth. It can represent a sound wave. This model makes the motion of the wave clear. It shows that matter compresses together in crests and spreads apart in troughs. But it does not show that sound waves traveling through air are moving through many particles. It also does not show that sound waves spread out in all directions. Still, the model helps show basic properties of sound waves like amplitude and wavelength.

These students are using a spring toy to model sound waves. They will use the properties they observe in this model to describe other kinds of waves.

A Pinhole Camera Model

A pinhole camera is another example of a model. It can represent the human eye. It shows that light passes through the opening in the front of an eye and that the light is projected onto a screen in the back of the eye. It also shows that the image projected is upside down.

Many human eye functions can be investigated using a pinhole camera. However, a pinhole camera is unlike an eye in other ways. It is not made of the same materials as a human eye. It is also not filled with liquid. Instead of being round like an eye, it is a cylinder. And it does not have a lens in the front.

But the pinhole camera model is useful for understanding certain properties of the human eye. It shows how light enters the eye. It also shows how the light projects onto the back of the eye. But, as with all models, it is not a perfect representation. So, it is not useful for studying things like the specific structure of the eye.

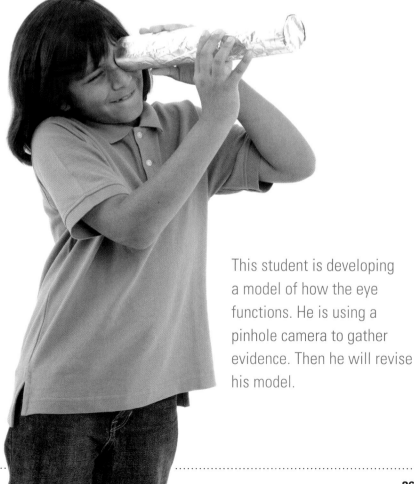

This student is developing a model of how the eye functions. He is using a pinhole camera to gather evidence. Then he will revise his model.

Planning and Carrying Out Investigations

Investigations are one of the main ways scientists and engineers gather evidence. This evidence supports their claims. Scientists use the evidence to construct and defend explanations and to answer questions. Engineers use evidence to identify problems or to decide between different solutions to the same problem. They also use it to determine how they can improve a solution.

Planning an Investigation

One of the key steps in successful investigation is planning. There are many different parts to plan. Here are a few important questions to ask while planning an investigation:

- What question am I trying to answer?
- What are my expected results?
- What data is the best evidence to answer my question?
- How will I collect and record my data?
- What errors are likely to occur during my investigation? And how can I prevent them?
- What safety issues do I need to think about?

These students are investigating how the height from which they drop a ball affects how high it bounces. They will use the data they gather to predict how high the ball will bounce in the future.

The Variables of an Investigation

The easiest way to do decide what data to collect in an investigation is to consider all the variables. A *variable* is a factor that can affect the outcome. Suppose you are testing a water filter. One variable affecting the test is the amount of water poured into the filter. Another is how quickly the water is poured.

Most investigations test the effect of one variable on the outcome. You might test how the rate of water being poured into the filter affects the effectiveness of the filter. In order to test just one variable, all the other variables must be the same in every test. So, you need to make sure you use the same amount of water and dirt in each test. But you need to change the rate that you pour water.

In most investigations, there are some variables that cannot be kept the same in every test. For example, the person holding the filter might shake a little bit. This makes the results change. So, scientists often repeat the same experiment many times. Each time is called a *trial*. They look at the average, or usual, results of the experiments. The more trials they do, the more confident they are that their results are correct.

These students are testing a design for a water filter. They consider variables to make sure their results are accurate.

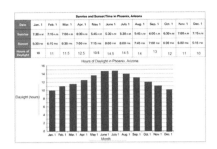

A bar graph can show patterns in data.

These students are analyzing measurements of the lengths of shadows during different times of the day. They will use their data to explain how the position of the sun affects the length of shadows.

Analyzing and Interpreting Data

Once you complete an investigation, you often have a data table full of numbers. But you might have pictures or words instead. How can you tell what all that *data*, or pieces of information, means?

Analyzing and interpreting data is the process of identifying patterns in data. It lets scientists turn their data into evidence. The evidence then supports their claim. Analyzing data might include graphing it to see a pattern. For example, you might make a bar graph that shows the length of shadows during different times of day. A graph will show the pattern of shadows better than a data table will. Analyzing data might also include identifying relationships between variables. Suppose you grow a bean plant. You might find that the plant grows 3 cm each week. Analyzing your data shows the relationship between height of the plant and time.

Scientists use many different methods to analyze data. They use many types of graphs. They also use mathematical formulas and tools. They compare data between trials and experiments. They even compare their data to data gathered by other scientists. They often use computers to help them find patterns in the data.

Finding Patterns with Graphs

Scientists use many different kinds of graphs and charts. These help them to find patterns. They use bar graphs to show how much of the data fits into a category. They might measure how much rain fell each month during a year. They could use a bar graph to show the amount of rain that fell in each month. The bar graph would show what parts of the year had more rain than other parts.

Line plots show a relationship between two variables. Line plots have two axes. There is one variable on each axis. They show how a change in one variable affects the other variable. A line plot might show how many hours of sunlight there are each day of the year.

These students are comparing the data each group gathered about rainfall in different years. They are looking for patterns in the rainfall during different seasons.

Using Mathematics and Computational Thinking

Mathematics plays a key role in science and engineering. Measurements and calculations provide evidence to support scientific explanations. The evidence can also disprove scientific explanations. Engineers use measurements to communicate their designs.

Using Measurements

One example of how measurements are useful in science is when you weigh things. You might measure the weight of cream before and after shaking it into butter. Without measurements, you may guess that the cream is about the same weight as the butter and buttermilk together. But by measuring, you can say with confidence that they are the same weight.

This student is measuring the weight of butter and buttermilk that she made by shaking cream. She also measured the weight of the cream. She will compare the weights before and after the change.

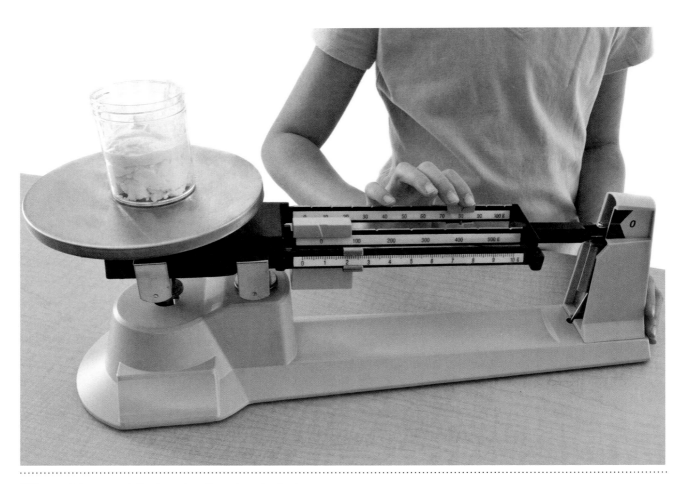

Graphing Data

Graphing is another example of how mathematics supports science. Often, scientists gather lots of data in tables. But it is difficult to see any patterns in the data. But when they graph it, they can see patterns more easily. These patterns suggest relationships between different factors. The data can then support explanations.

Graphing data also helps engineers. They use it to decide between different possible designs. They might test the amount of water several materials can absorb. Then they could decide which material will make the best sponge. By graphing the results of different designs using the same test, they can tell which design works best. Or they can see the strengths and weaknesses of each design.

This student learned that the weight of substances does not change. She is using this knowledge to predict how much an ice cube will weigh after it melts.

1. Use the data in the table to create a line graph showing how high above the horizon these four constellations are at different times of year in the Northern Hemisphere.

- Give the graph a title.
- Label the x-axis "Month."
- Label the y-axis "Altitude (degrees)."
- Graph and connect all of the points, using a different color for each constellation
- Add a key.

	Jan.	Feb.	Mar.	Apr.	May	June	July	Aug.	Sep.	Oct.	Nov.	Dec.
Leo	11°	35°	53°	62°	50°	28°	6°	0°	0°	0°	0°	0°
Scorpius	0°	0°	0°	12°	22°	21°	10°	0°	0°	0°	0°	0°
Pisces	5°	0°	0°	0°	0°	0°	0°	21°	42°	53°	46°	28°
Orion	44°	36°	19°	0°	0°	0°	0°	0°	0°	0°	19°	36°

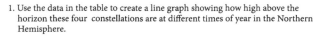

Graphing data helps scientists and engineers see patterns in their data.

Constructing Explanations and Designing Solutions

The main goal of science is to construct explanations for things observed in the world. An explanation is almost always a claim about the world. It can be a claim about two variables. For example, a claim could be moths with camouflage patterns that match their background are more likely to survive than moths with camouflage patterns that do not match their background.

Scientists Construct Explanations

While constructing explanations, scientists often investigate to gather data. Then they analyze the data. Often they use mathematics to do this. They usually use models to help construct their explanation. They use evidence to argue that their explanation is correct.

After constructing an explanation, scientists may ask more questions to clarify the explanation. They may have to change their models. Scientists also often communicate their explanations to other scientists. They might do this by writing papers or giving presentations.

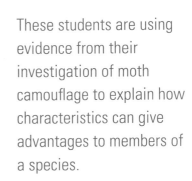

These students are using evidence from their investigation of moth camouflage to explain how characteristics can give advantages to members of a species.

One problem is converting energy stored in a battery into energy carried by light. So, these students design multiple solutions. They are using scientific ideas they learned about energy, electric current, and light to solve the problem.

Engineers Design Solutions

The main goal of engineering is to design solutions to problems. But the process has many of the same steps. Engineers still have to test their solutions. They also use evidence to show that their solution is the best one to solve the problem. After designing solutions, engineers often revise them. They ask questions about how they can improve the solution. Or they might ask what other related problems need to be solved. They communicate their solutions in similar ways as scientists.

The process of designing solutions has several steps. After defining the problem, engineers brainstorm many possible solutions. They compare the different possible solutions to decide which one is most likely to succeed. They may use models of the solution to compare them. After building the solution, engineers think about how the solution could be improved. They repeat this process several times to try to develop the best solution.

Engaging in Argument from Evidence

One process in scientific reasoning is engaging in argument from evidence. Arguments help scientists decide which explanation best fits the evidence. They help engineers decide which design solution best meets the criteria.

A Scientific Argument

There are three main pieces in a *scientific argument*. The first is a *claim*, which is the explanation that the argument supports. The argument claims that this explanation is correct. It is often a simple statement like "wolves eat meat."

The second piece is *evidence* that the claim is correct. This is the observations or data that support that claim. Evidence can be taken from investigations, research, or a model. For instance, one piece of evidence may be that "all wolves have sharp teeth."

The third piece is reasoning that connects the evidence to the claim. *Reasoning* explains why the evidence supports the claim. All evidence should have reasoning. Consider the example of wolves' teeth. The reasoning could be "animals that eat meat need sharp teeth for tearing the meat, but animals that eat plants need flat teeth for grinding plants."

This student is observing different kinds of animals' teeth. He will use his observations as evidence in an argument about how wolves and horses use their teeth to survive.

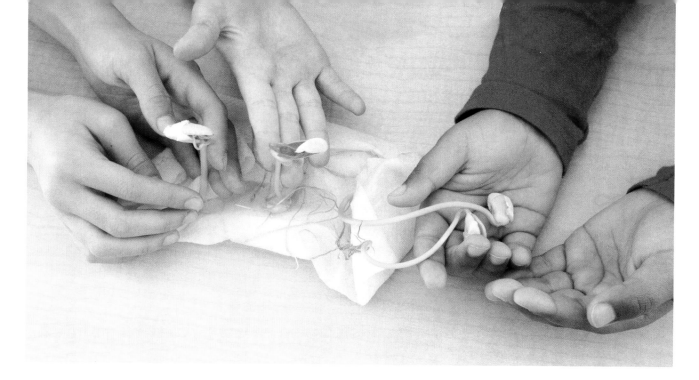

A Rebuttal to an Argument

Arguments are not very useful by themselves. So, they need to be in response to something or need to go against another argument. Because of this, there is often a fourth part to an argument. This part is called a rebuttal.

The *rebuttal* is a disagreement with the argument. It provides evidence or reasoning that shows that the claim is incorrect. It may directly show that the evidence in the argument is incorrect. Or it may point out a problem in the reasoning. It may also provide new evidence or suggest new reasoning that goes against the claim.

Consider the following argument.

Claim: Seeds need soil to sprout.

Evidence: Seeds sprout in places that have soil.

Reasoning: Plant's seeds can only sprout in places that have resources that meet their needs. Since plants live in places that have soil, soil must be needed for their seeds to sprout

Rebuttal: This experiment involved getting seeds to sprout on a paper towel. So, there is no soil. The seedsclearly sprouted on the paper towel. Therefore, the claim that soil is a need for a seed to sprout is incorrect.

This student is respectfully offering evidence to disprove his peer's argument that seeds need soil to sprout. His evidence is the seeds sprouted without any soil.

Obtaining, Evaluating, and Communicating Information

It is very rare for scientists and engineers to work alone. Almost all scientists work in teams, so they often communicate their investigations with each other. Many scientists are also often working on answering similar questions. This means that scientists share their results and information with each other.

How Scientists Obtain Information

Scientists make their results available in many ways so that others can learn from them. One way they do this is by writing up their results. Another is by presenting their research. In an investigation, you might present your research to your classmates.

While reading other people's research, scientists make sure that the information is reliable. They check to see if the data supports their explanations. They read about the methods used by the other scientists and look for possible errors. They also look to see whether the results of the experiment described match the results of similar experiments.

These students used a reliable source to find information about climates in different regions of the world. They are combining the information on one world map.

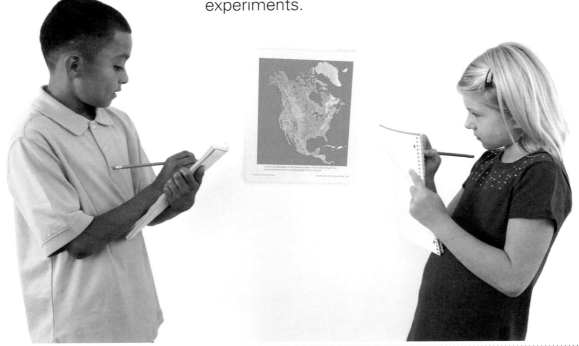

How Engineers Obtain Information

Engineers obtain information to help them define problems. They do research to discover exactly what the problem they need to solve. For example, many animals are killed while crossing roads. This is a big problem for some species. To solve it, engineers designed bridges that help animals cross the road without being hit by cars.

Before designing the bridges, the engineers researched the animals they were trying to help. There were many questions they had to answer before designing a solution. Here are a few of them.

- Why do the animals cross the road?

- When do the animals cross the road?

- How can engineers make the animals use their crossing instead of the road?

By obtaining information about these questions, engineers can define the problem they need to solve. Then they can design better solutions.

This student obtained information on the problem of deer being hit by cars. Based on this information, she designed a road crossing for the deer.

Using Science and Engineering Tools

The Metric System

The *metric system* is a system of measurement. It is used by scientists and engineers all over the world. Using the same system of measurement makes it easier to communicate scientific findings and engineering designs between different parts of the world.

Base Units

The metric system has several base units used for making different kinds of measurements. Here are a few of the most important ones:

Measurement	Base Unit	Symbol
Length	Meter	m
Volume	Liter	L
Mass or Weight	Gram	g
Time	Second	s
Temperature	Degree Celsius	°C

Prefixes

This chart shows you the prefixes of different units in the metric system. Each prefix makes a base unit larger or smaller.

The metric system also has prefixes that indicate different amounts of each unit. Adding a prefix to a base unit makes a new unit, which is made larger or smaller than the base unit by multiplying by a certain factor of 10. Each prefix represents a different factor of 10.

Prefix	Symbol	Word	Decimal	Factor of 10
giga	G	Billion	1,000,000,000	10^9
mega	M	Million	1,000,000	10^6
kilo	k	Thousand	1,000	10^3
hecto	h	Hundred	100	10^2
deka	da	Ten	10	10^1
deci	d	Tenth	0.1	1/10
centi	c	Hundredth	0.01	1/100
milli	m	Thousandth	0.001	1/1,000

The scientist measuring this panda's paw is using centimeters. This unit is part of the metric system.

Meters are the base unit for length. Millimeters have the prefix *milli*, which is 0.001. So a millimeter is 0.001, or 1/1,000, times the size of one meter. There are 1,000 millimeters in one meter. 1 m = 1,000 mm.

Similarly, there are 1000 meters in a kilometer. The prefix *kilo* means 10^3, or 1,000. So a kilometer is 1,000 times the size of a meter. 1 km = 1,000 m.

- 1 Gm = 1,000,000,000 m
- 1 Mm = 1,000,000 m
- 1 km = 1,000 m
- 1 hm = 100 m
- 1 dam = 10 m
- 10 dm = 1 m
- 100 cm = 1 m
- 1,000 mm = 1 m

You can also convert between units with different prefixes. Divide the size of the first unit by the size of the second unit. For example, to compare kilometers and centimeters you would divide 1,000 (the size of the kilometer) by 0.01 (the size of the centimeter). 1,000/0.01 = 100,000. So, there are 100,000 cm in 1 km. 1 km = 100,000 cm.

Try it yourself. How many decimeters are there in a megameter? How many hectometers in a gigameter?

Using a Hand Lens

Hand lenses are tools for making observations. They make objects and living things viewed through them appear larger. This allows scientists to see parts of an object that they cannot see with just their eyes. It helps scientist see more details of an object.

To use a hand lens:

- hold the lens close to your face in between the object you want to magnify and yourself. The object should appear blurry.

- slowly move the hand lens away from your face. When the object is no longer blurry, it is said to be "in focus."

- find the position where the object is in focus, and hold the hand lens still while you observe the object.

This student is holding the hand lens the right distance from his face to keep the leaf in focus. It helps him see the structures that make up the leaf in more detail.

Measuring Length

Small lengths and distances are measured in centimeters. Larger lengths and distances are measured in meters or kilometers. There are other units to measure lengths and distances. Some are even smaller than centimeters or larger than kilometers.

To measure lengths and distances, you can use a ruler. Rulers have marks that show length on them. Each mark is the same distance from the mark before it. The marks are usually one centimeter or one inch apart. Many have centimeters on one side and inches on the other side.

To use a ruler:

- find the 0 cm mark on the ruler.

- line it up with one end of the length you are measuring.

- hold the ruler along the length.

- find the centimeter mark nearest to the other end of the length.

- the number on that mark is the length measurement you should record.

Remember to record what units you used!

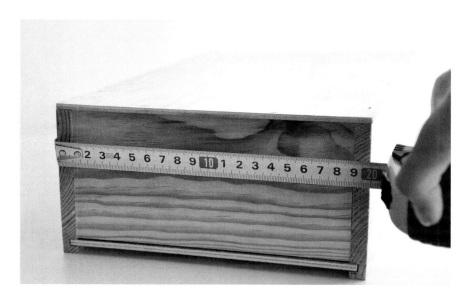

To measure length, you lay a ruler next to the length you are measuring. Find the 0 mark and the other end, and then record the length and units. This drawer is 20 cm wide.

Measuring Temperature

Temperature is measured in degrees Celsius. You can measure temperature with a *thermometer*. Many thermometers are glass tubes with red liquid inside. As the temperature increases, the liquid expands and fills more of the tube. The thermometer has marks on it that show the temperature. Since these thermometers are made of glass, you have to be careful while using them to be sure not to break them.

Digital thermometers have a metal tip that you put in the substance you are measuring. They display the temperature on a screen.

To read a thermometer with a glass tube:

- hold it near the top where there is not liquid.

- hold it so the top of the liquid is level with your eye.

- find the mark that is closest to the top of the liquid.

- record the temperature indicated by the mark.

Remember to record the units your thermometer uses!

This ice water is 0° C. You can see that the top of the red liquid is exactly at the 0° C mark.

Measuring Liquid Volume

Liquid volumes are measured in liters. Smaller volumes might be measured in milliliters or fluid ounces. There are 1000 milliliters in 1 liter.

A *graduated cylinder* is a tool that accurately measures the volume of liquids. It is a thin cylinder with marks on the side. It shows the volume of liquid there is in the cylinder below the mark.

To accurately measure volume with a graduated cylinder:

- make sure the cylinder is completely empty and dry.

- fill it with the liquid you want to measure.

- set the cylinder down on a flat surface.

- make sure the liquid is not splashing back and forth.

- crouch down so your eye is level with the top of the liquid.

- the liquid should be curved slightly, so it is lower in the middle than at the sides.

- find which mark is closest to the bottom of the curve. That is the volume of the liquid in the graduated cylinder.

Remember to record the units you used to measure the volume!

This graduated cylinder is full of liquid. Find the bottom of the curve in the top of the liquid. Which mark is it closest to? There are 96 mL of liquid in the graduated cylinder.

These weights can be used with a balance scale.

Measuring Mass or Weight

Small amounts of mass or weight are measured in grams. Larger amounts of mass or weight are measured in kilograms. There are 1000 grams in a kilogram.

Using a Balance Scale With Two Pans

You can measure mass or weight using a *balance scale*. Some balance scales have two pans.

To use a balance scale:

- put the object you want to measure in one pan. That pan should sink down.

- put weights in the other pan. You should know the mass of each of the weights.

- add weights to the second side until the two sides are balanced. So, neither side sinks down.

- add up all the masses on the second side. Their total mass is equal to the mass of the object on the first side.

To measure the mass or weight of this orange, first you would put the orange on one pan of the balance scale. Then you would put weights in the other pan. You would add and take away weights until the pans are balanced.

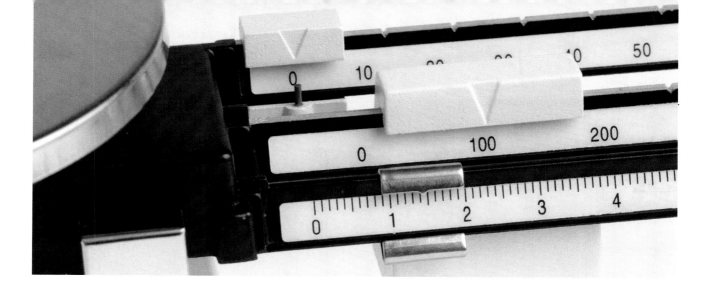

Using a Triple Beam Balance Scale

A triple beam balance scale is another kind of balance scale. It only has one pan, which is where you put the object you want to weigh. There are three sliders. One measures grams in hundreds, one measures them in tens, and one measures them in ones. There are also two lines, one on the beam with the weights and one on the frame. When the lines are lined up with each other, the scale is balanced.

Add up the weights to find the weight of the object. The scale reads 101.4 g.

To measure the weight of an object with a triple beam balance:

- place the object on the pan.
- slide the hundreds weight until the line on the beam falls below the line on the frame.
- slide the weight one notch back. The line on the beam should rise up above the line on the frame.
- slide the tens weight until the line falls down again.
- slide the weight one notch back. The line on the beam should rise up above the line on the frame.
- slide the ones weight until the beam is balanced, and the line on the beam is lined up with the line on the frame. Move the ones weight a little at a time to make sure your measurement is accurate.
- add up all of the weights to find the total weight of the object.

Remember to record the units you used!

GLOSSARY

A

air mass   A large quantity of air that has similar temperature, moisture, and pressure all through it.

air pressure   How much the air pushes on any surface.

apparent brightness   A measurement describing how bright a star looks from Earth.

astronomer   A scientist who studies objects and energy in space.

atmosphere   The Earth system that is made up of a mixture of gases that is air.

axis   The imaginary line that Earth rotates around. Earth's axis goes through the middle of Earth from the North Pole to the South Pole.

B

bacteria   One group of organisms that are too small to be seen without a microscope. Many kinds of bacteria are decomposers.

biosphere   The Earth system that includes all the living things found on Earth.

C

carbon dioxide   A gas found in air that is used to make food by photosynthesis.

circulation   The process of moving blood in a large, complicated loop through the body.

climate   The general weather of a place over a long period of time, such as many years.

compost   A mixture of soil and decaying matter that provides the materials that plants need.

conservation   The wise use of material and energy resources. Many conservation efforts involve reducing the amount of material and energy resources used.

conserve   To keep the same total amount of something.

constellation   A section of the sky that has a recognizable star pattern. Some star patterns, such as the Big Dipper, are part of larger constellations.

constraint   A limit that keeps you from doing certain things.

consumer   An organism that gets energy by eating other organisms.

contract   To get smaller.

criteria   The properties that you want a material or a solution to have.

D

decompose   When a material is broken down into smaller pieces.

decomposer   An organism that breaks down dead organisms and wastes to live and grow.

deposition   The dropping of weathered material in one place.

digestion   The process that breaks down food into simple materials that an animal's body can use.

dissolve   To mix completely with a different material.

disturbance   An event that changes an ecosystem for a long period of time. A disturbance can be caused by humans or by natural processes.

E

ecosystem   All the living and nonliving things that interact with each other in an area.

electrical conductivity   A property that describes how well a substance allows electricity to pass through it.

energy pyramid   A model that shows the amount of energy that is passed on at each level of a food chain.

erosion   The loosening and carrying away of weathered material from one place to another.

expand   To get larger.

F

food chain   A model showing the path of energy through a series of organisms in an ecosystem.

food web   A diagram that shows the many connected food chains and feeding relationships in an ecosystem.

full moon   The moon when it appears as a full circle. The moon is a full moon halfway through its cycle of phases.

fungi   A group of organisms that are not plants or animals and that act as decomposers. Molds are fungi.

G

geosphere   The Earth system that is made up of a thin surface layer of rock, soil, and sediments as well as the materials that are inside Earth.

gravity   A force of attraction that pulls objects without them touching. Earth's gravity pulls objects near its surface toward Earth's center.

H

hydrosphere   The Earth system that includes all of Earth's water.

I

invasive species   A non-native kind of organism that causes harm to an ecosystem.

L

landform   A natural structure on Earth's surface.

lens   A clear object that refracts light. Some lenses refract light so that light rays focus. Other lenses refract light so that light rays spread apart.

light-year   A unit of measurement used to describe distances between stars in space. One light-year is the distance that light travels in one year.

M

matter   Anything that takes up space and has weight. All matter is made of moving particles.

meteor   The streak of light that a chunk of rock falling from space toward Earth produces.

mixture   A combination of two or more substances whose particles are not joined together.

moon phases   The different shapes of the lit part of the moon seen from Earth. The pattern of changing moon phases is caused by the moon revolving around Earth.

N

new moon   The moon when it cannot be seen. The moon is a new moon at the beginning of its cycle of phases.

O

orbit   A curved path that an object makes around another object.

oxygen   A gas found in air that is produced as waste during photosynthesis.

P

particles   Tiny pieces that make up matter.

photosynthesis   The process that producers use to make food from carbon dioxide and water.

pollution   The presence of anything in the environment that can harm living things or damage natural resources.

precipitation   Water that falls to Earth's surface. Precipitation falls in many forms, including rain and snow.

predator   An animal in a predator-prey relationship that captures and eats other animals.

prevailing wind Wind that usually blows more often from one direction than from any other direction.

prey The animal that is captured and eaten in a predator-prey relationship.

producer Any organism that makes its own food.

property A characteristic of matter that can be observed or measured.

R

radio telescope A telescope that uses an antenna to collect radio waves.

reaction A process where one or more substances are changed into new substances.

recycling Taking materials from old discarded objects and making new objects from them.

reflecting telescope A telescope that uses a curved mirror to collect and focus light.

refracting telescope A telescope that uses lenses to collect and focus light.

rotate To spin. Earth rotates around its axis.

rotation A complete spin. Earth makes one rotation every 24 hours.

S

scrubbers Devices that remove dirt and harmful pollutants from smoke produced by burning high-sulfur coal.

sediments Tiny pieces of sand, rock, and shells that settle to the bottom in layers.

shadow An area of darkness that forms when light from any source is blocked. Shadows caused by the sun change in regular patterns.

solubility A property that describes whether a substance can dissolve in another substance.

solution A mixture in which the particles of a material are dissolved with the particles of another material.

space telescope A telescope that works in space, beyond Earth's atmosphere.

state change A change of a substance from one state of matter to another. Some common state changes include: melting, freezing, evaporation, and condensation.

state of matter The way the particles in a piece of matter move.

substance A material where each part of it is made of the same type of particle. No two particle types have exactly the same properties.

succession   The slow changes that take place in an ecosystem that has been disturbed. One group of organisms replaces another group until a stable community is formed.

sundial   A tool that uses the shadow cast by an object in sunlight to keep track of time during the day.

T

telescope   A tool that collects and focuses light to make images. A telescope makes large images of objects that are far away.

thermal conductivity   A property that describes how well a substance allows heat to pass through it.

time zone   A part of the world where the same standard time is used. There are 24 time zones in the world, one for each hour in the day.

toxic   Capable of causing injury or death to an organism.

W

waning   Getting smaller. The lit part of the moon is waning for about two weeks after a full moon.

water cycle   The continual movement of water between the air and the land.

water vapor   Water when it is in the gas state.

waxing   Growing slowly. The lit part of the moon is waxing for about two weeks after a new moon.

weather   The condition of the atmosphere at a place for a short period of time, such as a few hours or days.

weathering   The breaking down of rock by interactions with Earth's systems.

wildlife refuge   An area of land or of land and water that is set aside for the protection of wildlife.

constraints, 259
  identifying, 260, 264, 265
consumers
  carnivores, 38
  definition of, 29
  excess food storage, 32, 35
  in food chains, 55
  food for energy, 30–31, 35
  herbivores, 37
  humans as, 34, 35
  omnivores, 39
  as organism-eaters, 29, 35
  waste production, 33, 35
continental islands, 136
contour plowing, 149
contraction from cooling, 237
cooling substances, 235, 237,
    240, 241
  conservation of matter, 249,
    253
  contraction from, 237
copper wire, 213
coral islands, 137
coral reefs
  algae and, 24
  artificial reefs, 91
  food web in, 57
  restoration of, 91
corn tortillas, 155
cotton, 159
crescent moon, 334
criteria, 259
  identifying, 261, 264, 265
crust of earth, 112
cumulonimbus clouds, 124
cumulus clouds, 124
Curie, Marie, 207–209
currents
  ocean currents. *See* ocean
    currents

wind currents, 128, 129

D

dams
  beaver dams, 106
  biosphere, effect on, 106, 107
  rainwater, collection of, 166
dark side of the moon, 341
da Vinci, Leonardo, 178
day and night
  causes of, 296–301
  hours of, 300, 301
  rotation of earth and, 297–
    298, 301
  time zones, 299, 301
daylight hours, 300, 301
"dead" water bodies, 148
decomposers, 40
  bacteria as, 41
  bioremediation with, 48–50
  composting waste, 46, 47,
    142–145
  definition of, 41
  as digesters of food, 42
  earthworms as, 41
  electricity-producing
    bacteria, 51
  excess food storage, 44, 47
  fungi as, 41
  organisms as, 41, 47
  as recyclers of matter, 42–43,
    47
  scavengers as, 41
  as waste producers, 45, 47
decomposing material, 159
deep-sea vents, 60–63, 116–119
deer droppings, 37
dental plaque, 71
deposition, 139, 141

definition of, 139
desert soil, 114
digestion, 30–31, 35
digestive systems, 30, 34, 35
  as ecosystems, 72
dinosaurs
  droppings of, 84
  ecosystems of, 82–85
  Edmontosaurus's jaw, 84
  extinction, cause of, 85
  food of, 84
  T. Rex. See T. Rex
dissolves, 190
dissolving substances, 190, 238,
    241
  conservation of matter, 250,
    253
dormancy, 79
drinking water, 164–167
drizzle, 125
droppings, 36–39
  of dinosaurs, 84
ducks, 9
dung beetles, 327
dust storms, 75

E

earth's axis, 297, 301
earth's crust, 112
earth's layers
  crust, 112
  inner core, 112
  mantle, 112
  outer core, 112
earth's matter, 254, 256–257.
  See also matter
earth's rotation, 297–298, 301
  and the moon's rising and
    setting, 332

definition of, 120
weathering, 138, 141
  definition of, 138
weather maps, 123
weight
  of air, 193, 195
  changes to matter and,
      246–253
  and conservation of matter,
      246–253
  as the force of gravity, 280,
      281
  of matter, 187, 246–253
  mixing, changes from, 250–
      251, 253
  temperature changes and,
      248–249, 253
weightlessness, 280
whale migration (humpback
      whales), 329
white dwarves, 294
white stars, 290
wildebeest, 326
wildlife sanctuaries and
      refuges, 176, 177
willow trees, 22
wind, 193
  prevailing winds, 128, 129
wind currents, 128, 129
winter
  animals' preparation for, 79
  plants' preparation for, 78
  shadows in, 308
wolves, 38
  on Isle Royale, 66
wood, 203, 204, 215
worm bins, 145
worm farming, 142–145
worms. *See also* earthworms

composting waste with,
      142–145
intestinal worms, 72
pinworms, 72
as recyclers, 43
tapeworms, 72

Y

year, length of, 305
yellow stars, 290

Z

Zebra mussels, 92

CREDITS

Cover and Title Page
NASA/JPL-Caltech/Univ.of Ariz.

Front Matter
iii: Tristan3D/Alamy **viii:** ASSOCIATED PRESS **ix:** Trevor Smith/Alamy **x:** Monty Rakusen/cultura/Corbis **xvi:** Shaiith/Shutterstock **xvii:** Ethan Daniels/Shutterstock **xviii:** PhotoAlto/Frederic Cirou/Getty Images **xix:** Stocktrek Images, Inc./Alamy

Unit 1, Unit Opener
xx-1: Shaiith/Shutterstock **3 L:** Thinkstock **3 BR:** Thinkstock **3 TR:** Shutterstock

Unit 1, Lesson 1
4: Doug McCutcheon/ LGPL/Alamy **5:** Konstantin32/Dreamstime **6:** Lajos Endrédi/Dreamstime **8:** Chris Rokitski/Dreamstime **9 T:** Sergey Uryadnikov/Dreamstime **9 B:** Reinhold Leitner/Dreamstime **10:** Ukrphoto/Dreamstime **11 (#1):** Konstantin32/Dreamstime **11 (#2):** Lajos Endrédi/Dreamstime **11 (#3):** Reinhold Leitner/Dreamstime **11 (#4):** Ukrphoto/Dreamstime **12:** Thinkstock **13:** Thinkstock **14:** iStockphoto **15:** Stephen Alvarez/Getty Images

Unit 1, Lesson 2
16: Alexandre Fagundes De Fagundes/Dreamstime **17:** Michael De Nysschen/Dreamstime **18:** Meryll/Dreamstime **20:** Chiyacat/Dreamstime **21:** Lilittas1/Dreamstime **22:** Tofuxs/Dreamstime **23 (#1):** Michael De Nysschen/Dreamstime **23 (#2):** Meryll/Dreamstime **23 (#3):** Chiyacat/Dreamstime **23 (#4):** Lilittas1/Dreamstime **23 (#5):** Tofuxs/Dreamstime **24:** NOAA/NMFS/PIFSC/CRED, Oceanography Team **25:** LCDR Eric Johnson, NOAA Corps **26:** Durden Images/Shutterstock **27:** Matt Jeppson/Shutterstock

Unit 1, Lesson 3
28: Igorj/Dreamstime **29:** Robert Hughes/Dreamstime **31:** Dbajurin/Dreamstime **32:** 19838623doug/Dreamstime **33:** Russell Watkins/shutterstock **34:** Wisconsinart/Dreamstime **35 (#1):** Robert Hughes/Dreamstime **35 (#2):** Dbajurin/Dreamstime **35 (#3):** 19838623doug/Dreamstime **35 (#4):** Russell Watkins/shutterstock **35 (#5):** Wisconsinart/Dreamstime **36 R:** Tom Reichner/Shutterstock **36 L:** Blasch/Dreamstime **37 L:** Sue Smith/Shutterstock **37 R:** Thinkstock **38 R:** Thinkstock **38 L:** Remo Savisaar/Alamy **39 L:** Sorin Colac/Shutterstock **39 R:** lightasafeather/Getty Images

Unit 1, Lesson 4
40: Jan Podaril/Dreamstime **41:** Barbro Bergfeldt/Dreamstime **42:** Redwood8/Dreamstime **43:** George Bernard/Science Source **44:** Juan Moyano/Dreamstime **45:** sauletas/shutterstock **46:** Brad Calkins/Dreamstime **47 (#1):** Barbro Bergfeldt/Dreamstime **47 (#2):** Redwood8/Dreamstime **47 (#3):** Juan Moyano/Dreamstime **47 (#4):** sauletas/shutterstock **47 (#5):** Brad Calkins/Dreamstime **48:** RGB Ventures LLC dba SuperStock/Alamy **49:** Thinkstock **50 B:** Juan Gaertner/Shutterstock **50 T:** Shutterstock **51:** Thinkstock

Unit 1, Lesson 5
52: LOOK Die Bildagentur der Fotografen GmbH/Alamy **57 TL:** Matthias Weinrich/Dreamstime **57 TR:** Mark Doherty/Dreamstime **57 BL:** Steven Melanson/Dreamstime **57 BR:** Paul Vinten/Dreamstime **58:** Godfer/Dreamstime **59 (#4):** Matthias Weinrich/Dreamstime **59 (#5):** Godfer/Dreamstime **60:** OAR/National Undersea Research Program (NURP); Woods Hole Oceanographic Inst. **61:** Thinkstock **62:** NOAA **63:** Dorling Kindersley/Getty Images

Unit 1, Lesson 6

64: Michael Mill/Dreamstime
65: Paul Wolf/Dreamstime
66 B: Reino Jonsson/Dreamstime
66 T: Michael Thompson/Dreamstime **67:** Sauletas/Dreamstime
68: Rinus Baak/Dreamstime
69 (#1): Paul Wolf/Dreamstime
69 (#2): Michael Thompson/Dreamstime **69 (#3):** Sauletas/Dreamstime **69 (#4):** Rinus Baak/Dreamstime **70:** SCIEPRO/Getty Images **71:** STEVE GSCHMEISSNER/Science Source **72:** Juan Gaertner/Shutterstock **73:** Heather Davie /Science Source

Unit 1, Lesson 7

74: Vickymouse/Dreamstime
75: Cholder/Dreamstime
76 T: Thinkstock **77:** Andrew Orlemann/Dreamstime **78:** Daveallenphoto/Dreamstime **79:** BMJ/shutterstock **80:** Outdoorsman/Dreamstime **81 (#1):** Cholder/Dreamstime **81 (#2):** Andrew Orlemann/Dreamstime
81 (#3): BMJ/shutterstock
81 (#4): Outdoorsman/Dreamstime
82: iStockphoto **83:** Denis Kholyavin/Shutterstock **84:** NATURAL HISTORY MUSEUM, LONDON/Science Source **85:** iStockphoto

Unit 1, Lesson 8

86: Bidouze Stéphane/Dreamstime
87 B: Accent Alaska.com/Alamy
87 T: Peter Gudella/shutterstock

88: Shutterstock **89:** Prescott09/Dreamstime **90 B:** Tbe/Dreamstime **90 T:** Timothy Epp/Dreamstime **91:** Greg Amptman/Dreamstime **92 L:** Keithspaulding/Dreamstime **92 C:** Dale Mitchell/Dreamstime **92 R:** Oseland/Dreamstime **93 (#1):** Accent Alaska.com/Alamy **93 (#2):** Prescott09/Dreamstime **93 (#3):** Timothy Epp/Dreamstime **93 (#4):** Keithspaulding/Dreamstime **94:** Thinkstock **95 T:** iStockphoto **95 B:** Heiko Kiera/Shutterstock **96:** Heiko Kiera/Shutterstock **97:** National Park Service

Unit 2, Unit Opener

98-99: Ethan Daniels/Shutterstock
101 BR: Sian Cox/Dreamstime
101 TR: Thinkstock **101 L:** Hurst Photo/Shutterstock

Unit 2, Lesson 1

102: Thinkstock **103:** Thinkstock
105: Thinkstock **106 T:** Thinkstock
106 B: Thinkstock **107:** Thinkstock
108 T: Thinkstock **109:** Thinkstock
110: Thinkstock **112:** Thinkstock
113: Thinkstock **115 (#1):** Thinkstock **115 (#2):** Thinkstock
115 (#3): Thinkstock
115 (#4): Thinkstock
115 (#5): Thinkstock
115 (#6): Thinkstock **116:** Ralph White/Corbis **117:** NOAA Okeanos Explorer Program
118: NOAA Okeanos Explorer

Program **119 T:** NOAA Okeanos Explorer Program **119 B:** NOAA Okeanos Explorer Program

Unit 2, Lesson 2

120: Thinkstock **121:** Patryk Kosmider **122:** Thinkstock
123: Thinkstock **124 T:** Thinkstock
124 B: Thinkstock **125:** Roger Wissmann **126:** Thinkstock
127: Thinkstock **128:** iStockphoto **129 (#1):** Patryk Kosmider **129 (#2):** Thinkstock
129 (#3): Thinkstock
129 (#4): Thinkstock
129 (#5): iStockphoto **130:** National Geographic/Getty Images
131: Thinkstock **132:** British Antarctic Survey/Science Source
133: Radius Images/Alamy

Unit 2, Lesson 3

134: Thinkstock **135:** Thinkstock
136: Thinkstock **137:** Thinkstock
138 T: Thinkstock **139:** Thinkstock
138 B: Westend61 GmbH/Alamy
140: Thinkstock **141 (#1):** Thinkstock **141 (#2):** Thinkstock
141 (#3): Thinkstock
141 (#4): Thinkstock
142: Thingsofnature/Dreamstime **143 T:** Christian Kieffer/Dreamstime **143 B:** iStockphoto
144: Thinkstock **145 B:** iStockphoto

CREDITS

Unit 2, Lesson 4

146: Thinkstock **147:** Thinkstock **148:** koko-tewan **149 T:** Thinkstock **149 B:** Thinkstock **150:** Thinkstock **151:** Thinkstock **152:** Thinkstock **153 (#1):** Thinkstock **153 (#2):** Thinkstock **153 (#3):** Thinkstock **153 (#4):** Thinkstock **154:** iStockphoto **155:** David R. Frazier Photolibrary, Inc./Alamy **156 T:** Kabvisio/Dreamstime **156 B:** Thinkstock **157:** Sebastian Czapnik/Dreamstime

Unit 2, Lesson 5

158: Thinkstock **159:** Thinkstock **160:** Thinkstock **161:** Paul Doyle/Alamy **162:** Thinkstock **163 (#1):** Thinkstock **163 (#2):** Thinkstock **163 (#3):** Thinkstock **164:** Johnnymitch/Dreamstime **165:** Antonella865/Dreamstime **166:** Gillespaire/Dreamstime **167 T:** Lucian Coman/Dreamstime **167 B:** David Snyder/Dreamstime

Unit 2, Lesson 6

168: iStockphoto **169:** Thinkstock **170 T:** Thinkstock **170 B:** Thinkstock **171:** Thinkstock **172:** Thinkstock **173:** Thinkstock **174:** Thinkstock **175:** Thinkstock **176:** Thinkstock **177 (#1):** Thinkstock **177 (#2):** Thinkstock **177 (#3):** Thinkstock **177 (#4):** Thinkstock **177 (#5):** Thinkstock

178: iStockphoto **179:** iStockphoto **180 T:** Mikelane45/Dreamstime **180 B:** Vacclav/Dreamstime **181 L:** Henry Horenstein/Corbis/ AP Images **181 R:** Thinkstock

Unit 3, Unit Opener

182-183: PhotoAlto/Frederic Cirou/Getty Images **185 L:** Thinkstock **185 TR:** Thinkstock **185 BR:** Thinkstock

Unit 3, Lesson 1

186: Thinkstock **187:** Michael Flippo/Dreamstime **188:** iStockphoto **190 L:** Johnfoto/Dreamstime **190 R:** Danny Smythe/ Dreamstime **191:** Thinkstock **192:** Thinkstock **193:** Chung Jin Mac/Dreamstime **194:** Thinkstock **195 (#1):** Michael Flippo/ Dreamstime **195 (#2):** iStockphoto **195 (#3):** Thinkstock **195 (#4):** Thinkstock **195 (#5):** Thinkstock **196:** Thinkstock **197:** Jens Ottoson/Shutterstock **198:** Thinkstock **199:** NASA/ European Space Agency

Unit 3, Lesson 2

200: Thinkstock **201 L:** Deyan Georgiev/Dreamstime **201 C:** Anne Kitzman/ Dreamstime **201 R:** Bert Folsom/ Dreamstime **202:** Thinkstock **203:** Thinkstock **204 R:** Thinkstock **204 L:** Thinkstock **205 (#1):** Bert Fol-

som/Dreamstime **205 (#2):** Thinkstock **205 (#3):** Thinkstock **206:** Thinkstock **207:** Thinkstock **208 B:** Thinkstock **208 T:** Thinkstock **209 T:** Thinkstock **209 B:** Ocean/ Corbis

Unit 3, Lesson 3

210: Thinkstock **211 L:** Olga Kovalenko/Dreamstime **211 R:** Newlight/Dreamstime **212 L:** Kelpfish/ Dreamstime **212 R:** Denis Radovanovic/Dreamstime **213:** Bert Folsom/Dreamstime **214:** Duncan Noakes/Dreamstime **215:** Kaan Kurdoglu/Dreamstime **216:** Yarchyk/Dreamstime **217 (#1):** Olga Kovalenko/ Dreamstime **217 (#2):** Bert Folsom/ Dreamstime **217 (#3):** Kaan Kurdoglu/Dreamstime **217 (#4):** Yarchyk/ Dreamstime **218:** Thinkstock **219 T:** Martyn Chillmaid/Science Source **219 B:** Thinkstock **220:** Mark Hunt/Huntstock/Corbis **221:** iStockphoto

Unit 3, Lesson 4

222: Thinkstock **223:** Scott Griessel/Dreamstime **224:** Ben Heys/ Dreamstime **225 L:** Shutterstock **225 R:** Spfotocz/Dreamstime **226:** Photo Researchers, Inc. **227:** Marilyn Gould/Dreamstime **228:** Sandor Kacso/Dreamstime **229 (#1):** Scott Griessel/Dreamstime **229 (#2):** Ben Heys/Dreamstime **229 (#3):** Marilyn Gould/Dream-

stime **229 (#4):** Sandor Kacso/
Dreamstime **230:** Thinkstock
231 L: Thinkstock **231 C:** Thinkstock
231 R: Thinkstock **232 B:** Thinkstock **232 T:** Thinkstock **233:** Thinkstock

Unit 3, Lesson 5

234: bluesnote/Shutterstock
235: Banjong Khanyai/Dreamstime
236: Natursports/Dreamstime
237 L: Oleksiy Maksymenko/Alamy
237 R: Oleksiy Maksymenko/
Alamy **238:** Steve Lovegrove/Shut-
terstock **240:** Filipe Varela/Dream-
stime **241 (#1):** Banjong Khanyai/
Dreamstime **241 (#2):** Natursports/
Dreamstime **241 (#4):** Filipe Varela/
Dreamstime **242:** iStockphoto
243: iStockphoto **244:** Thinkstock
245: iStockphoto

Unit 3, Lesson 6

247 B: Oleksii Khmyz/Shutterstock
247 T: Ronald Kloberdanz/Dream-
stime **248 T:** Chatchai Somwat/
Dreamstime **248 B:** Rachwal/
Dreamstime **249:** Bagwold/Dream-
stime **250:** Michael Flippo/Dream-
stime **251:** Charles D. Winters/Sci-
ence Source **252:** Evan Robinson/
Alamy **253 (#1):** Ronald Klober-
danz/Dreamstime **253 (#2):** Rach-
wal/Dreamstime **253 (#3):** Michael
Flippo/Dreamstime **253 (#4):** Evan
Robinson/Alamy **254:** Thinkstock
255: Thinkstock **256:** Thinkstock
257: Thinkstock

Unit 3, Lesson 7

258: Trevor Smith/Alamy **259:** Guy
Sagi/Dreamstime **260:** Shutterstock **261:** Vladnik/Dreamstime
262: Andrey Yakovlev/Dreamstime
263: Dusty Cline/Dreamstime
264: Trossofoto/Dreamstime
265 (#1): Guy Sagi/Dreamstime
265 (#2): Vladnik/Dreamstime
265 (#3): Dusty Cline/Dreamstime
265 (#4): Trossofoto/Dreamstime
266: Thinkstock **267:** Paul Shamb-
room/Science Source **268:** Thinkstock **269:** Thinkstock

Unit 4, Lesson Opener

270-271: Stocktrek Images, Inc./
Alamy **273 BR:** moodboard/Alamy
273 TR: Rodolfo Arpia/Shutter-
stock **273 L:** iStockphoto

Unit 4, Lesson 1

274: 2happy/shutterstock
276 T: Jonathan Welch/Alamy
276 B: rgmeier/iStockphoto
277: Mikephotos/Dreamstime
279 T: NASA **280:** NASA
281 (#2): Jonathan Welch/Alamy
281 (#3): Mikephotos/Dreamstime
281 (#4): NASA **281 (#5):** NASA
282: NASA/Johns Hopkins University Applied Physics Laboratory/
Carnegie Institution of Washington **283:** Stocktrek Images, Inc./
Alamy **284:** NASA/JPL/University
of Arizona **285:** NASA

Unit 4, Lesson 2

286: Eraxion/iStockphoto
289 L: Claudio Balducell/
Dreamstime **289 R:** Thinkstock
290 T: Christian Darkin/Science
Source **291 (#3):** Thinkstock
292: Bill Frische/Shutterstock
293: NASA/Steele Hill **294:** NASA,
ESA, and The Hubble Heritage
Team (STScI/AURA) **295:** Shutterstock

Unit 4, Lesson 3

296: Health Head Images
Photograph/FotoSearch
297 T: Thinkstock **298 B:** Fotosearch
298 T: Lunamarina/Dreamstime
301 (#2): Lunamarina/Dreamstime
302: Titi Matei/Dreamstime
303 R: leonello calvetti/Shutter-
stock **303 L:** iStockphoto **304:** Shutterstock **305:** iStockphoto

Unit 4, Lesson 4

306: moodboard/Alamy
309 T: Flat Earth Photos/
Fotosearch **309 B:** IMAGE-
MORE Co, Ltd./Getty Images
311 (#3): IMAGEMORE Co, Ltd./
Getty Images **312:** Laurence
Delderfield/Alamy **313:** Stuart
Pearce/Alamy **314:** iStockphoto
315: iStockphoto

CREDITS

Unit 4, Lesson 5

316: Roger Ressmeyer/Corbis
317 T: peresanz/iStockphoto
317 B: Eckhard Slawik/Science Source **318:** Stocktrek Images, Inc./Alamy **319 T:** Gerard Lodriguss/Getty Images **319 B:** Elimitchell/Dreamstime **322:** Reed, Roland, 1864-1934, photographer
324: ALMA (ESO/NAOJ/NRAO)
325 (#1): Eckhard Slawik/Science Source **325 (#2):** Stocktrek Images, Inc./Alamy **325 (#3):** Gerard Lodriguss/Getty Images **319 B:** Elimitchell/Dreamstime **325 (#6):** ALMA (ESO/NAOJ/NRAO) **326:** Shutterstock **327:** CJWinch Animal World Photography/Alamy **328 L:** John L. Absher/Shutterstock **328 R:** Jonathan Blair/Corbis **329:** Luciano Candisani/Minden Pictures/Corbis

Unit 4, Lesson 6

330: Richard Linton/Dreamstime
332 L: Robert Gebbie/Dreamstime
332 R: eyecrave /iStockphoto
335: Shutterstock **337 (#2):** eyecrave /iStockphoto **337 (#3):** Shutterstock
338: Thinkstock **339:** NASA
340: NASA **341:** NASA/Goddard/Arizona State University

Unit 4, Lesson 7

342: National Geographic Image Collection/Alamy **343 T:** NASA & ESA, Acknowledgement: Gilles Chapdelaine **343 B:** yuriy kulik/shutterstock **344:** Don Farrall/Getty Images **345 T:** JOHN SANFORD/SCIENCE SOURCE
345 B: Procy_ab/iStockphoto
346 B: Hank Morgan/Science Source **346 T:** Photo Researchers/Alamy **347 T:** NASA, ESA, and the Hubble SM4 ERO Team **347 B:** NASA, ESA, and the Hubble SM4 ERO Team
348: Zack Frank/shutterstock
349 (#1): NASA & ESA, Acknowledgement: Gilles Chapdelaine
349 (#2): Don Farrall/Getty Images
349 (#3): Procy_ab/iStockphoto
349 (#4): Hank Morgan/Science Source **349 (#5):** NASA, ESA, and the Hubble SM4 ERO Team
349 (#6): Zack Frank/shutterstock
350: Martin Podzorny/Shutterstock
351: Radoslaw Lecyk/Shutterstock
352: Paulo Afonso/Shutterstock

Back Matter

355: Caro/Alamy **356:** Thinkstock
357: Radius Images/Alamy
359 T: weerayut ranmai/Shutterstock **375:** The Washington Post/Getty Images **376:** Cultura Creative (RF)/Alamy **377:** Thinkstock
378: Adam Hart-Davis/Science Source **379:** Thinkstock **380 T:** Asaf Eliason/Shutterstock **380 L:** JIANG HONGYAN/Shutterstock
380 R: Thinkstock **381:** Martin Shields/Alamy